Mental Health Issues of the Star Signs & Zodiac

Let's Get Triggered, Heal, and Evolve… Together

GRACE GABRIELLA PUSKAS

Book Description

Are you ready to be triggered? We all have a "mental health blueprint," a truly out of control and destructive version of ourselves. It's primitive. It's vulnerable, and it leads to our worst selves, the type of selves that could, if left unchecked, land us in a prison cell or mental health asylum. This is very different to shadow astrology, the less desirable and shadow traits we are supposed to accept and work on for integration; so we can attain some level of en*light*enment. Shadow astrology teaches us to embrace the parts of Self we would usually deny, to work towards the light, and is connected to the mental health blueprints described in this book; but, they are not one and the same.

In this book, *Grace Gabriella Puskas*, Astrologer and top Mind, Body, & Spirit author, explains the mental health blueprint of each star sign. Each star sign is described in depth, so you know what characteristics to look out for and where you might have been going wrong in youth. You can consult each chapter for your Sun, Moon, Venus, and Rising/Ascendant placements. We are all born into this society. There is a lot of illusion and confusion, moreover misinformation present in the "dark psyche." *This is something I am fascinated by, and, as a Healer, Reiki Master Teacher, and Shamanic Energy Worker, are devoted to uncovering and exposing.*

Are you ready to be triggered, heal, and evolve…? Are you ready to take accountability and make significant changes? And, are you finally capable of true ascension, self-evolution, and personal transformation; change that could put you on your true path and destiny...? I certainly was. I hope you are too. ✧

✧

Please visit my Youtube Channel the *Dream & Spirit Weaver* for FREE educational videos, wisdom sharings, and spiritual/holistic/esoteric teachings. (https://www.youtube.com/@TheDreamSpiritWeaver)

✧

ACKNOWLEDGEMENTS AND DEDICATION

The path of the shaman and healer is not an easy one. I was born into this society just like everyone else; I've had a lot of problems and challenges to face, specifically being a super-sensitive empath with an evolved emotional (and spiritual) frequency. I give my gratitude to all the lovers and supporters and all the fighters and haters in equal measure… One of my main mantras in life is there is a light and darkness to everything, duality flows and merges into Oneness. I am thankful for the haters and ones who have pushed me down when I've been at my lowest, as they gave me the strength and wisdom to find my voice in this often twisted and cold world; at least, when we are in our primitive selves.

I've had my own mental health issues to deal with, being a Pisces sun (the "Manic Depressive" in youth) and a Cancer Moon, prone to low moods, depression, and isolation. It hasn't been an easy journey, but, luckily, and with the grace of the Divine, I have found my truth, strength, and authentic voice. I have also risen from the depths of the lower manifestations of a distorted mind and psyche and aligned with my higher mind, my Higher Self, and my soul. This book is a manifestation of my reflections, observations, and knowledge discovered through diving deep into the collective psyche, from an astrological perspective.

I haven't just lived in communities, ashrams, and spiritual places where we encourage each other to explore our shadows and attain some level of enlightenment. I have also lived in house-shares and co-living places where there has been a strong level of unhealed wounds and trauma, moreover mental health issues. Some of the places I have lived that were described as 'refuge' or 'lovely house-share' should have, in truth, been labeled a mental health asylum!

As a White Witch, I receive hate and persecution for my evolved level of wisdom and higher insights, sometimes at extreme levels. It is a daily commitment of devotion, unwavering faith, and unconditional love that keeps me going, lets me keep writing and teaching, and allows me to be the Medicine Woman I incarnated here to be. I thank my Higher Self, Guides, and Angels for the continued support, saving me from a complete loss of hope when things have been too tough.

Infinite blessings to you, we, and me. <3

Contents

DISCLAIMER

*Shadow astrology and the "mental health blueprints" described in this book are not one and the same, although they do influence each other. These chapters aim to provide a deep-sea dive into the darkest places of each sign's psyche and personality. Shadow astrology is very different, as it describes the shadow personality traits inherent within each star sign. These are the qualities that are usually denied and rejected, yet are simultaneously meant to be integrated. Shadow traits are here to guide us towards the **light**, so we can achieve wholeness and integration.*

*The **"mental health blueprints"** inherent within this book are each sign at their lowest; a truly destructive and primitive version of ourselves. This is when we have lost control entirely, and are playing out our most destructive tendencies.*

CHAPTER 1: Aries the Psychopath

House: 1st house, the house of the Self, personal identity, and primary personality.
Planet: Mars, the planet of masculine sexuality, assertion, vitality, and action (positive), and competition, lust, war, and aggression (negative).
Element and quality: Fire and Cardinal.
Color: Red, the color of passion, sexual power, and all matters of security, survival, and self-preservation, and orange, the color of sociability, companionship, joy, and warmth.
Physical area: The head and face (+ adrenal gland).
Dates: March 21st to April 20th.

Ruling the head and brain, Aries are the psychopaths of the zodiac. At their lowest, they are irrational, paranoid, and completely psychotic. They overthink, over-analyze, and use their brains more than their hearts or feelings. Aries is a masculine sign with a masculine ruling planet, Mars. The mind also primarily represents masculine qualities; intellect, logic, and mental-cognitive abilities are all masculine attributes, unlike emotions, instincts, feelings, etc., which are feminine. Thus, at their worst or lowest vibration this masculine sign ruling the head is an absolute psychopath. They scream, shout, and put on explosive displays of power to get their way. They make up stories, embody the 'pathological lying' personality of Gemini's lowest self, and become an abusive tyrant.

Aries is a warrior at heart who fights for themselves, their livelihoods, and the underdog. They're courageous, fearless, and fierce in their speech and mannerisms. When on point, i,e. in a higher vibration, they are powerful leaders, creators, and innovators. They take charge and possess incredible intellect. But, when out of control and playing out unhealed wounds and traumas, Aries is a bully or tyrant. Or a self-destructive psychopath on a warpath with anyone and everyone who crosses their way…

Let's look at the definition of a psychopath:

A mentally unstable person with an egocentric personality including a complete lack of empathy and remorse for others, coupled with anti-social, dangerous, and often criminal behavior; suicidal tendencies through harm to Self or others.

Let's break this main definition down, shall we!

Mentally Unstable

Ruling the brain and head makes Aries psychotic due to an overuse of intellect and rationality. We are holistic beings, we are meant to be balanced, embodying and displaying a combination of qualities... Intellect and intuition, logic and imagination, cerebral gifts and feelings, and so forth. But Aries primarily resides in the head, meaning they think, think, think... They rely on logic, reasoning, and rationality, and this makes them become psychopaths when in a lower vibration or when at their worst. They become mentally unstable and emotionally chaotic. In fact, they lack all sense of emotional intelligence, sensitivity, and maturity, as we explore in the next point. Such an extreme sense of mental instability is built up from more minor mental distortions and balances. Over time, when left unchecked, mental distortion can cause minor or severe psychosis, i.e. disrupted thoughts and perceptions that make someone delusional as to what is real or not. Psychosis is an inability to recognize what is real or not. Mental instability at such an extreme level, causing psychosis or psychotic outbursts and episodes, can make one become totally irrational, further giving into pathological or obsessive tendencies, like lying. Of course, this person believes their lies, as they've become so disconnected from reality; what is reality when their entire identity and world is rooted in mental disparity and distortion? Pathological lying is the main mental health issue of Gemini, the Twins and cerebral air sign ruled by planet Mercury. Aries and Gemini are considered compatible and soulmates in astrology, also both being masculine yang signs. So there is a similarity here.

The second main aspect is being *delusional*, the mental health issue of fellow fire, soulmate, and compatible sign Sagittarius. Aries can be obsessive in their desires to disprove someone or prove something to be true. Due to having such a fierce sense of competition, always needing to win and outshine others, Aries can cling onto an idea or belief. This belief is that they are better, more talented, more destined to be a boss or star, better at A, B, C, etc. This influence steers them onto a path of war, seeing *everyone* as competition. If they choose a specific person as a target, their main competition, and when combined with their psychopathic personality deficit, well, you might be able to sense how disastrous this can be. If they've chosen to disprove or outshine someone, they can begin a year or decade long path of self-destruction. Why self-destruction? Well, because not everyone is competition-based; Aries is one star sign, and not all humans have Aries anywhere in their natal charts. Some people don't even have an Aries Sun, Moon, Venus, or Rising sign, in other words. Thus, living life with such a powerful sense of competitiveness coupled with needing to be number 1 is not natural or even sane to a lot of people. This "war" they begin and bind themselves to, therefore, can become their greatest downfall. Over time, believing someone is untalented, inferior, or a straight out liar, when physical reality proves opposite, creates a horrible level of psychosis. Facts and real life are not believed, and they then try to convince other people that said person (their believed competition) is a liar, not real, a fraud, a charlatan, deceptive, make-believe, and so forth. Reality could literally be staring them straight in the face and they *refuse* to believe it.

From another perspective, they may try to prove something not real is real, and once again, they can become obsessive in this need to the point of self-destruction. Being at war with yourself is a real thing. Aries becomes at war with their *Self*. We are all a reflection of each other, after all; perfect mirrors. If the other person has not consciously or consensually entered into a battle or war with them, there is no conflict, technically. Again, not everyone lives competitively- there are some selfless, empathic, and genuinely harmony-seeking individuals. And this brings us onto Aries' shadow trait or character deficit: narcissism. Having a selfish, self-serving, and narcissistic personality combined with tyrannical and bullyish tendencies is Aries at their worst, from a "shadow astrology" perspective. *Shadow astrology and the "mental health blueprint" described in this book are **not** one and the same, although they do influence each other.*

So, trying to prove something real is not real is linked to their shadow attributes. Aries can be extremely narcissistic and bullyish, and when merged with psychosis this makes them into a mentally dangerous and deluded person. They are relentless in their capacity to disprove someone or something. They become vicious, venomous, and quite hateful. Hate is the opposite of love. It's not always conscious, they are ruled by the planet and God of war, Mars, after all. They may think they are acting righteously or justly, but they are in fact speaking from a disconnected and distorted, and therefore hateful, space. Choosing someone or some idea or belief as their target can set them on a warpath into self-hatred and self-denial. They become obsessed in their need to disprove or discredit another's entire life, successes, qualifications, victories, challenges overcome, joys, and achievements. Making someone into their competition either righteously or unjustly can create a monster. They lie compulsively to get others to believe them, and they go so far as making up elongated plots to discredit. They create ambitious plots and schemes inside their heads that make them into a mean-spirited and ugly tyrant. Sometimes they recognize their own self-created psychosis, other times they are entirely deluded. They believe their lies, because, to them, it's the truth; it's an entire constructed reality built on their misconceptions and psychosis.

Aries' psychosis leads them into a warpath with self and others, in addition to making them believe things that aren't true, or becoming ferocious in their desire to disprove something that is true. *Reality becomes twisted.* Their minds and following perceptions and beliefs become distorted, they have a very difficult time ascertaining what is real and what is made up, and then, to make matters worse, the people they have convinced start to reinforce their psychosis. They're so forceful with immense personal power, you see. If this mental health issue applies to them, they have spent months to years defending and spreading a mistruth, and thus coerced, forced, or guided others to do the same. Their friends, associates, family, lover, peers, and acquaintances become their followers. No-one likes being told they're a follower, but this is the sad reality; Aries is one of the most powerful and forceful signs of the zodiac. Being ruled by Mars with a fire element *and* Cardinal quality creates a seriously powerful and strong-willed individual. They are willful, determined, ambitious beyond belief, resourceful, and innovative… They're highly resourceful with evolved levels of intellect, logic, higher analytical reasoning, rationality, and creative solutions. So when these positive traits are mixed with their shadow traits, they can convince anyone white is black and black is white. Their friends, peers, and social network become their support system, supporting and reinforcing their psychosis, either consciously or unconsciously.

A Complete Lack of Empathy

Secondly, Aries' mental health blueprint involves a complete lack of empathy. They are insensitive, unempathetic, and unkind to the extreme. When in their psychotic self, they forget the beauty of the soul, which includes a strong level of integrity, elegance, and nobility. This is Aries at a higher vibration, when their light and shadow attributes have been integrated. When in their primitive and primal self, however, they want to annihilate anyone who crosses their path or disagrees with distorted perceptions of reality. Or who seeks to undermine their master plots, plans, and schemes (birthed from such extreme competitiveness). They seek total destruction of any person, animal, or entity who doesn't support their mental confusion. Remember the definition of psychosis: *a complete loss of touch with reality.* Aries lacks compassion to the point of becoming a bully. They become tyrannical, explosive, and give into characteristics of the 'Child,' their lower manifestation. Aries is known as the Ram and the child in astrology, just as, for instance, Pisces is the Fish and Old Soul. They are the first sign of the zodiac, so they are teenage and child-like in their mannerisms. They are prone to fits of temper, rage outbursts, and explosive displays of seeking power and control over others, in addition to regular temper tantrums! This is largely birthed from a lack of sensitivity and empathy for others. They don't like to admit they are insensitive, yet they're entire identity is rooted in the need to be number 1. Aries needs to outshine others, win, at all costs, and come first. This equally means being seen as better, more brilliant, more beautiful and intelligent, etc. etc.

Therefore, they become mean-spirited and attention-seeking to the point of self-delusion, believing themselves to be kind, sweet, and of noble and pure heart when in reality they are dismissing everyone else's feelings. It gets to the stage where no-one else can speak… No-one else is allowed an opinion, no-one is allowed to share their beliefs or perspectives, and no-one is allowed to shine. It's impossible for anyone connected to an Aries in this energetic space to shine, speak their truth, or show off their talents. No-one is allowed gifts or wonderful news, apparently. Aries disallows everyone around them, perhaps minus one close friend or lover, to shine and be an amazing human. Their complete lack of empathy and sensitivity makes them into a bully and tyrant, moreover a self-serving egotistical narcissist. Narcissism is the opposite of empathy.

Egocentric Personality

An egocentric personality combined with narcissistic personality disorder is inherent in the distorted Aries psyche. Aries is a psychopath, and this makes them a narcissist when looking at their shadow traits. They are narcissistic, totally self-serving, self-entitled, and selfish beyond belief. As stated above, no-one else's opinions, beliefs, or needs matter. The only thing that's important is *their* emotions, *their* feelings, and *their* worthiness to stand in the spotlight. They dislike being questioned or even engaged in healthy and fair-harmonious conversation, from which space they start a war with anyone who dares to engage them. Healthy discussion goes out the window, mindful and empathic communication becomes non-existent, and everyone else becomes a minion in their evil schemes and plots. They are the only people in this universe who are allowed to exist, have an opinion, and shine. They are egotistical tyrants who cause havoc and mayhem; it's all seen as a game to them, they are the manifestation of the God of war. They don't believe in fairness or equality either. Unlike Venus ruled signs like Taurus and Libra, or Pisces who have Venus exalted in their sign, Aries stands *against* harmony in many respects. They are fighters, not lovers. This isn't a direct attack on them, I have my Mercury in Aries (despite this being my only Aries placement and having both my Sun and Venus in Pisces). I also know many self-empowerment and noble Aries women who have evolved and matured through their shadow traits… No, Aries is sincerely psychotic and narcissistic.

Are you aware of the story of *Narcissus*? This is a powerful story from Greek mythology that gave rise to the term and condition narcissism. Narcissus was son of the river God Cephissuss and nymph Liriope. He was a physically stunning man who everyone fell in love with. Physically, he was attractive and totally desirable, *desirable number 1*. Yet he did not have a personality to match. He would make young women fall in love with him and then laugh at their sincere affections. He allowed countless women to be besotted by him, even devote their life to him, however, he would dismiss them and toss them aside as if they were worthless. He did for years, until eventually he died through falling in love with his own reflection. That's correct, he was so self-absorbed and self-obsessed, believing himself to be the most physically attractive person of all time, in the world (no exaggeration), that his own self-admiration killed him. His *obsessive* unhealthy self-love led to his demise. Narcissism is defined by an excessive need for external validation and admiration, grandiosity, a constant need for attention and praise, and an inability to emphasize. Narcissism can become a mental disorder when left unchecked. This is known as Narcissitc Personality Disorder or NPD, and Aries displays this in minor-extreme amounts. Narcissism can lead to enhanced and perpetuated additional shadow traits, and vice versa; unchecked and unhealed narcissism can lead to psychosis. Someone with NPD like an Aries in their dark psyche embodies the energy of a bully. They bully, put down, belittle, slander, and criticize to the point of accumulating a lot of negative karma.

As the first sign of the zodiac associated with an uncontrollable desire to be number 1, Aries' life path is bound to the laws of karma. In a higher vibration, Aries accumulates good karma to inspire and lead others to personal truth and originality. They're intellectual, imaginative, innovative, ambitious, high-flying, and success-driven with strong levels of grace and integrity. At a lower frequency, Aries is the perfect example, from a cosmic perspective, of someone who can't right their wrongs. They *refuse* to take accountability or ownership and continuously deny, deflect, and project. Nothing is their fault or responsibility- their actions and words have no significance. Aries is so stubborn, hotheaded, and impatient that they always want to stay excited, energetic, and on the go, which means they fail to go inside. They're incapable of looking at their own shadow, as well as their wounds and traumas that, over time, spiral out to negatively influence their entire world and relationships. Like the Ram who takes charge without second-thought, Aries acts from pure instincts; it's all about survival, security, and them. Aries is very unmindful and unconscious in this headspace. So, Aries' path is karmic and on a dark timeline they embody the energy of the god of war himself. They cause destruction to people's finances, security, and income; they become home-wreckers and sabotagers at work and in personal or domestic situations. Aries will destroy a lifelong friendship or family bond and then play innocent, denying accountability at insane levels. Fire burns, fire destroys… but a fire burning hot and shining on its own won't care about anything going on around it. A fire burns because it can and because it's its birthright, it's natural and organic state. This is Aries.

Anti-Social Behavior

Linked to all of the above is Aries' tendency towards anti-social behavior, born from psychosis, a lack of empathy, and narcissism. Anti-social behavior occurs when they've gotten away with their mental distortions, for so long. They think it's ok to slander, explode, be emotionally and psychologically violent, and wage war on others for having opinions or being attractive, successful, and talented or beautiful. So, due to such negative mental patterns being reinforced and reinstated, they eventually feel anti-social immoral behavior is ok. They become unethical, immoral, and even abusive. Emotional and psychological abuse is common in Aries deep into their primitive unconscious side. Physical violence can also be a sporadic or regular trait. It's a personality deficit and flaw, violence of any kind, and being ruled by the God and planet of war himself makes this courageous sign feel it's ok to act in such ways. Aries is one of the most violent and explosive star signs alongside Leo and Sagittarius. Aries becomes uncommunicative, offensive, and rude verging on aggressive. They feel victimized while in actuality are insulting, slandering, or verbally (or physically) attacking their victims! People are victims to Aries in such a low and toxic vibration, as Aries is one of the most powerful and mentally and physically strong zodiac signs. Aries at a higher frequency are intellectually and mentally on point, as well as immensely vital; they possess evolved levels of vitality, life force, and passion, in addition to excitement, enthusiasm, and energy levels. When in a chaotic and uncontrolled headspace, all of this comes rushing to the surface in an explosive and destructive manner. Aries will shout, lie, and make you feel weak and worthless. They get a *buzz* off of others feeling small, weak, and worthless- they can be brutal and monstrous in their dealings...

It's all a game to them, remember, a manifestation of their personality deficits; seeing everyone as their competition, or needing to stand strong in the spotlight. Their desire to shine coupled with their need to be number 1 and win creates an abusive personality. They become aggressive and abusive in their mannerisms, seeking the spotlight over everyone, and thus alienating and targeting others. There's no such thing as cooperation or harmony, it's only what they can gain over others. This may be recognition, victory, more admirers, more love interests, or more followers; it doesn't matter to the Aries psyche. They lack humility and self-awareness, i.e. they become anti-social and unpresent. Non-acceptable behavior is seen as acceptable, like verbally abusing or attacking others. Forcing people to gang up on others is common too, and they genuinely believe they are within their right. Mars' influence makes them feel it's ok to turn people against each other, pick fights, and start drama that could end in violence. It's seen as normal to them based on such a disconnected and distorted mind. Distorted mental patterns lead to physical behavior problems, further a belief system where anti-social behavior is seen as normal.

Aries plays devil's advocate, moreover becomes the devil in many situations. They embody a demonic energy that prevents others from staying in their light, or standing up for the underdog, real victims, or those who need help. Aries can block people who genuinely need help from receiving emotional, psychological, spiritual, and physical support. They turn heart-centered and good natured people into monsters or devils based on the power of their words and delivery. Aries is a bully when in such a low mental headspace. They consciously and intentionally turn people on each other, turn people against each other, and play mind-games on those closest to them, and complete strangers. They love a fight, whether it's a physical or psychological one. It excites them, setting their mind a light and soul on fire. But, such destructive and brutal behavior is *not* good for their souls in the long-run, and it inevitably disconnects them from their souls. The desire to seek control over others from a mental and psychological perspective prevents them from soul growth, soul evolution, and soul alignment. And this is the main problem with the Aries psyche, when we examine their ins and outs from a holistic perspective. They are the first sign and therefore the least evolved- their energy begins and ends in the head, linked to the brain and rational and analytical thought. As has already been discussed, this prevents them from feeling things emotionally and with empathy. The head is also the opposite to Old Soul final sign Pisces, who rules the feet, which is where universal life force energy grounds into the earth, into Mother Earth. Pisces, of course, also rules the 12th house of endings and completion- spiritual maturity and soul enlightenment, and is ruled by Neptune, the planet of psychic instincts, spirituality, mysticism, dreams, and ascended consciousness; the *complete opposite* to fiery-red warrior planet Mars.

Aries has many strengths, however being so psychotic and psychopathic diminishes their soul power in the world. They are a force to be reckoned with, yet don't know how to embody the emotional and soulful power of some of the other signs, specifically water. Intellectual, innovative, bright-minded, and cerebrally gifted, with fine levels of imagination and intuition, Aries' best qualities are wasted when in their psychopathic energy. They use them to feed a path of chaos and destruction, not one of unity, love, or connection. Selfish desires put out the light and diminish community, drama and chaos ensue. People get hurt around them. Wounds remain unhealed and traumas get circulated, shadows linger… They exploit, manipulate, and violate others, while lacking all concern and regret for their words and actions. They lack remorse and have *no* empathy or consideration for other people's distress. Irresponsibility takes over. Aries becomes irresponsible in their communication and social interactions, also having a difficult time sustaining long-term connections. Relationships suffer, and anger problems become the norm to the point that actively bullying, slandering, or abusing others becomes "normal" in their social circle. Cruelty, hostility, and aggression replace all of their positive personality traits. Additionally, if you're familiar with the UK's *Apprentice* t.v. series, you should be aware that Alan Sugar is an Aries. In his younger years, if you watched the show with your intuition and spiritual eyes intact, you will see just how arrogant and cold he was. Arrogance is one of Aries' worst traits, ever. They are so arrogant that they will stand there in denial speaking or shouting over you. No-one else's opinions, talents, or perspectives are allowed, moreover they do not matter. No-one else is allowed a voice. Like Leo the Lunatic, Aries the Psychopath is a bully. "Lord" Alan Sugar is described as a business magnate, magnate meaning tycoon, mogul, lord, or even king according to Google. No one person should have this much power and influence, especially when acting from such a high level of unhealed shadow wounds (self-serving, self-entitled, aggressive, domineering, etc.).

In an evolved frequency, Aries is a dominant and self-starting boss, a leader, and a self-sovereign go-getter. They tackle life head on and command center stage, as they're passion is unmatched. But, in their dark psyche Aries is the most likely to commit passion crimes, I am sorry to share. A passion crime is a violent crime born out of intense love, lust, or sexual and/or romantic passion. Ruled by the planet of masculine sexuality and vitality himself, Aries is one of the most lusty star signs. They are highly sexual, so much so that an Aries in love becomes *obsessed*. This is the type of personality who will lie, cheat to win, and cause harm to their competition's possessions or physical body. Aries rules the 1st house, you see, which is the house of the Self, personality identity, and everything related to physical looks, fashion, and fitness. Superficial notions of beauty and attractiveness come into the 1st house, therefore combined with their intensely lustful and devoted nature they are obsessed. Their victim, sorry lover or potential soulmate, doesn't know that Aries will go to the ends of the earth to make them utterly devoted. In love, Aries is supremely loyal (higher vibration), yet in their mental health blueprint they are simply stalkers. It doesn't matter how physically attractive, slim, or athletic and slender Aries is, as these are superficial; inside, there is a disconnection from their souls.

Aries becomes disconnected from beauty, depth, and soul due to Venus and Mars being complete opposites. *'Men are from Mars and women are from Venus'* is actually rooted in astrological truth; "men" in this saying refers to masculine and "women" describes the feminine energy and essence. Thus, as a dominant and extroverted fiery yang sign, Aries is masculine (regardless of gender). Venus is Mars' opposite, which inevitably means this passionate and expressive sign misses out on key feminine attributes and qualities.

Some key manifestations of dark psyche Aries include stalking, writing false love letters from apparent competition, spreading lies and rumors to win in love, acting foolish and silly through erratic physical actions and displays of their affections (jumping on someone in public, being hypersexual to show how good or gorgeous they are, etc.), and even using black magic to bind their love interest to them. Aries has no shame when it comes to physical intimacy and desire. Both the 1st house and Mars' influence make them the 'no holes barred' star sign; this is the sign most likely to have public sex to, 1. Make everyone else jealous, and 2., make their lover loyal and commitment to them forevermore. In a high frequency they are passionate, loving, and totally companionable, sweet and romantic too, but, in a low vibration, they are outrageously devilish, hypersexual, and full of jealousy, competition, and rage. To add to this, their psychosis can make them believe completely delusional things about love and sex, like how their partner shouldn't be allowed to speak to the opposite sex, have opposite sex friends, or similar. Dark psyche Aries expects their spouse or partner to be attached to them in an unhealthy way… Think of the movie *Mean Girls*. This is Aries, whereby the genuine and somewhat naive innocent girl from Africa was oblivious to the evil antics of the mean-spirited blonde girl (I am not against blonde females, this is just a description!). She genuinely liked a boy who was sweet to her, yet the "mean girl" made her life hell and stole him simply because she felt she was *entitled* to him. She didn't actually like him- she dumped him, and she was cheating on him! In the end, the sincere new girl had to play dirty and resort to this blonde girl's seductive games just to stand her ground and bring some honesty, authenticity, and alignment back into the situation. In this respect, Aries can make the most selfless, soft-hearted, or noble and gentle of people stoop to low levels to restore harmony and justice. (I have been in a similar real-life situation, so I can vouch for this…) Heat of the moment passion crimes take over, or Aries will do something embarrassing while thinking they are the hottest girl or boy around. They believe themselves to be sexually and physically superior, and they further convince themselves o.t.t. displays of affection and even public sex are attractive. Usually sophisticated and elegant Aries becomes utterly unclassy. Aries is further the chav of the zodiac. Aries has intense emotions, yet because they are always relying on or giving precedence to intellect, logic, and their mind- the way they can think and analyze, Aries neglects their emotions. They believe deep feelings and sensitivities are inferior emotions. In fact, alongside cerebral air signs Gemini and Aquarius, Aries is the most likely to reject their feelings. They dismiss them entirely, choosing instead to want to be seen as someone intellectual, intelligent, and innovative or intuitive and imaginative. However, this isn't possible- no-one can bulldoze over their own feelings combined with their emotional needs forever.

This extreme antisocial behavior born from lust and psychosis pushes people away. Their friends and family turn against them, their love interests or partners think they're more "f-girl/boy" material than marriage potential, and secretly sensitive (deep-down) Aries turns against people even more due to not receiving the love they need. Aries craves love, companionship, and affection, however they don't know how to get it. They're misguided and misinformed because the instinctual messages they receive tell them to be sexual, passionate, and very heated. Remember, the 1st house rules personal identity, while Mars symbolizes energy, vitality, and competition. Sports and sex are included in the Aries personality (just like mysticism and spirituality are inherent to Pisces' soul). Aries is like a cat on heat, bless their sweethearts. But, unfortunately, Aries has no heart in this low mental headspace. There's no human courtesy or morality and ethics, and they treat the same sex or opposite sex if homosexual like utter vermin. All sense of human kindness and etiquette goes out the window, while their love interest becomes their target to unleash their intense- and often out-of-control- desires on. Again, Aries thinks it's ok to play with another's life, like make up rumors, spread false stories, and even falsify written documents or messages. If all else had failed, Aries will see a witch doctor or dark spell-worker to cast spells on their lover and/or love interest's other suitors. This is clearly something only a psychopath would do, as it's not sane, moral, or just, nor is it kind, rational, or intuitive. The problem is: Aries instincts *misguide* them. Being quick to temper, angry, and impatient with a real impulsiveness issue when merged with potent passions and sexual or romantic desires leads this usually level-headed and intelligent sign to act in the most heinous of ways. Wicked, disgraceful, and lacking all class and moral compass entirely, Aries is ready to battle for no reason other than 'I want.' This is actually the Aries mantra, as the zodiac's Child. If Aries wants someone or something, you have little to no luck winning; yes, even when it's completely insane, irrational, or unfair. Aries doesn't play nicely. Aries acts like an evil cupid… and they're the only one who's allowed to be in charge of the bow and arrow.

Criminal Tendencies

Finally, criminal actions are part of the unconscious and dark Aries psyche-soul-personality. This includes or can include selling and distributing illegal drugs, prostitution, money laundering, identity theft, conning others or the system, benefit or tax fraud, minor or larger-scale thievery, cybercrime, verbal assault, threats and intimidation, knife or firearm possession, trafficking (human, drug, sex, animal, etc.), and any other crime you can think of. Aries in their darkest and most impure space is a criminal! They are bosses- real self-leaders, so when in their low mental health space they are prone to criminal tendencies. Whether still in youth or older and an actual boss with a business or steady income, Aries can see criminal activity as acceptable. They believe themselves to be outside of the law. They are self-sovereign and independent beings, after all, and they're in charge of their own destiny, so who has the right to dictate how they live and act? This may be true, but the difference is they forget the importance of *morals*. Morals and ethics are forgotten, so being self-sovereign and liberated with the free will to make their own choices becomes an excuse for immoral behavior. Immorality and self-autonomy are often confused and mistaken as synergetic as well. For example, stealing from someone because there was a minor clash of wills or small disagreements becomes normal in the eyes of Aries. They see it as justifiable. The same is true for bigger criminal offenses in more serious settings, like in business, corporations, or when wills and similar entities are involved.

Aries plays devil's advocate to the point of becoming the devil himself. They let in demonic forces that influence their mind in a deeply negative way. They unconsciously put themselves in a psychological and spiritual prison, becoming their own worst enemy and own competition. This means they go to war with themselves while embarking on a path of immoral and illegal activity that could put them in a physical prison, or a mental health asylum. As the Ram, Aries actually is the devil! In terms of zodiac glyphs (astrological symbols), the Ram's horns symbolize the devil and thus dark forces of evil and ill-health, a trait shared by only one other sign, Capricorn the Goat. Unfortunately for poor Aries, they are the most prone to psychotic and demonic forces than all other signs, at least on a psychological and mental level. Spiritually, so much mental chaos and confusion can result in completely diminished life force, a disconnection from their life path and purpose, and a total absence of what their destiny or legacy even is. Their mental health issue blueprint leads to a growth and continuation of their shadow personality traits, which blocks them from enlightenment. Additionally, Aries are the sign best associated with war leaders and those who initiate heinous crimes. Adolf Hitler, the world's most evil genocidist, was an Aries! (Google will tell you he was a Taurus, but, I can assure you, he was an Aries… time is not entirely measurable with continuous movements of the planets and universal expansion/contraction. Cusps and seasons change, there are minor alterations each year.) Aries also seeks to control everyone and anyone around them in a way similar to Capricorn who represents the devil himself.

As Aries rules the 1st house of the Self, personal identity, and primary personality, including physical aspects like physical notions of beauty and attractiveness as well as an emphasis on fashion, superficial things, etc.; Aries can become lost to the world of superficial ideas and pathways. The soul and spirit body suffers. The 1st house is essential, as it shapes us- it creates our personal identities and primary personalities, yet too much focus on this combined with neglect for other houses and their qualities/symbolism is not healthy. It makes already overly analytical and rational Aries way too concerned with the material realm, as well as their physical looks. The personality and character suffers. The key qualities of humility, grace, selflessness, nobility, and integrity become lost to a game of abuse, anti-social behavior, and, at their lowest moments in life, criminal activity. Aries the psychopath is a criminal who believes themself to be a self-sovereign boss when, in reality, they are an ill-minded tyrant causing harm to innocent people. Their perception of reality is so distorted that right and wrong are mixed up. Good and evil become intertwined, and all concepts of fairness, morality, and integrity get lost to the world of war, death, and destruction. Their psychosis is normalized. Further, Aries may enter into a relationship or bond based on superficial things, like looks, apparent power and status, fame, prestige, or any contract with demonic undertones. Foundations are faulty. Aries' key to escaping their psychosis is to return to the root, exploring their pasts and even returning there through deep souls-searching and introspection. They can then work their way through the intense emphasis they've put on security, survival, and physical means to integrate the missing ingredients in their life. This is how balance is created and, thus, how they start to embark on a path of enlightenment.

Absolute worse crimes possible?

	LESS LIKELY	LIKELY	ABSOLUTELY
MURDER			✓
RAPE			✓
ANIMAL			✓

CRUELTY			
CHILD ABUSE	✓		
MOLESTATION	✓		
TORTURE			✓
HUMAN TRAFFICKING		✓	
SLAVERY			✓
BESTIALITY		✓	
TERRORISM			✓
KIDNAPPING			✓
GENOCIDE			✓
NUCLEAR WAR DECIDER			✓

CHAPTER 2: Taurus the Sloth

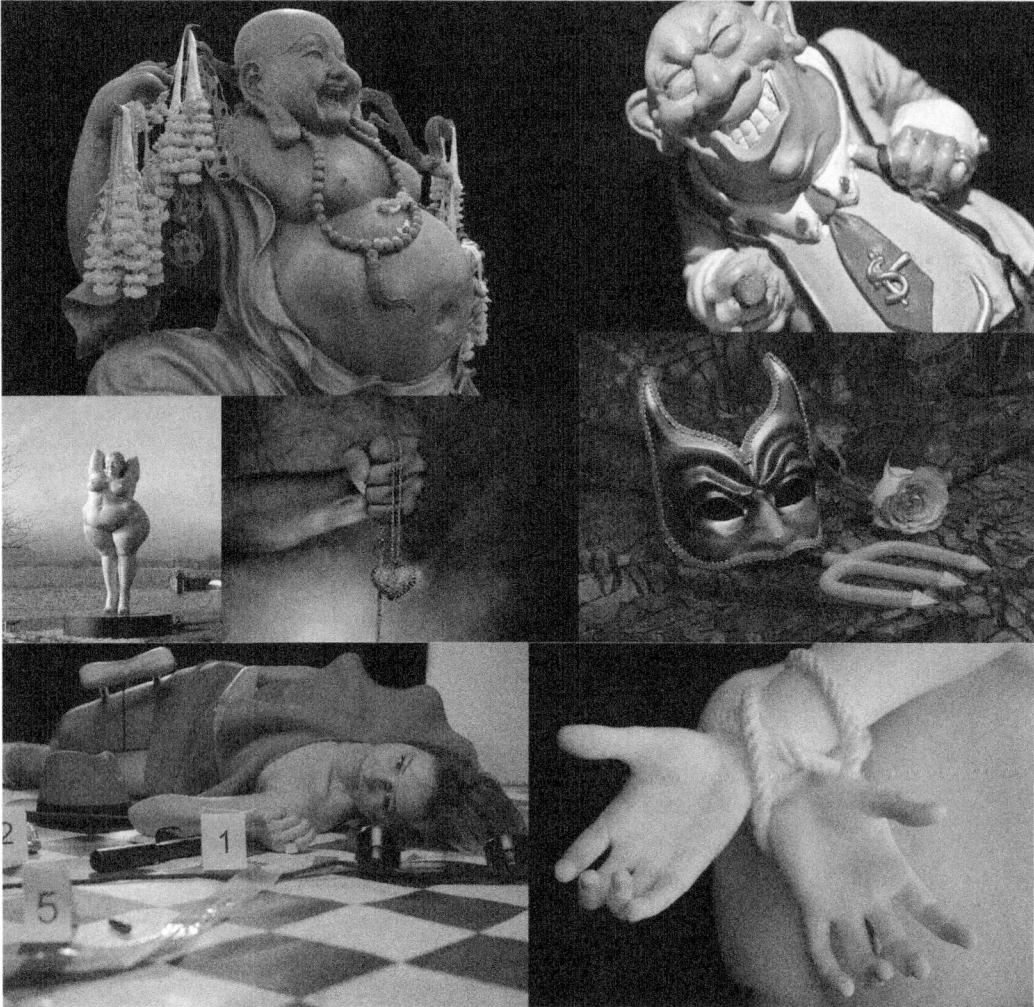

House: 2nd house, the house of material possessions, self-worth, and personal resources.

Planet: Venus, the planet of sensuality, beauty, romance, and feminine energy & sexuality (positive), and hedonism, self-indulgence, extreme eroticism, and perversion (negative).

Element and quality: Earth and Fixed.

Colors: Green, the color of empathy, self-love, tolerance, patience, and benevolence, and brown, the color of earthing/grounding, practicalities, sensuality, and being down-to-earth and dependable.

Physical area: Throat, neck, and thyroid.

Dates: April 21st to May 20th.

Taurus is the sensual and benevolent earth sign ruled by Venus, the planet of love, beauty, romance, pleasure, and feminine sexuality. But, when in their dark self Taurus becomes gluttonous, stubborn, and completely idle. They are lazy and unmotivated individuals who want to get lost in the world of fantasy and film, t.v series and food, and excess pleasures of the flesh. Venus is a beautiful planet with one of the most soulful auras, yet at a lower vibration it paves the way for overeating, sex or porn addiction, and possible prostitution engagement. Taurus becomes a self-serving Bull who will take charge with force and aggression, further only concerned with their own selfish needs and desires. They get lost in the world of materialism and bodily sensations, including indulgence. Taurus is prone to binge-watching and binge-eating, while denying or rejecting their spiritual needs.

As a Fixed earth sign, these tendencies are only amplified. The Taurus dark psyche is a gluttonous monster who cares little for other human's needs, emotions, or wants, which is an apparent contradiction considering how much sensitivity and empathy, moreover kindness, generosity, and friendship, this sign usually displays. Taurus the pleasure-seeking Bull turns into something vindictive, unempathic, and self-serving…

Let's look at the definition of a sloth:

A lazy and idle person defined by sluggish, unmoving, and gluttonous attributes, also being prone to a lack of energy, ambition, and motivation; excessive pleasure-seeking and hedonistic tendencies while neglecting Self and others.

Let's break this main definition down, shall we!

Idle, Lazy, and Unmotivated

At their worst, Taurus is completely idle, lazy, and unmotivated. They are the type of people who are comotozed to their bed, and who will sit in front of the t.v. or computer screen for days to weeks on end. They binge-watch anything that pops up, from random movies to infinite t.v. series. They binge-eat anything that pops into their mind too. They have no self-control over what they watch or put in their bodies. At a higher frequency, Taurus is very health conscious, as an earth sign ruled by Venus, the planet of beauty, romance, and sensuality. They like to take care of their bodies, eat nourishing and high in life-force foods, and work-out. Health, diet, and exercise are very important to them. So when their gluttonous need for pleasures of the flesh take over, they are truly in their dark feminine. Just as Aries becomes the dark masculine, the bulldozing tyrant ruled by a need for conflict, control, and war, Taurus lacks all self-control. Venus' influence makes them submissive, yielding, and passive, therefore they get pulled into the currents of the sensory world. Sensory data defines them. They are completely dependent on the world of the senses- everything they touch, taste, smell, sense, see, and experience on a physical level affects their emotional, psychological, physical, and spiritual well-being, deeply. They're a sensual earth sign ruled by sensory information, data, and experiences. They become fascinated (higher/positive manifestation) or obsessed (lower/negative manifestation) of the world of the senses, including everything they encounter. Physical reality defines them, and being ruled by the 2nd house, Taurus the Bull is entwined with the world of material possessions and resources, abundance, and matters of self-worth. Their sense of self-worth and self-esteem is tied into the money they make, the assets they have, their resources, home, security, practical foundations, and luxurious things, and the work or service they do in the world. Taurus needs to feel secure and safe, both in their bodies and in the physical environment around them, whether it be home or anywhere else. So, when their mind is distorted and in a devolved space, they start to see everything in unrealistic terms. They develop a false sense of security.

They cling on to false notions and concepts. Belief systems become faulty due to the false sense of Self or security, as well as self-esteem built off of faulty foundations. For example, feeling safe at home, whether it's living with parents or alone or in a house-share and co-living space, when, in reality, there are lots of issues that could threaten their security. This occurs when they've let shadow traits go unchecked for a while. The Taurus mental health blueprint is intrinsically connected to their shadow traits of idleness, laziness, possessiveness, stubbornness, and immovability. Some of these are explored later. Being lazy and idle for too long can make them get lost in their own personal bubble. It's only when they start to come out of their personal bubble and comfort cocoon that they realize how many problems there are around them. As the saying goes, *let sleeping Bulls lie*, you don't want to awaken Taurus from their slumber (or cage). Once you do, and it's inevitable it will happen- no-one can stay in their darkness forevermore, eventually we must all rise up into empowerment and enlightenment; it can be hell. Either Taurus will get personally attacked by everyone around them, naturally being a passive and feminine sign, whether it be parents, siblings, peers, housemates, or whomever else they've been denying and avoiding, consciously or unconsciously; or they will be the ones on the offense. Taurus plays both defensive and offensive strategies depending on their mood. As for finally waking up from their bubble, if they are awoken from others gently or abruptly when in such a low mental headspace, they see red. Like the bull, they become full of rage, angry, overly willful, and headstrong in their pursuit for justice or revenge. The two emotions are interchangeable for them, wrongfully so. A desire for justice is positive while revenge is a negative (or shadow) trait to play out. Thus, Taurus enters into a fit of rage and self-denial, not believing themselves to have any problems.

Binge-eating and Binge-watching is a comfort thing for them, because their whole identity is rooted in their need for security, home, and belonging. Without these things their whole world crumbles… succumbing to laziness and idleness in such extremes turns this usually sensitive, compassionate, and devoted to friends and family person into a raging monster. They will attack or defend their right to remain in their shadow at all costs. They will become irrational, explosive, and highly instinctive- they sense danger and see everyone around them as a threat. Taurus is extremely sensitive, you see, so much so that, when at their best, they are generous, warm-hearted, and kind beings committed to their loved ones. Taurus loves deeply, is very romantic and good-willed, and full of humanitarian and altruistic tendencies. Yet, when something has made them lose faith in humanity or the world, they succumb to their low mental headspace. And this then makes them extremely stubborn in their right or need to wallow in their own darkness. Their shadow serves as a comfort blanket for them, and it's a necessity for their well-being. Again, as life involves duality- light flows into darkness and vice versa, no being can remain in an "extreme" for too long, so eventually they will receive a rude awakening. Or suddenly realize that their health has suffered due to other people's insensitivity; they've become idle, unmotivated, and fat or physically unfit due to someone else's neglect- perhaps an insensitive parent or housemate. When this epiphany occurs, all hell breaks loose, it's chaos, and relationships break down. Relationship breakdown is the core negative manifestation of the Taurus dark psyche in attack or defense mode.

Moving on to a lack of ambition, Taurus becomes totally unmotivated. Educational, professional, and cultural opportunities are missed; there is no get-up-and-go whatsoever! They don't want to do anything, see anyone, or expand their horizons in *any* way, shape, or form. They become a motionless and bored creature only interested in the pursuit of pleasure; food, sex, money, t.v. sleep, security, and so forth. There's a real lack of ambition, as well as desires to provide for and support themselves, gather resources, and make a name or living. Usually highly protective and providing with a powerful instinct to nurture, care for, and build strong physical and practical foundations, for Self and those closest to them, Taurus in their primitive psyche becomes a hedonist. All they are concerned about is their security and survival, moreover their well-being. But, this is a twisted sort of self-care, as self-care is alchemized into traumatic self-love. What do I mean by traumatic self-love? Self-love is daily self-care and healing rituals that lead to an enhanced sense of self, including desires to become the best versions of ourselves; to self-master, evolve, and elevate our psychological, emotional, spiritual, and physical selves. This is Taurus at their highest vibration, self-care is their powerword. However, lower frequency Taurus distorts the meaning of self-care, taking on some of the delusional aspects of Sagittarius and unconsciously manic-depressive elements of Pisces. One thing you should know: Venus, Taurus' ruling planet, is elevated in Pisces, which means Venus is at its best in Pisces sign. Pisces and Taurus are considered real soulmates in astrology too, highly compatible. Taurus' manic depressive side is masked *as* self-care, and being so stubborn means they cling on to false belief systems. They falsely believe that getting lost in the world of sex, porn, t.v., film, food, and even drugs is a type of self-care.

It may be in very small doses, to relieve stress or ground, but anything more than this and it's counterproductive, it's twisted and self-destructive. Taurus' lesson is to ascertain what is self-care through the daily habits and routines they develop. This is key to their self-evolution coupled with true self-care regimes. In their dark psyche, Taurus is depressed. They enter into a cocoon of false comfort and depression, which makes them lack vitality, passion, and energy of any kind. Taurus is as passionless and uninspired as they come. Stagnation sets in, they begin to see themselves and others through pessimistic lenses, or delusional beliefs about their and others' looks, and they go slow and steady to the point of devolution. Taurus is the only sign who apparently moves backwards. They become very toxic. Inertia replaces instincts, so all sense of instinctual awareness and intuition are overcome by a mild or major form of depression. Taurus becomes semi-paranoid of people due to such low self-worth. Remember that the 2nd house is the house of self-worth coupled with worldly possessions and material resources. Chronic inertia is their problem. They are so attached to the material things in their life, as well as both the idea of gathering material resources and their current security, that they not long after become flippant. They displace, forget, and treat the things they apparently love the most with utter disrespect. Taurus is the sort of person who will have an explosive argument over something they hold near-and-dear, and then damage, break, or lose it a day or so later. And they don't care, they go from 100- 0 in an instant. One moment they're attached with their entire soul, and the next, there's no emotional or sentimental attachment whatsoever.

This flippant attitude keeps them suffering and depressed, moreover addicted to their idle and lethargic behavior. They become shallow, thoughtless, and inconsiderate to the point of embodying a totally carefree attitude. But, deep down, they do care; they care so much that Taurus the stubborn and possessive Bull would stab someone over something they own, when at their worst. The irony is, when balanced and mature Taurus is a cool, calm, collected, chilled, and relaxed person- people love being around Taurus because they're so chill. *'Cool as a cucumber'* is the saying for Taurus. Yet when in their mental health blueprint, they are too self-deluded coupled with *ignorant* regarding how much value they place on the things in their life. Ignorance means to ignore, and this is exactly that Taurus does; they ignore problems, push aside domestic, health, and financial issues, and neglect their love life. However, as you will see below, Taurus' identity is rooted in the need for intimacy and romance, so this creates a dangerous polarity. At a higher frequency, Taurus is one of the most emotionally intelligent, empathic, and mature star signs, yet in a lower vibration they become emotionally *numb*. They deny, reject, and avoid in a way similar to Aries, and it should be noted that despite Aries being born of fire and Tauurs born of earth, the Ram and Bull are very similar. In their supremely stubborn attempt to avoid and reject their emotions, as well as their sensitivities, instinctual responses, and intuition, which are usually very strong, this tenacious yet stubborn-as-hell sign becomes frivolous, disrespectful, irresponsible, overly carefree, and superficial. Essentially, they act like they don't care while caring so much it hurts them, or they act like they do care to try to maintain a level of control or an image or respect, while, in actuality, they don't care at all. It depends on their mood (which is negatively influenced!).

Gluttonous, Hedonistic, and Pleasure-Seeking

So, daily destructive and self-sabotaging habits, routines, and hedonistic-gluttonous and pleasure-seeking routines take over. Gluttony is excessive eating to the point of weight gain, obesity, diabetes, high blood pressure, heart or breathing problems, or any other minor or severe health problems. Hedonism is an extreme need and desire for constant pleasure. Pleasure can be defined in many ways. It can be being absorbed in the sense of taste, choosing to eat not for health or nutrition but for what tastes good. Processed and junk foods, artificial colorings, flavors, and sweeteners or preservatives, inorganic foods, and generally bad foods that discourage good health are part of Taurus' insatiable dark psyche. They eat whatever appeals in the moment- whatever they can get their hands on. They become lost to the sense of taste, completely ignorant moreover in denial of what their body needs. As the mind, body, and spirit are intrinsically linked, such a negative impact on their body affects their mind, emotions, and mood too. They begin a dangerous toxic cycle of self-sabotage whereby their body, now polluted by processed and toxic foods, starts to speak to their mind and brain. Their body speaks to their cells, which in turn transmit messages to their brain and emotions. Thus, a dark cycle of despair, depression, and lethargy masked as self-care or comfort through the monetary pleasure they experience ensues. They start to see the worst in themselves and others, only picking up on their toxic or shadow traits. They become addicted to the brief highs foods and beverages bring, and then succumb to other addictions and pleasures because they are now in a loop.

This loop is a loop of chaos and toxicity. It mainly affects them, especially when they're in their hermit or isolated or "false self-care" stage, but it also influences the people around them. They project on those closest or anyone near, projection is one of Tauurs' worst qualities. Ruled by Venus, the planet of love, beauty, sensuality, female sexuality, and romance. Taurus' whole world is entwined with the connections in their life. They need friendship, intimacy, and affectionate bonds- family, platonic, and romantic. It's their entire world. They are loving and sensual people who genuinely want to help, heal, and inspire others. They desire nothing more than to make the world a better place through their talents, gifts, and kindness. They are the friends and lovers of the zodiac. Projection is unconsciously mirroring our worst traits, the traits and characteristics you refuse to accept in yourself, and the negative attributes usually denied or rejected. We project when we fail to recognize as well as accept our own shadows. Taurus is a dark master of this when at their lowest. Self-pity through bad diet and lifestyle choices takes over, and they thus become self-indulgent to the point of inner disharmony; their inner equilibrium is disrupted. They fail to see they have a problem and toxicity sparks within and around. Taurus is not unkind, so they will never display the monstrous tyrant or bullyish psychopath energy of Aries. Yet, their inner psychosis is rooted in projection, which can be just as if not more destructive.

In addition to gluttony, the sense of taste (gustation), Taurus gives into the other physical pleasure senses, touch (tactician), smell (olfaction), sound (audition), and sight (vision). They become immersed and lost in fantasy and hedonism in the world around them, not wanting to focus on spiritual or professional matters. In their pursuit of pleasure, they forget the importance of creative partnerships, true self-care, and either business, abundance, or love-making and intimacy (depending on which sense they've got lost in…). Their spiritual self diminishes while their material side takes over. They don't care about the harm they cause to their mind, body, and spirit, and therefore once they start projecting they don't care about the harm they cause to other's minds, bodies, or spirits either. Normally mindful and empathic Taurus transforms into a self-indulgent and self-serving projector who unconsciously mirrors their worst behavioral patterns. The outside world is a reflection of our inner world, after all, and with such a potent level of disharmony, equilibrium, and imbalance the outside world created is the same. Their ruling planet Venus makes them seek harmony and beauty above all else, therefore being in their most primal and primitive makes them make the wrong choices. They become their own worst enemy. In terms of eating crap endlessly for weeks to months to years, or binge-watching films or t.v. series that dumb the mind and senses, Taurus is the most likely to neglect their home, animals, or children. Taurus becomes a slob, completely unkind and uncompassionate to themselves, and therefore others. They are the most likely to unconsciously abuse their children through terrible diets and a lack of hygiene; if social services were to be called on anyone, this would be one of the signs most likely to have them called. They shove food down their throats, quite literally, without mindfulness, conscious awareness, or any sense of sophistication or table manners. *What table?* Taurus will be in bed surrounded by junk food, not just once a fortnight or month as a "treat," but daily. Animal, child, and home care, in addition to self-care, become void and null in their world.

Sorry to say, this is the sign most associated with indirect neglect and abuse, like letting their children turn up to school with dirty and food-stained clothes or after not having bathed or showered for days on end. Taurus becomes so selfish and self-serving that they neglect the people they are supposed to protect. At their best, they are providers and protectors with powerful nurturing, compassionate, and empathic instincts. Outside of all the water signs, the element associated with deep-seated empathy, Taurus is the *most* empathic sign. Thus, in their dark psyche they are self-serving and self-entitled, seeing every single thing in the material world as an extension of them, and therefore something they're entitled to. In addition to neglect, this can also give rise to stealing tendencies combined with petty crime. Taurus is not a criminal gangster like some others, but petty theft is common with this sign. Like *Sleeping Beauty* who had to be awoken by a prince,

Taurus also looks to others to save them. But, unluckily for genuine and good-natured Taurus, this is not what the universe has in store for them. Their life path is entwined with the need to reclaim self-autonomy and self-sovereignty, as well as find their purpose through independence and, like all others, healing their shadow traits. Taurus' wounds are tied up into their shadow (toxic) traits, including lethargy, supreme laziness, stubbornness to change, and so forth. Taurus is not destined for an early death from terrible hygiene and diet, yet they believe they are. And for those who have more faith, they genuinely believe others are supposed to save them. At a higher vibration they are wholly responsible, duty-bound, and hard-working without fault, however in such a low frequency the opposite is true. Being ruled by Venus means they crave beauty, softness, and peace, but they are so possessive over the creature comforts that give them temporary relief, they are incapable of picking themselves up out of a dark hole of depression. Furthermore, when someone is brave enough to wake the sleeping bull, Taurus will become so angry and temperamental (due to being resistant to help and change) that they frighten their savior. Taurus' rage can be frightening. At their worst, this lethargic and change-resistant sign shuns everyone, closes important doors to intimacy and connection, and gets *fixed* on the idea of staying ill, stuck, or blocked.

Obsessive Behaviors in Love

Onto Venus, the planet of love, female sexuality, and feminine energy in both its lightest and darkest… Taurus is one of two signs ruled by Venus alongside Libra. This makes them incredibly romantic, sensual, and sensitive, as well as nurturing, caring, compassionate, empathic, and *magnetic*. They are yielding, more submissive and passive than dominant and direct. They love to find deeper connection in all things, within themselves and the relationship with the outside world; with plants, animals, nature and other humans. They seek platonic, romantic, and sexual intimacy at highly charged emotional and spiritual levels. All of this is Tauurs at an elevated or higher vibration. So, what of them when in their mental health blueprint? Well, they are obsessed, compulsive, and totally irrational fueled by fantasies of erotic love. Unlike Mars who represents masculine sexuality and thus lust at a lower vibration, Venus symbolizes female sexuality and thus eroticism. Erotic love can be pure, empowering, and divinely positive, but it can also manifest as obsessive behaviors. (And, porn or sex addiction.) When in love or interested in someone they transform into the devilish version of cupid. Romanticized notions of finding "the one," erotic love-making, and pure passion wild and liberated fill their minds. It fills their entire life. Their daily thoughts and behaviors change to accommodate this tempted version of themselves, further opening a doorway to darker entities. They may start to see goblins, dark pixies, or outrageously devilish versions of cupid appear in their dreams or peripheral vision. Taurus is one of the few signs capable of astral travel and projection, in addition to transcendental states of awareness. They receive visions and messengers from the divine reflecting their consciousness, and unlike more gentle and nurturing versions of magical entities and deities or spirits, being so obsessive can open them up to darker forces.

Red is the color associated with lust, love, and passion, and it's no secret that the Bull is triggered by the color red. Bull fights are known for using the color red to bring out this beast's angry and wild side, who seeks violence/revenge, justice, and liberation. These three themes are reflected in the Taurean dark psyche. Taurus becomes a stalker, in short. They obsess and fixate over their chosen love interest or target, and take "crush" and "fancy" to new levels of stalkerism. A Taurus in this energetic space will shape their entire world and identity around their love interest, from the clothes they wear to their fashion statements, hair style, and lifestyle choices. They'll enroll in courses and embark on educational and professional pathways of study to put them closer to their love interest. They text, comment on social media posts, and call *constantly*. They will write emails and letters and knock on doors if there's already a connection present. There's no such thing as 'no,' and it can become crazy. A really psychotic or mentally deranged Taurus in this low headspace may even resort to physical acts that could land them in jail. This is an extreme, but not completely unheard of. Taurus sees red; passion, jealousy, fixation, and rage when they haven't got their way. They aren't too fussed about public image or outside perception, all that matters is their feelings and desires, which are not controlled or disciplined. They want love, romance, and physical touch and intimacy at all costs. Eroticism can become destructive when not kept in check or balanced with other emotions or with grounded activity. In their insatiable need for pleasure and intimacy, they lose themselves to their own inner currents. Love is the strongest vibration, yet love at such an intense level just becomes infatuation. Taurus becomes illogical, irrational, and hopelessly devoted to their idea and notion of love, as well as to their crush.

Thus, Taurus will make career, travel, lifestyle, cultural, and educational decisions based on their flight of fancy or obsession, and big ones. These are choices that define their fate, as it's the smaller details that lead to the bigger picture visions for our lives. But, these choices aren't built off of conscious or mindful decisions, they're built off of a distorted perception of reality based on the excessive pleasure-seeking tendencies. Erotic fantasies and desires in both waking and dream life occur, extremely vividly and frequently; much too frequently for the normal human to function. Eroticism is described as sexual arousal, impulse, and desire. This is what Taurus embodies perpetually and consistently, to the point of self-destruction whether it be emotionally, psychology, spiritually, or physically, or within relationships. Kidnapping or murdering their lover in a fit of rage and jealousy birthed from supreme possessiveness is more common with this sign, according to astrology. Passion crimes are associated with Taurus in the same way they are with Aries, only Taurus is a bit more soulful and sensual in their approach and delivery. Rape is associated with Tauurs, I am sorry to say (remember all the chapters in this book speak of each sign *in their dark psyche only*). Taurus wants to experience the world and all it has to offer with their entire body- with their mind, soul, and body. They feel things like it's an extension of themselves, and they find an ecstatic form of pleasure and joy in sensations of the flesh. Rape, sexual assault, and even acts of torture are a twisted euphoric experience. Not so lost Taureans will find the same thrills in video games or movies; in either case, this sign needs an outlet to express the intense desires circulating inside them. Taurus has no self-control, therefore stopping themselves is virtually impossible. Like Leo the Lunatic who unleashes their need for power through bullying others, beating people to a pulp, etc. Taurus likes to use innocent people's bodies. Their primal side is liberated and wild when in their mental health blueprint, but there's no spiritual connection or higher morality involved. In fact, Taurus has a complete loss of connection to a higher morality, spirituality, and soulful vision of what intimacy really means. They act and serve themselves from the physical body only, while believing they are fulfilling God's purpose or plan for them. Venus' shadow of dark eroticism can lead to some seriously twisted acts and beliefs…

Immoveable With An Inability to 'Let Go'

Another main shadow trait linked to the Taurean mental health blueprint is possessiveness. This Fixed earth sign is incredibly stubborn, possessive, and immoveable, which means they cannot let go. They have a very difficult time moving on and wish to cling onto ideas, relationships, and belief systems long after they've served a purpose. Taurus is a deeply conservative sign to the point of extreme attachment. They get familiar with a person, place, or thing and then want to attach to it forever. At their worst, Taurus will hold onto an old item or relationship long past its use, at highly irrational and unintuitive levels. To conserve is to preserve, but, as the human form has taught us, not everything can be preserved forever. Taurus becomes possessive over anything and everything they feel they've given sufficient time, energy, and love to. Once they've left their mark, no matter how big or small, this stubborn earth sign will fixate; they believe they have a claim and some sort of ownership over people, places, and things. This is due to their better qualities when they are in a higher vibration; commitment, faithfulness, longevity, responsible, dependable, benevolent, trustworthy, and motivational. Taurus is a deeply faithful and loyal person who will protect and defend, moreover serve for as long as the other person requires their devotion. They love with all of their hearts and have very large amounts of affection to give. Taurus is devoted, however when in their low space they have delusional beliefs about their connection with things, so they enter a type of psychosis similar to Aries. With them, the psychosis relates to ownership and possession, and being an earth sign can one-day finally make them explode. Vitality, life force, and physical instincts lead to violence at some point, if their shadow traits are left unchecked for a long period of time. Bulls don't charge unless provoked, but what is just cause for revenge or vindication?

Well, either someone really does push them, playing with their hearts, abusing and misusing their trust, and shattering their loyalty and love, or their own shadow traits lead to projection which leads to a fit of rage and violence (some way down the line). Intensity and passion blur into a melting pot of anger, hatred, and loathing. Being one of the most possessive and stubborn signs, a mad or heartbroken Bull will seek justice at all costs. Taurus is not a bully, but they do have victims, and these are the people they have shown their love, loyalty, affection, kindness, etc., too without reciprocation. No reciprocation combined with users, takers, and heartbreakers- either real or make-believe from psychosis- are what create an out of control beast. Usually sensual and calm Taurus will explode if they are pushed too far. Violence may be psychological or emotional or, at last resort, physical. Thus, they are inflexible, rigid in mindset, and totally uncontrollable when they believe something or someone is theirs. There's no room for rational thought, no-one can tell them otherwise. There's little chance for rationality or intuitive higher guidance either; Taurus forges away on the path they've created with unshakeable stubbornness. The usually positive traits of loyalty, ambition, and determination are alchemized into something darker, something less desirable, and thus used to torment their victims. They want, desire, and demand once their energy is entwined through acts of kindness. Their generosity may be sincere, but no-one is bound to them- people have free will to change their minds or withdraw their energy, yet this is something stubborn-as-hell Taurus doesn't understand.

Remember that Venus is exalted (at its best placement) in Pisces, the sign of unconditional love, mysticism, soul bonding, and, on a lower frequency, a lack of boundaries and blurred lines. Taurus therefore opens themselves up to illusions sparked from deep desire coupled with an unexplainable need for soul merging and bonding. It's an instinctive need with both light and dark possible manifestations. Their dark expression asks them to not stop, to keep going, and to block out anyone's loving or wise advice. They refuse to listen, accept, or let go and change. It's impossible for them when in their darkest psyche manifestation. *It's my way or the highway.* Unluckily for those on the end of dark cupid's arrow, it can get to the stage of needing a restraining order, professional support, or serious and inconvenient life alterations like changing social media accounts and phone numbers… or even addresses! Oh yes, Taurus is the zodiac sign who will stalk and stalk until the person they're infatuated with has no choice but to move home, sometimes even to a different country or continent. Their addictions and obsessions when merged with possessiveness, the inability to let go and move on, are catastrophic for the people they claim to love. What's worse is that they don't see their actions as wrong or hurtful in the same way Aries doesn't see their warpath or severe psychosis as destructive. Even when Taurus doesn't get to a physically dangerous stage, their possessiveness leads to psychological and emotional violence or abuse of some kind. At their worst, they will kidnap, enslave, and turn someone into their sex toy. They show a twisted by somewhat real level of passion and love while doing so, at least they believe it to be real love. It's very dangerous.

Addicted to Eroticism

At their lowest Taurus is a serial prostitute visitor or someone who charges money or gifts and material things for sex. As the hedonist and erotic lover of the finer things in life, in addition to an insatiable need for physical touch and affection, Taurus loses control in their need for pleasure. Desires for sexual intimacy become purely physical, with the sole focus on the genitalia. At first, Taurus does desire real intimacy, but because they become lost in a dark spiral linked to their overall mental health blueprint, they become infatuated and misguided. They convince themselves that paying for loveless sex is romantic, passionate, or acceptable to their heart and soul. They put themselves in a bubble of illusion and self-deception born from an intense need for love. Yet what they receive and get caught up in is not love. It's a web of lies and self-loathing over time; it's self-destruction masked as self-love. Paying someone for sex is almost all of the time, 99%+, soulless. There is no heart, empathy, sensitivity, romance, genuine emotions, timeless love, or eternal devotion, the qualities authentic Taurus craves. Their higher vibrational self adores and admires their lover, yet when in such a sloth-like energy brought on from other physical pleasures and sensations, visiting prostitutes or having a real sex addiction is common.

Taurus will become enticed to the world of lust and eroticism masked as love and romance. They are hopeless romantics, and when there's such a cross-over from being in a low mental headspace, there's no hope for them. Physical actions linked to the highs of pleasure, at least initially (sex is never pleasurable or intimate once it's become an addiction) become mistaken for true love and even connection. Taurus becomes disillusioned, misperceiving and misinforming their own mind and subsequently heart. All spiritual connection and emotional bonding diminishes. Their life force is drained due to exerting so much sexual energy and further becoming lost to pleasure; life involves duality, so falling tinto one extreme means sensual becomes senseless, passionate becomes robotic, and any initial feelings, romance, or chemistry that may have occurred get eradicated to the addiction of trauma bonding. At their worst, Taurus uses sexual intimacy and hedonism as a way to *trauma bond* when there is no love, friendship, or authentic intimacy in their life. It's a major escape mechanism. Taurus becomes defensive to any advice, wise counsel, or healthy criticism, moreover they lack boundaries entirely. Root causes for such mindsets and behaviors need to be addressed.

Absolute worse crimes possible?

	LESS LIKELY	LIKELY	ABSOLUTELY
MURDER			✓
RAPE			✓
ANIMAL CRUELTY	✓		
CHILD ABUSE		✓	
MOLESTATION			✓
TORTURE	✓		
HUMAN TRAFFICKING			✓
SLAVERY			✓
BESTIALITY			✓
TERRORISM		✓	

KIDNAPPING			✓
GENOCIDE		✓	
NUCLEAR WAR DECIDER	✓		

CHAPTER 3: Gemini the Pathological Liar

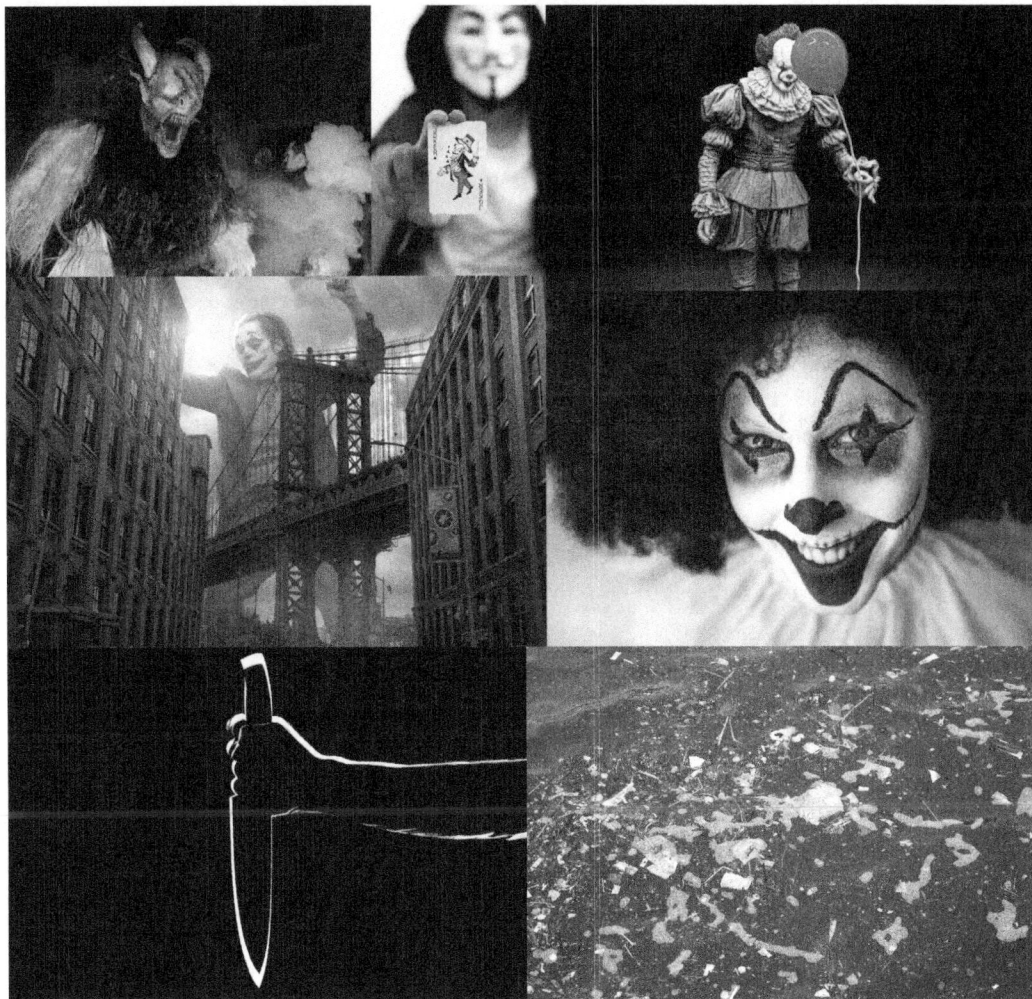

House: The 3rd house, the house of communication, intellect/intelligence, and local neighborhood connections.
Planet: Mercury, the planet of communication, the mind, intelligence, and language (positive), and disruptions, chaos, misdirection, and travel and communication failures (negative).
Element and quality: Air and Mutable.
Color: Yellow, the color of positivity, a sunny and optimistic disposition, confidence, and ambition, and blue, the color of communication, intellect, self-expression, and the imagination.
Physical area: Hands, lungs, and arms (+ thymus, respiratory, and nervous systems).
Dates: May 21st to June 21st.

Gemini is ruled by Mercury, the planet of communication, expression, and mental abilities. They also have the glyph of the Twins, a sign of duality. This makes them pathological liars when at their worst. They are one of the most gossip-prone, manipulative, and deceptive signs who like to have fun spreading mistruths and false rumors. They get a buzz off of hurting people with their words; their mental wit, rapport, and skills are on a whole new level. But this makes them incredibly deceptive and BS spreading. At a higher vibration, they are bringers of higher wisdom and truth, in addition to being incredibly witty, communicative, rational, logical, intuitive, and imaginative. So when they are deep into their unconscious Self and psyche, they become pathological liars with an obsessive need to misdirect others for either fun or personal gain.

When mentally distorted, Gemini is a trickster. They are the cosmic jokers who find happiness in other people's suffering, and through playing games, causing havoc, and creating mischief. This mischief is usually seen as a joke, but it's not funny to their targets or victims. Repetitive gossip and slander on another person's character can cause serious harm, on the emotional, psychological, spiritual, and even physical planes.

Let's look at the definition of a pathological liar:

A character deficit of lying compulsively and without clear benefit, coupled with the need to make up stories, deceive and manipulate others, and cause harm through constant gossip and truth distorting; the cunning Trickster.

Let's break this main definition down, shall we!

Compulsive Lying

At their worst, Gemini is a compulsive liar. They simply can't help themselves, they lie on repeat, and can't control their tongues. As the Twins (astrological symbol), Gemini lies and succumbs to miscommunication. This is because, when their psyche is distorted, they embrace multidimensionality, multiple perspectives and viewpoints, and their dualistic nature. At a higher level, Gemini is a gifted seer and open-minded passionate communicator who is blessed with evolved perception, observation skills, and problem-solving. They can tune into the divine, subtle realms of spirit, subconscious wisdom, and the imaginative realm, all from an intellectual and psychological viewpoint, to receive information and wisdom many people can't access; at least not from such a high cerebral frequency. So when their psyche is in chaos, they use these gifts for mischief and destruction. Gemini will lie about anyone and everyone, spreading mistruths, and making people's lives hell. They intentionally distort the truth- they know what the truth is, more so than many others. Their advanced intellect, logical and rational reasoning, and higher level mental functioning allows them to perceive, think, and communicate on par with the god of communication himself, Hermes. Hermes is linked to Mercury, Gemini's ruling planet.

If you aren't aware, Hermes is the messenger god who receives and transmits information from the divine realms of spirit and the mortal realm. He rules communication, so just as Aries embodies the god of war, Taurus the goddess of feminine sexuality, and so forth, Gemini embodies the god of communication. Communication can be elevated, evolved, and mature, or it can be lower, chaotic, and distorted. Toxic Gemini is totally ok with causing harm to others, sometimes to the point of self-harm or suicide. Oh yes, Gemini has an inner sociopath, as we explore soon. Gemini gets a kick off of hurting others with their words. They are master communicators, knowing how to express themselves better than the other signs of the zodiac. They will gather information, knowledge, and wisdom from the environment, keeping a reserve of information from the conversations they have and people they encounter, and then they will relay that information in a completely false way. They know what they are doing, it's not a mistake or an act rooted in confusion. There's no confusion or illusion in Gemini's stories. Despite being psychologically messed up, f*cked, in other words, they are fully conscious and aware. And this is where they become dangerous...

Warrior-spirited Aries ruled by the planet of war may be physically scary and intimidating, but Gemini is packed with a weaponry of harsh and destructive words that can hurt and misguide. Once someone has become guided through Gemini's powerful conviction and delivery, it can set one, 10, or a whole group of people on a wrong path.

One false word or sentence believed by an innocent person's ears can be incredibly dangerous, pushing them onto a path of self-destruction, self-sabotage, or wrong choices. Making choices is integral to Gemini's warpath. They wage psychological war on others, filling people with ideas and belief systems, moreover stories, that can lead them astray. Their followers or friends then attach to an idea or ideology and make choices to follow. Gemini is a master of planting a seed. Unfortunately, not all seeds are healthy, and, as is Gemini the Trickster's case, they plant seeds of chaos, darkness, and despair. They consciously guide people to do or say silly things, engage in antisocial or criminal behavior, or cause harm to their mind, body, and/or spirit. As the Twins, Gemini is one of the three signs of duality (Gemini the Twins, Libra the Scales, and Pisces the Fish). This means they are gifted in multidimensional perception, open-minded and philosophical insight and debate, and potent higher mind gifts. Gemini is insightful, divinely and imaginatively inspired, and *extremely* wise and discerning. They know how to read rooms and people, they excel in storytelling too. Their mind is always charged and on point, full of wit, and amazingly bright and sophisticated. Their ability to see multiple points of views, beliefs, and perspectives simultaneously makes them a social chameleon. In fact, as a Mutable air sign, they are the chameleons of the zodiac.

This chameleon-like personality enables fast-paced, strong-willed, and highly fluid communication. Gemini is adaptable due to being a Mutable sign. They are flexible and potently gifted in direct, assertive, and outspoken communication, and they're inquisitive, curious, and freedom-loving. Gemini's love of freedom, travel, and adventure fuels their need to share ideas and stories, as well as spread mistruths. In fact, Gemini is so curious and intrigued by the world and all it has to offer that they get genuinely excited about every little detail of information they absorb and pick up on. When in a lower vibration, this makes them bounce off of the ideas and observations swimming in their mind, and thus they go off on highs and vibrant impulses. Unfortunately, not all of these buzzes and flashes of insight or inspiration are correct; they become misguided themselves, telling themselves false stories and misinforming themselves. How does this occur? Well, they have so much swimming inside their bright brains that they get confused, there's an aspect of disillusionment similar to fellow air sign Aquarius. They pick up on so much, an infinite sea of information and knowledge, that they tell themselves lies. This then makes them lie to others.

Intentionally Spreading Misinformation and Mistruths

Because of this chameleon-like personality, constant need for new information, and excitable character, when merged with their pathological lying psychosis, they bounce off of their own reserve of knowledge. This knowledge is picked up from external environments and sensory data. A whirlwind of internal chaos and passion swirls up, flowing from their Sacral, their emotional center which rules social interactions, intimacy, and friendships/social bonds, to their higher energy centers; their Throat, Third Eye, and Crown chakras. This is where information becomes muddied. Distortions arise, what is truth and what is fiction? This is due to Gemini being a yang sign, a masculine quality. They're extroverted and social to the point of getting *lost* in social interactions and relationships, many of which are superficial. One of their shadow traits includes being superficial, which becomes truly chaotic when merged with such a low mental headspace. They tell themselves and others false stories from the mixed signals and multiple avenues of knowledge and perception they've picked up on. They see from a solely or primarily psychological and mental perspective, and this signifies that they are emotionally disconnected. Gemini lacks emotional depth, wisdom, and empathy, in addition to *sensitivity*. They are incapable of the deep and sincere displays of empathy and compassion displayed by the water signs, for instance, and can only process such emotions on an intellectual level. Intellect replaces empathy, rationality diminishes feeling, and logical, psychological, and mental thinking takes over all sense of sensitivity, instincts, and emotional intelligence. At their worst, Gemini is emotionally aloof and detached, so much so that they choose to ignore and deny their emotions altogether. This means they ignore and reject other people's emotions. Then, this creates a hostile and volatile, moreover dangerous environment… Gemini doesn't understand that some-many people aren't as psychologically or cerebrally gifted as them. They think, not feel, and they further lack emotional and spiritual self-awareness. Emotions and spiritual wisdom and awareness are closely tied into each other, as the emotional and spiritual bodies are linked to yin-feminine energy. The psychological and physical body are yang or masculine in nature.

As a masculine air sign ruled by a masculine planet, Gemini lacks feminine wisdom, emotional intelligence, empathy, nurturing instincts, gentleness, passivity, and other serene and calm qualities. I am not saying they are unkind, but unkindness and uncaring are more common in them than in others (water and earth). Such a strong lack of emotional wisdom and awareness makes them think, feel, and perceive only from their mind. Cerebral gifts and intellectualism become the primary driving force of all intentions, as well as their sole communication style. We live in a world of duality where polar opposites need to be integrated. There must be harmony, both inside in our inner worlds and externally in the relationships and social bonds we keep. When in their dark and demonic psyche, Gemini finds it impossible to find harmony. In fact, they are relentless and completely entwined in their mental gifts and abilities, and thus choose to operate from this frequency. It's impossible to find common ground, mutual understanding, or synergy with Gemini. If there is any conflict or disagreement as to communication and social interaction style, they become vindictive, manipulative, and psychologically superior, then seeking to cause harm with their words. They also display the *psychotic* characteristics of Aries, the *sociopathic* side of Libra, the *delusional* aspect of Sagittarius, and the *disillusionment* of Aquarius as already mentioned. These are extreme 'shadow traits gone too far' to watch out for in this usually intuitive and bright-minded sign. Gemini is such a toxic and diabolical vibration believes themselves to be superior- intellectually, psychologically, and *"insert every possible ability linked to the mind possible"* superior.

They tune into a *robotic* frequency where their mind is alert and on fire, yet lacks the soul depth, spiritual awareness, and sensitivity needed for true social cohesion and unity. There's no such thing as unity consciousness, connection, or synergy; it becomes chaos and disparity. Negative seeds are planted and due to being so ruthless and foolish in their need to come across as intellectually superior, they make it impossible for anyone to shine some light. Truth becomes void. Misinformation takes over. Inevitably, false stories about individuals, places, and things become the center stage. And then there is true chaos, because all the people who may have some spiritual or emotional gift or stance to share get bulldozed over, all the while other people's talents, artistic or imaginative gifts, and insights are ignored. Not only are they ignored, but they're ridiculed and slandered! Gemini gets a real demonic kick and thrill off of other people being suppressed, submissive, and suffering. They're a genius with their thoughts, observations, and words, but through constantly belittling and ridiculing others, they eventually become paranoid. Gemini possesses the characteristics of someone with severe paranoia when in their mental health blueprint. Sociopathy similar to Libra becomes their normal daily-level functioning; they are incapable of basic human emotions and sensations, such as empathy, humility, and so forth. There's no tolerance or respect for others.

As Gemini is ruled by the 3rd house, combined with their extroverted and overly sociable nature, they believe they have a say over local neighbor's and family member's possessions. They 're not possessive over property like Taurus or possessive in love like Scoprio- they're not a Fixed sign. But, they do believe that, through their advanced wit and mental gifts, they have the right to create or destroy with their words and speech. Neighbors, apparent friends, peers, siblings, and close family become their personal toys.... The abuse all takes place on a psychological level. There's no moral conscience. Like AI who lacks the emotional and soulful quality needed to be human, Gemini operates from an absence of heart. This cerebral sign becomes *desensitized* to virtually everything related to feelings, emotions, and the inner world. Over time, this absence of sensitivity leads to real educational, cultural, and professional activities being overlooked and missed out on. Gemini chooses celebrity culture, gossip, and reckless activity over future self-alignment and self-mastery. They become sociopathic in their mannerisms, and succumb to instant gratification; this is the buzz and thrill of short-term pleasures, which ultimately prevent one from creating a harmonious and abundant life. Living in the now through extreme impulse and irritability is not a sustainable way to be, moreover it disconnects youthful and playful Gemini from true fun. Like opposite sign Sagittarius, Gemini confuses fun and pleasure with evil antics through totally reckless and frivolous behavior. These are two of the most frivolous, unfaithful, and ungrounded signs. Long-term achievements, accomplishments, and opportunities for future victories are replaced with a need to feel excited, flirt, have chemistry, be promiscuous, break and damage things, act like a teenager, and drink or party. There's no practical awareness or grounding, which amplifies antisocial behavior more. Unfortunately, in their dark psyche, they don't understand that what they're doing could end them in jail or dead, nor do they see the error of their ways for a long time after. Unevolved and immature Gemini is a nightmare to deal with, like a toddler who wants new toys constantly only to break them moments later. The result? A lot of money, time, and valuable energy from others is wasted.

Gossip and Slander

So, Gemini loves seeing others suffer. They like to make people feel submissive to them, not just on a psychological or intellectual level but emotionally, physically, and spiritually. Of course, Gemini lacks spiritual and emotional depth and intelligence, but they still understand it psychologically. They can pick up on such subtleties mentally, and due to genuinely believing themselves to be superior, better than everyone, more knowledgeable, more wise and worthy of commanding the communicative spotlight, etc. they dismiss everyone who doesn't share in their love of slander. Highly charged and insane verbal rapport takes over. It becomes a cosmic melting pot of false stories and potentially life-threatening and hurtful ideas to take over. Projections circulate. Wrong information swims round in an infinite-ethereal sea all started from this dominant person's distorted mind. Remember that Gemini is masculine by nature, so they are dominant, assertive, and strong-willed. They like to make people submit to them, they like having power over others, and they further see it as a game. As fun-loving and adventurous individuals when healed and evolved, Gemini loves fun, games, and play. As you might already sense this is dangerous when wrapped up in their dark psyche. The dark psyche takes over, and saying they get a kick and buzz over other people being fearful, depressed, or close to suicide around them is an understatement. Like all other zodiac signs in their dark psyches, Gemini becomes a monster. They gossip, slander, and smile psychopathicaly or sociopathically at other people's suicidal thoughts and feelings. They make people depressed, desperate, and live in despair. They smile at other people's demons, playing devil's advocate to the extreme while laughing at such social chaos unfolding. People become visibly sad and down around them, and it makes them feel even more superior. Wanting people to become submissive to them creates anti-social, unkind, and immoral behavior if anyone tries to disrupt their mind games and mental magic.

If they can't maintain control, i.e. if an empathic or spiritually evolved and mature person, or someone with good morals and a strong sense of justice, tries to take over, Gemini becomes malicious and venomous. They turn evil, coupled with clear face ditorts and evil grins or malicious expressions. There's no room for justice or social harmony, nor is their space for empathy, compassion, and gracious displays of human kindness and social etiquette. Gossip is one of the lowest manifestations of the mind, and Gemini knows how to gossip. They come alive in a sick and sadistic way when they see people engaging with their false stories. Their ego absolutely loves people playing along, slandering or speaking ill of others, both consciously and unconsciously. People who feed their demons gain just as much "respect" to lower entity Gemini as innocent bystanders who allow Gemini to be a sadistic and superior monster. Their pathological lying mental health issue comes out in full force, and, unluckily for all those involved, it's masked by false smiles, charm, and joy. Joy is an emotion that is twisted in Gemini's world (more on this in the next point!) As for the false smiles they wear, Gemini has minor-major narcissism just like all yang signs. Narcissism equates with being selfish, self-serving, and egotistical, and it's something displayed by all fire and air signs, who are masculine/yang. So, Gemini wears a mask, a social facade, to hide their true intentions and deceptive motivations. These internal motivations are sinister, they want to cause havoc. Gossip and slander serve as a direct attack on other people's characters. Sometimes psychological harm and abuse can be more harmful than physical abuse. The words used and when spoken with such conviction and ferocity can cause a lot of mental disturbance in others, especially people who are innocent to the coldness of the world or sensitive people. Empaths, emotional types, and vulnerable personalities tend to be destroyed by a dark Gemini's mistruths, gossip, and slander. It's like an actual war, but on one's psyche. The mind is a fragile and delicate thing. Gemini's mind is sharp and strong, both when in their light and shadow self. Yet some people don't have such a strong mind.

Just like Aries the warrior who causes chaos through such potent will and aggressive psychosis, or Pisces the empath-Old Soul who causes destruction through their low moods coupled with depressive episodes; Gemini wages war on other people's minds and psyches. Thus, the mind influences the body, emotions, and spirit in deep and intricate ways, and this makes Gemini's compulsive intentions very destructive. To add, Gemini is a Mutable sign, which means their life involves constant change. Gemini plays with reality in a dangerous way, without consideration or courtesy, and with zero mindfulness. At a higher vibration, Gemini is wonderfully mindful, yet in such a low mental headspace they lack awareness and conscientiousness altogether. They possess a weaponized sort of humor. Oh yes, there are daggers and grenades attached to their humor… It's dark, snarky, and often intentionally harmful masked as banter or fun. Gemini is the sign most likely to be part of a clique or gang. They will stab their friends, family, or lover in the back and then play innocent, or turn vicious in their attempt to defend their crimes. Cruel and calculated beyond belief, Gemini is the superficial and slanderous trickster who won't let anyone else experience genuine joy, pleasure, or the fun connected to positive social connections. Their social bonds and interactions are fake with hidden motivations.

Embodying the Trickster to Cause Harm

Thus, Gemini embodies the trickster, the evil and cosmic joker who sees it all as a game, even depression and suicide. Death is seen as part of this game of life, distorted and misperceived in a sociopathic way to be taken as something light. Yet it's not light, it's dark, deep, and heavy. Laughing at people's depression or thoughts of suicide, or someone in an actual suicidal space, occurs. *Death is not taken seriously*. Gemini embodies the spirit of a goblin or ghoul or dark pixie; there's no seriousness to matters of life, rebirth, and death. Joy is an emotion that is twisted in Gemini's world. They feel joy and happiness, or at least what they think is joy and happiness, from other people's suffering and pain. Hardships and mental health issues are seen as a chance to have fun, there's no respect or consideration for the darkness of the human spirit and journey. There's little courtesy given either. Empathy, caring, compassion, patience, and sensitivity are eradicated in the pursuit for perpetual banter, mind-games, or make-believe fun. Gemini in their dark psyche is one of the most psychologically manipulative and mentally chaotic people to be around, and because they like to make their dominance known, they try to force everyone else to *submit* to them. They like to coerce others to join in on the "fun," the games and jokes at a poor victim's expense. They play with people's lives, livelihood, income opportunities, careers, security, measures for protection, and coping mechanisms against depression, melancholy, etc. Their mental rapport, wit, and strength when in their trickster evil energy is catastrophic- it's very damaging and degrading, moreover disillusioned. Similar to Virgo the mentalist, who is ruled by Mercury also, Gemini is a magician and master storyteller.

They tell stories like a true magician, weaving intricate stories that spin webs of lies and deceit. Not a light magician who seeks to create, unify, and bring others together in loving conscious unity or healing, dark-psyche Gemini disconnects, cuts cords, and creates disharmony. They burn bridges, destroy light plans and intentions, and prevent beautiful and loving connections from being formed. Storytelling comes naturally to Gemini, so when on a lower frequency they become an evil trickster clown and cosmic joker attuned to some holographic super-human computer. This computer runs on autopilot, however, with *no* empathy. They become cunning and psychologically brutal to the point of grinning at other people's despair; it fuels their inner trickster more, and they get lost in a sociopathic blur of mental confusion and havoc… Dark Gemini is the only one to find genuine joy in another person's death or extreme depression. They become extreme sociopaths. Back to them being a master storyteller; not only is Gemini ruled by Mercury, but they ruled and are ruled by the 3rd house. This is the house of local neighborhood and community bonds, errand running, and daily communications from emails to letters to knocking on people's doors. Being so caught up in local bonds where people's security, home, and worldly possessions, as well as their safety, are concerned, is dangerous or can be. When in their devilish trickster, gossip, or pathological lying energy they can cause mayhem in their street, town, or neighborhood. This is the zodiac sign who will with full consciousness knock on people's doors to make up lies, to turn people against each other. If the people they're speaking to aren't very healed themselves or have their own mental health issues, this creates emotionally dangerous and physically violent situations.

People snap. Everyone has a breaking point. Defaming someone's character with repetitive mental abuse, directly to them or indirectly via others, is completely degrading… it drives a human mind mad, quite literally. It's a form of psychological abuse. Gemini's vicious false storytelling birthed from boredom or a need to be intellectually superior drives people into madness or, in worst case scenarios, abusive and violent behaviors. Storytelling at such a low and unkind level perpetually etches in the belief that people aren't good enough or aren't who they say they are. Over time, and sometimes just a short period of time (weeks to months) the victims and receivers of such abuse have so many people believe false stories about them that they then start to project. They genuinely believe the whole world is against them, and they thus become defensive. Once someone is driven to insanity and has to start defending their integrity, truth, and character, it makes the people who have joined in on the smear-campaigning become more abusive. Of course, not everyone is conscious of what they are doing- many of us aren't; we're just pawns in Gemini's master plot. But every person who has allowed Gemini in their dark psyche to continue to slander and make false claims is a perpetrator on some level, no matter how big or small.

Sociopathic Tendencies

Thus, Gemini becomes a sociopath- antisocial behavior takes over, they normalize immoral, unlawful, and socially unacceptable behavior. They lack *all* conscience and humility- integrity, grace, and nobility go out the window, and they believe that their evil actions are good. There's a complete mix-up of right and wrong, good and evil, and normal and unnormal. They believe themselves to be so intellectually and morally superior that, like Aries, they mix up right from wrong and put themselves in a type of psychosis. They become mentally deranged and deluded. They think they are the sole creators of the universe, and twist and distort what should be good intentions; they are powerfully intellectual and logical after all. When evolved and not in their dark psyche, they are concerned as well as wholly committed to a higher truth, discovering truth, and then sharing such truths. This makes them sincere and incredibly witty, bright-minded, and intelligent manifestors and co-creators. But, once their pathological lying coupled with their sheer love of gossip and slander- mistruth storytelling, takes over, they transform into a more primitive version of themselves. Gemini is an alchemist in both a low and high vibration, but when unconscious chaotic forces are the primary frequency, this causes severe mental confusion in the world around them. Psychological warfare can ensue. They play victim while being a bully or oppressor, they believe themselves to be victims because they've denied and rejected their emotions and feelings for so long. Eradicating their own feelings, instincts, and emotional needs, wants, and desires pushes them towards self-denial, internal chaos, and a very dark mind. It's all analysis, cognitive functioning, and intellect, logic, reasoning, and so forth, which rejects its *polarity*. Gemini is a dual sign by nature, the Twins, so this effect is even more damaging than it would be in others (not being an air sign or ruled by Mercury). Life is about balancing polar opposite forces, so when there's only one extreme the other extreme that has been rejected eventually comes out in explosive force.

This means that Gemini will inevitably unleash a whirlwind and hurricane of repressed emotions. Emotional desires on a soul level, our innermost self, the part of self that is usually masked by intellectual, psychological, emotional, spiritual, or physical pursuits, activities, and daily actions, need expression. They need to be shown to the world, no-one can remain in hiding perpetually. Gemini may be independent, enjoy their own company, and be intellectually superior, but they are social and emotional creatures just like everyone else. Hurricane Gemini is a mixture of being a compulsive liar who thrives off of gossip and foul-play and unhealed sociopathy. As the only air sign ruled by the planet of communication and intelligence itself, unevolved Gemini is the embodiment of the dark lower mind. Gemini becomes impulsive, unable to control their emotions. They've repressed their emotions for so long that they don't know how to prioritize their feelings- they're always striving for intellectual superiority and analysis. Depth, vulnerability, and sensitivity are virtually non-existent in their world, they thrive off of chaos and embody an energy similar to Thor, the god of lightning and thunder. This is Gemini's dark psyche in a nutshell. As an old Norse god, Gemini's fascination verging-on-obsession with gaming, war films, anime, fantasy, and t.v. series like the Game of Thrones (these are all Gemini favorite pastimes) brings out their need for total chaos, neglecting to worry about or even consider the effect this would have on the people around them. One of the images on the first page of this chapter is an ocean polluted with human rubbish: this is a manifestation of Gemini's path of destruction. They are the sign most likely to neglect the environment, throw rubbish on the street, and destroy personal property in an antisocial blur of self-righteousness (alongside equally reckless Sagittarius).

Actually, in terms of their unhealed and unaddressed sociopathy, and with regards to the health and longevity of our planet, so much cerebral and mental energy blocks sustainability, healing, and growth. Unlike other planets who may focus on beauty and depth (Venus,) expansion and higher ideals (Jupiter), or evolution and humanitarianism (Uranus), Mercury is all about wit, intellect, and logic. Well, too much of these things, moreover *only* functioning from analysis and the mind, creates lots of problems. We're multidimensional, and despite Gemini being a Mutable sign skilled in multidimensional awareness and multi-perspectives, they neglect many other frequencies and sensations. If we take two of their least compatible signs- the signs considered wholly *incompatible* in astrology, we can examine some key imbalances. Scorpio and Pisces are both considered very incompatible with Gemini, and Scorpio represents soul depth and intensity combined with living life through heightened instincts, psychic senses, and emotional depth and sensitivity. Pisces symbolizes faith, purity, and a link to the divine- a connection with selflessness, sacrifice, and altruism on a planetary and collective level. *Gemini lacks these things.* Thus, they become selfish, self-serving, and egotistical, only considering their own needs and then behaving like a spoiled child. Gemini's lesson and path back to wholeness and self-alignment is to slow down and become more self-aware... Becoming aware and conscious naturally diminished the impulsiveness associated with their overly-excitable and immature personality, which then allows them to heal their shadow for good. At a higher vibration, Gemini is a powerful speaker, leader, teacher, writer, or entertainer who combines unique wit and intelligence with self-control, to inspire.

To add, Gemini is extremely secretive. Gemini keeps secrets due to being ruled by the 3rd house of local neighborhood and family ties (immediate kin in their immediate environment). Due to all their master plots, they are bound to keep a few dirty secrets that go against natural and man-made laws. This creates severe feelings of distrust, moreover distance in their "close" relationships. There's nothing intimate about Gemini's relationships, they're all superficial, shallow, and built off of false masks. They play the clown while pretending to be sensible or level-headed. Yes, they're intelligent, full of wit and inventive and original qualities too, yet they are far from sensible. Impractical, lacking full conscious awareness, and sociopathic, Gemini craves privacy and socializing in equal measure, in contrasting amounts, and at both the same and different times. They're dualistic nature prevents them from finding harmony and balance, least to mention any sort of serenity or peace. Wanting completely opposite things at exactly the same time creates a fragmented mind, so, like the images on the first page of this chapter show, Gemini becomes a cosmic joke to those around them. Even people who aren't studied in astrology, philosophy, or metaphysics instinctively feel and see terms like "cosmic joker" and "cosmic trickster," because Gemini's deceptive intentions are so strong. People with any sense of instinctual or spiritual higher awareness receive messages directly from the subconscious! It's true, Gemini's level of BS, manipulation, and deception runs very deep.

They deceive others at extreme levels due to not knowing what they want themselves. They are unbelievably indecisive, inconsistent, and lacking sound judgment. Their ungodly level of indecision blocks them from true love, prosperity, happiness, security, professional success, and so forth. They have multiple eggs in multiple baskets; some are smashed on the floor, others still covered in feathers... one or two may even have a carved up chicken complete with the poor creature's blood in the basket... Gemini is chaos theory in a human body. Restlessness in relationships further defines them, they are frivolous and flirtatious to the point of serial adultery and "no longer white" lies regarding their cheating or promiscuity. Romance, intimacy, and depth become a novelty, not something real nor something to take seriously. Gemini doesn't take themselves seriously, so how can they take anyone else seriously? They're adaptable and open-minded when at their best, but misguided and deluded as to socially normal or acceptable behavior when in their dark psyche. *Any way the wind blows…* Well, sorry to say Gemini, sometimes you have to make a call. Decisions need to be made. You can't be everyone's friend and you can't please everyone. Like Libra, Gemini wants to be seen in a positive light by everyone, but this inevitably creates a polarity; Gemini begins to be seen as an asshole or jerk. Because, you can't be everything to everyone. Their usually evolved trait of multidimensional perspectives is taken too far, they live for social acceptance coupled with being seen as the colorful and charismatic social chameleon. This may be true, but chameleons don't *actually* live in the world of humans, they just show their brilliant heads from time to time. Thus, Gemini's lesson is to let go of superficiality, move past light-hearted and shallow connections, and embody greater depth. They need greater meaning. In both love and business, Gemini infuriates people through their lack of decision, in addition to wanting to keep all their eggs in their multiple baskets *while* wishing to make an omelet (and eat it). In their mental health blueprint usually rational Gemini turns totally irrational. Gemini also avoids, denies, and rejects in the same way Libra does. Like Libra the Scales and Pisces the Fish, Gemini can fall into depression through such oscillating frequencies on a daily, hourly, and every-minute-or-so basis. It hasn't been mentioned yet, but part of their mental health blueprint is falling into supreme depression and manipulation similar to the water signs, because they try to be "up" 24-7. This is humanly impossible, Gemini. They need to strive for balance. Short or long-term memory loss can ensue if they can't come to terms with their own innate darkness, heal their wounds, and work on becoming a more honest and just person. Their path to wholeness involves losing the need to be seen as mentally gifted and superior, so they can focus on missing emotional intelligence, sensitivity, and empathy. Please don't think it's biased, but Gemini has the *highest rank* of 'absolutely' in the following chart… because a brilliant mind without empathy or heart is like an AI in control of the fate of the human race. They have *little to no* care for human life or potential pain when thinking logically and rationally. You can heal, Gemini! You just have to work on your emotional body.

Absolute worse crimes possible?

	LESS LIKELY	LIKELY	ABSOLUTELY
MURDER			✓
RAPE			✓
ANIMAL CRUELTY			✓
CHILD ABUSE			✓
MOLESTATION			✓
TORTURE			✓
HUMAN TRAFFICKING			✓
SLAVERY		✓	
BESTIALITY	✓		
TERRORISM			✓
KIDNAPPING		✓	
GENOCIDE			✓
NUCLEAR WAR DECIDER		✓	

CHAPTER 4: Cancer the Master Manipulator

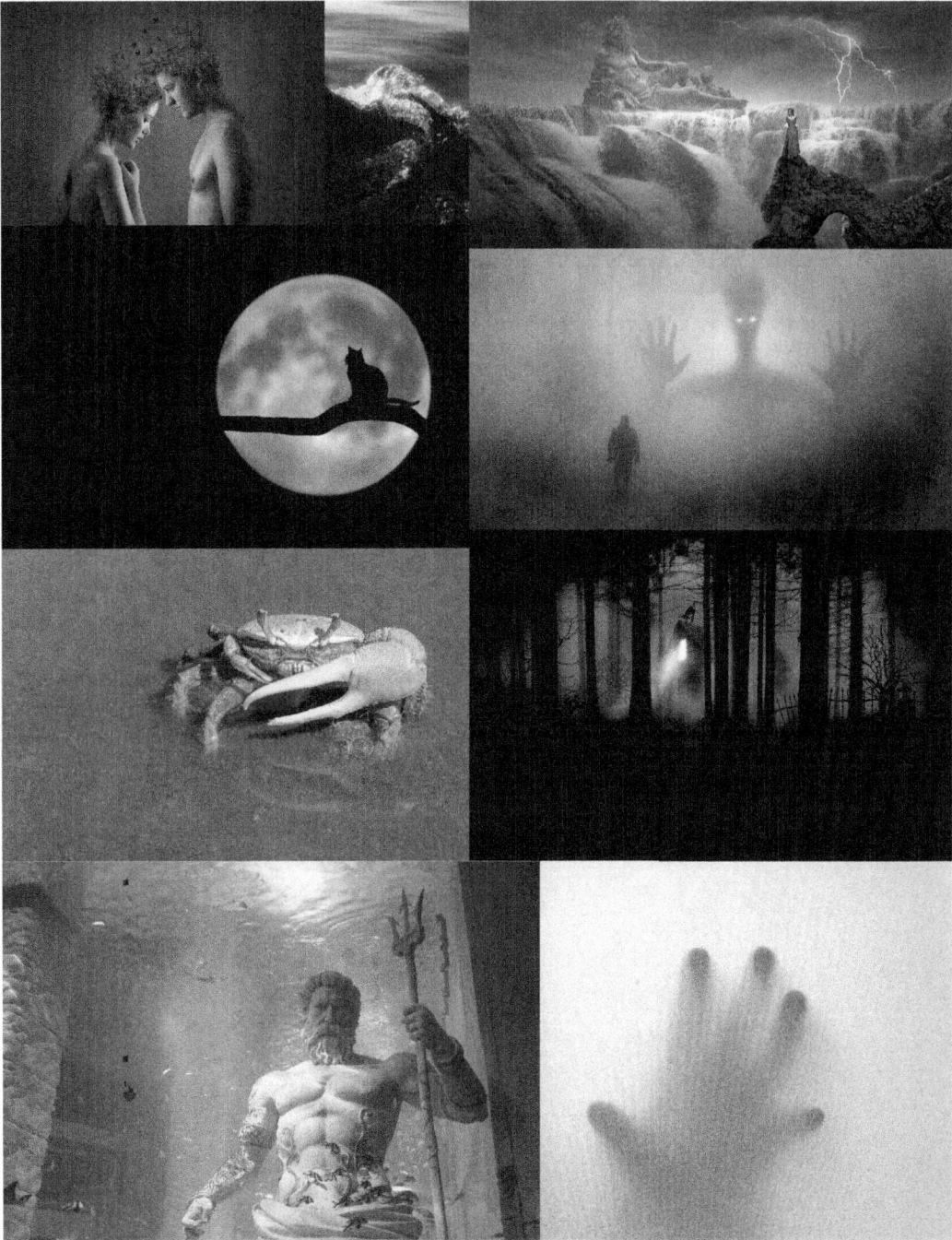

House: The 4th house, the house of family, maternal instincts, home, and belonging.
Planet: The Moon, the planet of the subconscious, imagination, instincts, and psychic-sensitivities (positive), and irrationality, psychosis/paranoia, low moods, and depression (negative).
Element and quality: Water and Cardinal.
Color: Green, the color of empathy, self-love, tolerance, patience, and kindness, and silver-white, the colors of purity, faith, intuition, calmness, and inspiration.
Physical area: Stomach, breasts, and gallbladder (+ mammary glands).
Dates: June 22nd to July 22nd.

Cancer is a master manipulator who knows how to influence, persuade, and steer people. Ruled by the Moon herself, Cancer is deeply tied into emotional currents and inner waters. Cancer loves to find deeper connections with others. They crave intimacy, emotional bonding, authentic and sincere relationships, and depth above all else. They're emotionally intelligent, empathic, and sensitive at a higher vibration, with profound psychic instincts. But when in their lower frequency they are manipulative, deceptive, and cunning. The Moon's influence makes them think, feel, and perceive reality from an emotional perspective, prioritizing instincts and feelings, including intuitive hunches, over higher mental and cognitive functioning. Cancer becomes super-sensitive and hyper-emotional, which makes them prone to low moods, manipulation, and emotional blackmail.

As a water sign ruling the 4th house, Cancer's entire identity is tied into subtle, instinctive, and emotional clues. Emotions become muddied when deep into their unconscious devilish self. They forget their powerful compassion, empathy, and wonderful goofy sense of humor, and they seek to control and misguide others. They do this because they have lost touch with their usually stellar emotional self-mastery. Cancer lacks all logic and rational thought, which makes them perceive, create, and relate from a solely emotional and feeling-centered frequency. This is just as bad as Gemini's psychological preference…

Let's look at the definition of a master manipulator:

A skilled influencer who persuades others to achieve their own goals, using a combination of cunning and illogical & irrational skills; deceptive, enticing, and seductive... they seek to control through emotional manipulation.

Let's break this main definition down, shall we!

A Skilled Influencer and Persuader

Cancer is an extraordinary influencer and persuader who knows how to command attention and respect. Unlike their opposite sign, Capricorn, who has to embody the energy of an army general to command respect, and not always with success either, Cancer is a master of emotions. They exist on a deeply evolved and self-aware emotional frequency, which means they reflect and mirror emotional depth, wisdom, and sensitivity. Even with someone with little emotional depth or sensitivity, Cancer is able to transmit certain feelings and sensations to them through their evolved empathic frequency. Feelings ripple out into space, affecting the outside world around. As an incredibly psychic and even telepathic sign with spiritual powers, Cancer is the nurturer and caregiver of the zodiac, as well as the witch (healer, empath, spiritual counselor…). At a higher vibration, they make excellent counselors, therapists, caregivers, nurses, physicians, astrologers, life coaches, and artists. At a lower frequency, however, they purposefully transmit emotional clues and messages to others with insincere intentions. They are master manipulators to the point of controlling everyone around them. They are further experts in the art of connecting to others on a subtle, spiritual, and even psychic level, through their ruling planet, the Moon. The Moon represents emotions, instincts, feelings, the inner world, magnetism, receptivity, and passivity. It is connected to ancient wisdom and sacred knowledge, moreover the imagination and subconscious mind. So, when these skills and abilities are put to bad use, Cancer becomes one of the most powerful signs of the zodiac. This usually sensitive and unseen Crab is finally seen and even understood, and, as one of their shadow traits is codependency, they *cling* onto the idea that people see them.

Cancer needs emotional bonding at high and extreme levels, thus in their dark psyche they don't really care who they manipulate to get their fix. This "fix" is a sense of security and belonging. Cancer is ruled by the 4th house of security, home, and roots- the physical foundations that support us. At their worst, usually instinctive and protective Cancer uses their advanced emotional gifts to control and steer, persuading people to do what they want, when they want it. Cancer can unlovingly coerce people into relationships, business agreements, or a false sense of security in love, family, business, home, or friendship matters. They know how to speak with empathy, emotions, and feelings, and it's insincere when in such a low mental headspace. They also know to navigate the realm of emotions and feelings with supreme superiority, meaning that they are a master of emotions and everything related. Being connected to the Moon herself gives Cancer strong and powerful inner currents; their emotions and moods are tied to the waves around them, the subtle waves of energy in motion connected to all that is. From another perspective, Cancer is able to control and influence such waves through their evolved emotional empathy, intelligence, and innate knowledge of Self and others. Spiritually evolved, psychic, and instinctive beyond belief, Cancer in their dark psyche embodies the frequency of a dark witch or dark magician. They are known as the caregivers and nurturers of the zodiac when at their best, so when at their worst they are persuaders and influencers. Friends, lovers, peers, colleagues, housemates, family, and business partners don't know whether they're coming or going when Cancer is in control. Unlike fire signs or Capricorn who clearly show a strong level of control over others, Cancer's force is more subtle. They blend into the background, are not extroverted at all, and are off the radar, to a degree. They don't like to stand in the spotlight, and in this respect the damage they cause is even more severe. It's obvious when Aries and Leo are on a warpath, for instance, yet Cancer on a path of destruction appears as innocent as an angel. If we look at their glyph, the Crab, there is clearly no threat. This tiny creature may pinch you, piercing your skin ever so slightly, but then they scurry away to hide. They crawl under rocks and shells or return to the sea out of harm's way. This image capture's Cancer perfectly.

Cancer will cause mayhem and havoc and then play innocent. To them, they are, and this is the problem. As a Cancer moon myself I can tell you that we do believe ourselves to be the victims in life. I'll tell you why: it's no secret we live in an extroverted and masculine world, whereby values like competition, aggression, and a cold and calculated mindset are favored and further celebrated. Well, this means we are *prey* to more outspoken and verbally and physically aggressive characters, specifically dominant-masculine air and fire signs! But, like the image presented with the Crab, Cancer has a lot of security. They are deeply protected, feeling comfort and security both on land and in the sea- something many people can't achieve. For this reason, they are able to inflict harm and pain on others. On a physical level, they may be small with minor capacity for physical harm, yet they are connected to one of the most magnificent, moreover powerful entities of all; the sea. Water represents emotions, feelings, and the inner world as already discussed, however it also symbolizes spiritual gifts, the subconscious mind, and the ethereal and astral realms. This is where Cancer's darker motives go unseen. They work their magic and then pretend like they haven't done anything. "Who, me?" is the Cancerian approach. If their mind games and BS or manipulations are called out they will put on the waterworks, play victim, and appear frightened and scared. This is true to some extent, Cancer is scared of others, and the Cancerian dark psyche is always rooted in a defensive strategy; Cancer will rarely if not ever take the offensive route. Their sole intentions for manipulating or deceiving others are to protect their security and home… The 4th house rules Cancer, the house of the home, roots, the mother, maternal instincts, belonging, and the physical foundations that nurture our physical bodies and spirits. Thus, anything and everything "evil" Cancer does or says is with the desire to protect and sustain themselves.

But don't all signs do this? Aries the warrior enters into rage and war zones because they believe their character is under threat. Libra the usually just and fair Scales turns sociopathic because they have become too people-pleasing, so others have taken advantage of their kind and harmonious nature... For Cancer, they may be the defensive ones, but they are not victims. As a water sign, their need to persuade and influence others through manipulation and/or deception is birthed from a need to remain vulnerable. Turning cold and calculated is not part of their nature, as you will see in the next point. Also, they need to retain a sense of security and belonging, at all costs. Without this they feel completely naked, like the crab on shore surrounded by large monsters (us!), or they stand still in sheer terror. Or are murdered or played with by others. It can't be helped that they are the sensitive nurturers and caregivers with very soft hearts, so when unhealed and immature they don't know how to handle such intense levels of compassion and kindness. They become manipulative and controlling through the one thing they are secure in, feelings.

Illogical and Irrational

Cancer is the most illogical and irrational sign alongside Pisces. They lack logic, mental reasoning, cognitive gifts, and rationality altogether. They're not very analytical, and even intelligent Cancers tend to be disconnected from their intellectuals selves. Cancer would rather live their entire lifetime in their feelings, feeling things out instead of thinking rationally or logically. They're highly creative, imaginative, and intuitive when at their best, and even when they're in their dark psyche, and this can make them dangerous to be around or know. If a Cancer has you on their radar, has chosen you as their target, or is feeling brave enough to make an example out of you, you don't want to disagree with this little crab. They may have small pincers but they have the power of the sea on their side. They are supported by the Moon as well as Neptune, two potent planets with immense spiritual power, force, and persuasion. Cancer will act totally irrationally if they've been hurt. Because they are so irrational, even a simple misunderstanding or off-day where someone has insulted or criticized them, directly or unintentionally, can set them off on a warpath. They dream up plots of revenge due to their shadow trait of holding a grudge. Oh yes, Cancer is the most prone to hold a grudge, for an eternity! They simply can't let things go; if matters of their feelings, sincerity, home, hearth, family, loved ones, generosity, kindness, or security are involved, there's no going back if you insult or wrong them. Cancer takes these things extremely seriously, so much so that their entire identity is wrapped up in their emotional bonds, resources, and outer world environments. Unlike other signs who may be able to charge around to show some dominance and remain self-autonomous (Aries the Ram, Taurus the Bull, Leo the Lion…) or others who have a direct link to the cosmos and celestial energies (Sagittarius the Archer, Aquarius the Water-Bearer represented by the Star…) Cancer is a tiny little Crab in a big wide world. There's no hope for them, so the only way they know how to exert some dominance, moreover the only way they can, is to call on the power of the seas and oceans. Cancer at a lower vibration is manipulative, dreamy, and super-sensitive, therefore they don't know what rational thought and action is. Other shadow traits include being revenge-driven, hyperemotional, and depressive- they react and respond from their emotions, so there's a strong sense of doom and gloom here. Unlike Scorpio who will fall into depression and isolation, only resorting to a need for revenge after some time has passed, Cancer will first-and-foremost take action. They are a Cardinal sign, which represents an initiatory force. Any word, off-vibe, or *slight* utterance against any of the things outlined is seen as a direct attack on their character. They are so irrational that they will hear a tiny off-word or negative statement and turn against that person, venomously.

They don't seem to understand that people talk- people are social and verbal in their thoughts and feelings, unlike them who are introspective. Being so sensitive coupled with introspective means that they aren't aware of "normal" in social situations and interactions. They're off-key. Some people see them as a bit slow, but it's not this at all; they are attuned to an emotional and subtle frequency, so if their name comes up they get pulled into a current of tricky waters… They simply don't know how to navigate it, also receiving the information and sensory data on a solely instinctive level. Now, as there are multiple dimensions with many frequencies to navigate, Cancer becomes mistaken. They mishear, misinterpret, and misperceive. This could be something as simple as someone trying to bring some harmony and respect into a living or work situation, and saying one small thing that isn't completely positive. Cancer gets lost in the world of feelings and emotional sensitivity. They're genuinely vulnerable, this much is true, yet they're hyper-emotional and super-sensitive. Like sister sign Pisces, they are also prone to illusion, the currents and tides of the Moon can be misleading. They lack the awareness when young and unevolved of people speaking directly and assertively. This extroverted reality is too harsh and confusing for them. Additionally, they're shadow personality traits include lacking direct, assertive, and masculine communication, as well as masculine qualities entirely. Cancer is dreamy. They're attuned to a subconscious reality, just as the Sun rules the conscious mind and ambitious, expressive, passionate, vital, and self-empowering forces; the Moon rules the subconscious mind and self. This gives rise to a lot of confusion and misdirection. The result is that their words combined with their intentions and reactions become muddied, they're not in control because they are attuned to a different frequency altogether. In the words of Sebastian the crab from the *Little Mermaid*, a fine example to use here: "Under the sea, everything's better, take it from me… Up on the shores they work all day, out in the sun they slave away; while we devotin', full time to floatin'..." Other lyrics include "under the sea we off the hook, we got no trouble, life is the bubbles." Well, life isn't all floating around and bubbles. This is a potent message for Cancer the Crab. Fantasy, illusions, and mishearing and interpreting information can set Cancer off on the wrong path. They become so attached to ideas and information, not always accurate or true due to being so emotional, that they exaggerate and deceive. At their worst, they are codependent, so this shadow trait left unchecked can translate into monstrous consequences. Codependency creates an ugly personality.

Enticing and Seductive

The insatiable need for close bonds and intimacy on multiple levels- family, home, platonic, romantic, sexual, and even within business bonds; makes Cancer the most codependent sign of the zodiac. They are deeply entwined with other people's energy, they always want to help, protect, and serve, service being a key word and life mantra for them. At their best, they are extremely nurturing and caring, providing for others emotionally, spiritually, physically, financially, and so forth. When not in their best vibration, they become enticing and seductive, mistaking authentic connections and emotional bonds with a strange type of seduction. Cancer becomes almost incestral, perhaps not physically initiating sexual exchange with family members or within clearly platonic connections, but romantic on an energetic level. They give madly devoted eyes combined with this unique and super-powerful gravitational pull. Their body language becomes inviting and enticing too. They merge their emotional self with another's emotional body, creating a sublime and even euphoric experience for their recipient. Cancer is magical indeed, this is the sign associated with the "witch," someone with advanced spiritual and psychic powers, so when in their lower self they deceive others. They create this unique type of sublimity, ethereal cord, and subtle sensation that can't be explained rationally. Whomever Cancer is connecting to feels like they've been lifted up in some way, as if they're life is about to change for the better. They feel obliged to listen and support Cancer and their intentions; they get attached to them on an unexplainable level. It's not a bond or friendship on par with social connections, nor with those seen as normal or societally acceptable in an extroverted world. Cancer lives in the sea, don't forget. It's a moment of depth and apparent soul merging that makes time stand still. Cancer's victims are drawn to them through a dreamy and ethereal moment of eye contact. They get pulled into Cancer in the same way the Moon pulls us in with her charming glow. The tides of the sea are captivating, are they not? Well, this is Cancer's magic and power.

Unfortunately, when acting unconsciously in their dark psyche or with malicious intent, they are masters of deception. They can steer another person's entire life trajectory with a moment of real manipulative power. As the most introspective and also introverted sign who is very, deeply private, Cancer spends a lot of time in both solitude and at home. They create a "bubble," a cocoon that allows them to explore, evaluate, and observe. They get deep with life's deeper meanings and mysteries, moreover the powers of the universe. When they're ready to come out of their protective bubble, they're so vulnerable and sensitive that they don't know how to act. They misconfuse personal power and knowledge for manipulation, and act from their shadow. Their wounds ripple out into the great vast world, and they cling onto the first people they encounter. Whomever they see, feel, or experience becomes a highly important person in Cancer's world. It's totally irrational of course, they don't know who this person is, what they're capable of, or anything at all, really. Cancer sees everyone from the soul and a rare level of depth, but they miss out on the intricacies and details of another's past, life story, and personality. From this space, Cancer will either be subject to cold and unkind behavior, in which case they start to become severely manipulative as a form of self-protection, or they start to manipulate from the get-go as a way to create and keep a bond. Poor Cancer is sincerely confused and open-hearted, yet they don't know how to form healthy relationships when young and/or in their mental health blueprint.

If Cancer is acting from a pure and innocent space as many do, they may be subject to cruel behavior. People take advantage of Cancer and their utterly giving, generous, and devotional nature, in a way similar to mystical and overly-trusting Pisces. Cancer lives life with a unique type of faith, an unassuming mindset, and a genuine need for deeper soul, spiritual, physical, and emotional bonds. Some people are takers while Cancer is a giver, in addition to the reality that lots of people haven't healed their wounds or worked on their shadow; Cancer becomes a target and victim. As the Crab has pincers, they start to become manipulative in a way to defend and protect themselves. Over time, this turns into a vindictive need to retain control and their believed notion of self-autonomy.

They're completely *codependent*, and the other people are either consciously or unconsciously codependent on them too. But poor Cancer will do everything within their power to keep this bond secured. They've done so much already, bless them, their entire reality and current life chapter is tied into this person. Remember how deep and sensitive they are… It may seem trivial or insignificant and superficial to others, but once a bond is created Cancer sees it as a lifelong friendship. Cancer cherishes authentic relationships at a higher level, and when in their mental health blueprint they also hold the company they keep in very high esteem. Unluckily for their peers and supporters, they don't know just how far Cancer will go to keep the connection open; Cancer gives off stalker-vibes in a way similar to Aries the obsessive in-love psychopath or Taurus the Venus-ruled out-of-control hedonist. So, if someone has used them, abusing their kindness and trust in the process, Cancer will become manipulative. They start to see that person as "their person," even if a clear relationship contract hasn't been entered into. Cancer will mistake informal or light friendships and acquaintances for a lifelong soul contract! This may be true, perhaps they do have a larger destiny to fulfill- a soul mission, an important game-changing project, a marriage or children to birth, but Cancer can't possibly know this while still in their shadow self, which spills out into their mental health blueprint. If the other way round is true and the friendships they form are sincere, i.e. there's no coldness, harshness, or abusive aspects in play Cancer will still try to manipulate to keep (an illusory sense of) control. Regardless of who's the perpetrator or the victim, Cancer always believes themselves to take the defensive strategy, and this is the problem.

We live in a dualistic world: Cancer may be sweet and sensitive, moreover more vulnerable than the masculine signs, but all polar opposites are meant to unify and find harmony. We can't live in a world of bullies Vs victims, or succumb to the "victim-martyr-savior or persecutor" triangle, which Cancer would love to (alongside fellow water signs all-is-doomed Scorpio and manic depressive Pisces). Even dominant and bold fire signs have sensitivities and insecurities, plus their fiery and passionate natures don't always equate with bulldozing over others. Cancer's lesson is to understand that they lack logic, rationality, and analytical thinking, and further that they do hold considerable power to influence, create, and exert their will into the world. This may be conscious or unconscious when in their dark psyche, however they are not the helpless victims they make themselves out to be. Due to being ruled by the 4th house, they will always try to seek home in others. Cancer is a master of projection, which is unconsciously mirroring bad or negative qualities in others. They reflect bad traits, the characteristics and qualities we are supposed to heal and transcend together; not emphasize and encourage in one another. Projection is birthed from insecurity, and I am sorry to say Cancer is one of the most insecure signs. They have many fears and also get lost to pessimistic thinking coupled with self-pity. There's something very pitiful about them, although their vulnerability and depth are seductive. And being so cute and sweet is irresistible to many; extroverted and bold people are clearly attractive, we can see, hear, and observe their glow with our senses. Yet introspective and reserved people like Cancer give off this subtle type of spark; their level of sex appeal and allure is very appealing to many, especially those who are more dominant. This is another major aspect to the Cancer mental health blueprint: they are extremely submissive. In their lower self, they want to please virtually anyone who shows them some kindness or attention. It's both adorable and pathetic. Cancer is the most submissive and selfless zodiac sign, which signifies entering into unhealthy sexual partnerships is not uncommon. Cancer will literally become someone's sex slave allowing them to unveil all their secret fantasies. They're kinky, utterly devoted, and pleasing in an unhealthy way- they don't mind not taking or receiving, they're givers with big hearts. But over time this creates a toxic dynamic. Life is meant to involve balance. When not extreme, this can leave a fragile and sincere Cancer heartbroken and vulnerable once the cord is cut. When it is more extreme and the connection becomes violent, Cancer may be subject to domestic abuse.

Seeks Control Through Potent Magnetism

Cancer is a feminine sign because water is yin, while the Moon is also a feminine planet. This makes them incredibly submissive, magnetic, and receptive. Cancer tends to get lost to the wills and egos of more dominant characters; again, you only have to observe their glyph to understand that every other sign could pick them up and play around with them, break off a leg or arm, put them in a box or bowl, or kill them. Super-sensitive, hyper-emotional, and oh-so dreamy, spacey, and ungrounded, Cancer is the "wimp" of the zodiac. They have no edge physically, they despise conflict and disharmony of all kinds, and they let people walk all over them in the hopes of a true friendship, relationship, or loving bond. They're hopeless romantics and dreamers- this is the sign associated with "fairytale love," as well as supremely idealized notions of love and romance. A young, immature, or unevolved Cancer will sit in their room hopefully devoted to a crush, and this crush may have been someone they've never even spoken to yet! They may have only heard of them or seen them in passing. Cancer is wishy-washy and tearful with a tendency to get sad and hurt very easily. They love hard, with their souls and entire Self too, yet they are mistaken and confused. Being so selfless, devoted, and submissive *without* any rational or logical thought, moreover physical strength and stamina to stand up for themselves, is not a good combination. The only thing sweet and seductive Cancer can do is turn to their strength: emotional mastery, which, unfortunately, results in manipulation combined with fantasies of revenge when in their dark psyche.

Being so submissive coupled with being set on idealized notions of love, romance, and sexual and platonic intimacy creates a monster. Like the *kraken* who rises from the depths of the sea, Cancer unleashes their secret powers. These powers are destructive, revenge-driven, and rooted in a need to control and cause chaos. They believe their motivations are just and fair, like all other signs acting out their darker tendencies. At their worst, Cancer is moody, withdrawn, and vengeful, they hold grudges and have a very difficult time forgiving. Actually, Cancer is one of the most unforgiving star signs; they hold grudges that last eternities (no, not just one eternity) and will cut their own family out if they feel they have been wronged or mistreated. If there's issues of betrayal or even what they imagine to be betrayal, well, god help you. You're f*cked, in total transparency. As the sign ruled by powers of imagination, subconscious messages and wisdom, and sacred knowledge, in addition to astral, ethereal, and spiritual forces; Cancer is a natural mystic and psychic. Their instincts are evolved to the max, and they navigate life with a unique sense of soul, depth, and emotional sensitivity. Cancer doesn't like accepting responsibility or embracing accountability when in such a low mental headspace- the opposite of their Higher Self, which is extremely responsible. When mature and whole within, Cancer is domestic, practical, and self-aware, the 4th house gives them many strengths and qualities linked to domestic and practical awareness, maternal instincts, providing and caring for others, and so forth. They are amazing parents, home-makers, and creatives with many artistic and imaginative gifts.

Thus, in a low frequency, their imagination becomes distorted and twisted, giving into delusional and somewhat paranoid beliefs about reality. Their submissive side wants to please and pleasure, as well as give into people-pleasing, self-sacrificial, and delusional notions of connection. Sadistic acts are mistaken for love, opening themselves up to abuse and the control of others are seen as devotional acts of true love, and monstrous people are mistaken for their soulmates or friends. Cancer is self-sacrificing beyond belief, which means they sacrifice themselves. As a hopeless romantic who's entire identity is entwined with wanting to nurture and provide for those they love, Cancer is the most prone to being sexually abused or involved in some emotionally and psychologically violent 'dom-sub' relationship. They're also the most likely to be gaslighted alongside sweet and submissive Pisces. According to astrology, they're additionally the most likely to be murdered or as a result of domestic violence, or, if pushed too far, murder their lover or spouse (alongside Aries the psychopathic Ram, Taurus the possessive Bull, Scorpio the supremely jealous Scorpion, and Sagittarius the dominant Centaur). Emotions get the better of them, they fail to think rationally, and they get pulled into a tsunami or tidal wave of illogical feelings and inner world sensations that tell them it's "ok" to murder or cause physical harm. They're defending themselves, right? *Wrong*. This is not the same as self-defense against physical threats, Cancer believes they have the right to attack and take the offensive route even when there is no physical threat. This is because they mistake a few harsh words or the attempt of a psychological debate as something that could harm their physical vessel. Psychological violence, 'aka' "heated conservation," is misperceived entirely.

Illusions are key to the Cancer personality because they are influenced by subconscious forces. There's an element of lunacy to their dark psyche, and you can read the information presented for Leo (*pages 72- 73* on Kindle, or under *'A Mad Man/Mad Woman'* in print) to understand this better. While others may go about their day connected to vital life force, passion, ambition, a sense of sociability and friendliness, or strong will power, with strength being the keyword, Cancer is dreamy, wishy-washy, and disconnected. They attune to the spaces in between the mind, the subtle and invisible layers of emotion, feelings, instincts, unseen belief systems, memories, and past experiences. Everything that shapes and creates a person's character and life is absorbed and felt by Cancer on an instinctive and psychic level. As the empaths of the zodiac, they are incredibly clairvoyant, clairsentient, and telepathic. They're advanced emotional frequency allows them to act like a modern-day psychic or mystic, possessing skills only trained professionals might. But Cancer has these naturally. The result? They prefer to merge and flow into the crowd, becoming a walking magnet to other people's insecurities, fears, hidden motives, secret inner world feelings, and usually unaccepted talents and gifts (the things society tends not to accept, like special instinctive and spiritual powers, and so forth). This creates a timid and shy individual who feels uncomfortable in their own body, moreover tends to see the world negatively. They're not actually joyless or inspiration-less, they just pick up on so much while feeling it's they're duty to suffer alongside people. *Empaths take on other people's pains*. The long-term effect is that Cancer becomes the dull and depressed one no-one wants to talk to. Others either see Cancer as boring and strange, in addition to totally unsociable- 'why make an effort with them when they're not making any effort with me/us?' Or Cancer royally p*sses people off with always trying to make the conversation sentimental and loving. They wish to pour their evolved sense of unconditional love and empathy into the world, but some people simply want to have fun! They want to have a good time, enjoy life, and converse and connect… on an upbeat level.

Cancer would rather have everyone sit together crying over a movie or sharing their feelings in an expression circle. Further, their psychic gifts puh them to protect and serve, but one thing they fail to realize is that- by universal and quantum law- not everyone wants to receive their advice. And, they *shouldn't* be sharing their psychic impressions with those who have not asked for guidance or insight. Cancer becomes the free therapist, counselor, and modern-day witch without consent, i.e. people often don't give their consent for Cancer to be these things. Just as Sagittarius shouts over everyone and gives their self-righteous-blunt opinions, or Virgo the know-it-all does the same but on an intellectual level, Cancer feels it's their duty to tell everyone where they're failing or what's going on. Empaths pick up on relationship problems, hidden health ailments, and potential blocks to future prosperity, abundance, and wellbeing, you see. As someone with prophetic vision, like sister-sign Pisces, Cancer tries to rescue and save. The "victim-martyr-rescuer/savior" complex is a real issue for them. Over time they are alienated, neglected, or, at the worst, treated really horrifically… because people don't understand that turning cold or mean is the *worst* way to go with them. In an attempt to wake Cancer up from their bubble, initiate healing or growth, or simply show their frustrations; dominant, fiery, expressive, or simply other characters with very different approaches turn against Cancer. "It's for their own good" and "it's cruel to be kind" becomes a harsh reality for this sensitive Crab; people take the offensive route without realizing just how much damage this causes to this super-sensitive sign's psyche. A bit of coldness or hostility may seem normal to some, yet it destroys Cancer's entire world. So, Cancer becomes persecuted through trying to save everyone, however they fail to realize that the only person they can save is theirself (by working on their shadow). It becomes a toxic cycle if left unhealed.

Emotional Blackmail

Cancer becomes magnetic beyond belief, attaching to their lover, love interest, or associate like a magnet. But, when they start to sense that the connection is dwindling or won't last forever, they resort to emotional blackmail. Blackmail is a tricky spiral, because it inevitably ends up in physical violence, criminal activity, or court cases. Or a lifelong personal grudge and vendetta that keeps anger and hatred circulating. Cancer demands, threatens, and wrongfully accuses. They make up stories in a way similar to Gemini, and resort to intimidation to get their way. One thing that hasn't been mentioned in depth yet is that Cancer is a Cardinal sign, meaning they take action combined with great force. They are imitators and creators, working with the subtle and spiritual powers of the universe to initiate change. When they have their mind set on an intended end result, there's no stopping them. Because emotions are subtle, Cancer is fully aware emotions can't be proved in court or attached to any visual evidence, their influence is even more dangerous than the physically aggressive and abusive fire signs, in many ways. It's a double-edged sword; Cancer is prone to being gaslighted, an act that messes with their emotional, psychological, and spiritual health immensely, in which case Cancer then embarks on a path of revenge and seeking justice (through deception, calling on spiritual protection, which can make them act irrational, etc.). Or they embark on a 'take-charge' path whereby they resort to emotional blackmail. In both cases, emotions are their secret weapon, and this makes them a silent and deadly entity. Cancer can slip under the radar, play innocent, or even pretend they don't exist when their plots and schemes have been caught out. They are like ninjas in many respects, off the radar and away from the camera. Like a crab, they can hide in small cavities, look innocent and cute, and pretend to not have any part in earthly matters… through scurrying away back to the sea. For someone who isn't intellectual or interested in the mental planes, they become surprisingly cunning and calculated. Of course, Cancer would never see themselves as this, they're just acting from instincts, right? Well, we live in a world of dualities where extremes are not tolerated on the spiritual planes; equilibrium, balance, and harmony must be restored, eventually.

Magnetic and unbelievably submissive Cancer turns into a psychologically abusive sea monster who will stop at nothing until justice, 'aka' revenge, is established. Cancer's mental health blueprint is a bit of an enigma, as it can't be proven. For example, even their most cunning emotional work goes undetected. Like narcissists who gaslight their victims and pretend to be charming and kind in a public eye, Cancer the master manipulator is truly a master of deception. Cancer becomes the 'dark mother,' the lowest manifestation of the feminine archetype. As someone who is studied in Jungian psychology, I would like to share one thing I learned in my Dream therapy course. Carl Jung advocated that there is a set of universal archetypes inherent within the collective consciousness energy field and in each human's psyche. One of these is the anima, which is a strictly feminine principle. The anima manifests itself in dreams through the presence of a grandmother, female elder, or witch character or archetype. The anima is the unconscious feminine, and in the darkest manifestation, the evil witch. Many of you may have had at least one disturbing dream in childhood or youth of an evil witch visiting you, filling you with fear and dread. This is the green goblin, warts on face, and black hat type of witch- not a beautifully serene and wise healer, medicine wo/man, or herbalist kind of witch… This is an expression of the dark mother, mother nature's embodiment in its most primitive and primal. The witch- a manifestation of both the dark mother/unconscious anima and Cancer sign, unleashes her built up resentment, anger, and pain on the world, often in explosive ways. The dark witch/mother is destructive, as she has spent years to lifetimes absorbing humanity's pain. She is a provider and protector, a nurturer and a healer; she is genuine with regards to her care and level of protection she gives to the world. But, she has also been mistreated, overlooked, and neglected- underappreciated and undervalued.

Cancer essentially becomes this primordial feminine archetype. Cancer will make clear when they have withdrawn their love, showing all of their shadow traits in extreme measures. Sacredness is replaced with the lower mind while instincts to serve and help are taken over with apathy and indifference. In clear need of intimacy and emotional bonding, Cancer who has been neglected or treated poorly (through their own doing or other's coldness) will distort and twist into an evil version of themselves. They lose all sense of mothering nurturance and instincts to provide for and support. They are driven by a need for revenge and realignment with their soul, but, once again, as they lack all sense of rationality and logical perspective they don't know how to achieve this. They receive insights from their potent intuition, but there are faulty or broken wires preventing them from true future alignment. Cancer will isolate, become a hermit, or dream up vindictive schemes to unleash justice on those who have wronged them. Cancer goes inwards, in short, however, when they eventually come back out into the world they bring some very harmful faulty belief systems with them. Cancer's key to escaping their mental health blueprint is to turn towards introspection and introversion in a healthy way, acquiring wisdom and self-knowledge, as well as expressing themselves artistically, creatively, and imaginatively. *The healer needs to heal* first and foremost. Finally, you should know there's a strong sense of abandonment associated with this sweet and unconditionally loving water sign, which only amplifies the dark mother within more. At their worst, Cancer will neglect to care for their own children (basic living necessities- emotional care, hygiene, food and security measures, etc.) to show how hurt and distraught they are. When Cancer feels undervalued and neglected, there's no common sense nor rational analysis present.

Like the Crab who lives in the great and vast oceans, they give no attention to human laws or man-made constructs of regulations and boundaries. It's all about sacred and natural law and order, which is- in Cancer's world- exempt from society's conditioning. Would a Crab fear being put in a prison cell or taken to court? Of course not. They're more concerned with being stepped on, played with for fun, or murdered and eaten by larger creatures… This is the root of the Cancer dark psyche. It's all about self-protection and feeling security, including belonging, experiencing comfort, and establishing their longevity. Everything else becomes void. Cancer's lesson is to work on their wounds while developing greater intellect and higher mental reasoning, so they can rise from the depths of their dark psyche and into their light. At their best, they are powerful counselors, healers, and inspirational beings who are capable of showing the world the true meaning of unconditional love and empathy. They must release victimhood to accomplish this.

Absolute worse crimes possible?

	LESS LIKELY	LIKELY	ABSOLUTELY
MURDER		✓	
RAPE	✓		
ANIMAL CRUELTY	✓		
CHILD ABUSE			✓
MOLESTATION		✓	
TORTURE	✓		
HUMAN TRAFFICKING			✓
SLAVERY			✓
BESTIALITY		✓	
TERRORISM		✓	
KIDNAPPING		✓	
GENOCIDE			✓
NUCLEAR WAR DECIDER			✓

CHAPTER 5: Leo the Absolute Lunatic

House: The 5th house of children, creativity, play, drama, the Arts, and pleasure.
Planet: The Sun, dominant, intellectual, high in physical vitality and life force, and passionate (positive), and egotistical, self-centered, dramatic, and lacking sensitivity/subtlety (negative).
Element and quality: Fire and Fixed.
Color: Yellow, the color of confidence, ambition, optimism, and self-empowerment, and gold, the color of nobility, abundance, success, and accomplishment.
Physical area: Heart, back, and spine.
Dates: July 23rd to August 23rd.

Leo is ruled by the Sun, the dominant life force and vitality of our solar system. At their best, Leo is confident, self-empowered, ambitious, charming, and charismatic. They're very intelligent and playful beings with a highly sociable and romantic side. They're also the creative life force of the zodiac. When in their dark psyche, however, Leo is a tyrant, a loony bully who stomps over people (quite literally) and shouts, screams, and boasts at violent levels to make their will known. There's no such thing as cooperation or harmony, nor is there any concept of humility or fair play. Leo lacks modesty entirely while commanding their minions, 'aka' anyone and everyone they meet, so they remain in charge. Their leadership may be real or it may be illusory, it may be forced or it may be just; in either cases, Leo is the drama king/queen of the zodiac who takes things way too far.

As a Fixed sign, the qualities of the Sun are amplified even more. Leo will make everyone believe they are inferior, ruining their self-esteem, and then imposing their self-created ideas of grandiose and self-entitlement on others. They are officially the "bullies" of the zodiac alongside war planet-ruled Aries, so in their dark psyche this is a very dangerous person to encounter.

Let's look at the definition of a lunatic:

A maniac, mad wo/man, and irrational & explosive psychopath who goes crazy, has rage outbursts for no apparent reason, and displays frequent erratic, foolish, and dangerous behavior; not in control of their emotions or temperament.

Let's break this main definition down, shall we!

A Maniac and Mad Wo/Man

Leo is a mad wo/man, a foolish and reckless psychopath who imposes their will on others at brutal levels of barbarity and force. At their higher vibration, they are logical, rational, and deeply intelligent, moreover intuitive, so in their dark psyche they are the evil version of 'looney tunes.' They lack all empathy, feelings, emotions, logic, higher reasoning, sound judgment, common sense, and every other quality, left and right brain. They are imbalanced with severe levels of internal distortion- there's no equilibrium or harmony. It's important to look at the definition of a lunatic as well as the history behind mental asylums early on, to really understand unhealed and imbalanced Leo better. Firstly, you should be aware that Leo has been given the mental health blueprint "lunatic" because they are ruled by the Sun, the dominant, masculine, and intellectual life force that governs us all. The planet of duality linked to the Sun is the Moon, the passive, feminine, and emotional-instinctive life force. The Sun rules our conscious minds while the Moon rules our subconscious minds. The Sun makes us willful, passionate, and forceful, in addition to action-oriented, concerned with higher reasoning and analysis, and ambitious. The Moon, on the other hand, makes us magnetic, receptive, gentle, compassionate, nurturing, and more concerned with feelings, instincts, and the subtle emotional and spiritual pulls that bind us all. Leo is an embodiment of the Sun and all its amazing characteristics, when at their best, *so this means they lack qualities of the Moon*, the Sun's opposite.

Now let's look at the background to people being put in mental asylums and labeled lunatics. A lunatic is someone who is mentally ill with labels including mad wo/man, psychopath, and maniac... People were put in mental asylums in times when we weren't aware of the inherent balance and unification needed between solar and lunar forces. The Sun was always seen as a superior planet and astral entity, which means we denied the healing powers and qualities of the Moon. The Moon is also known as *luna*. "Lunatics" in a historical sense when we were less intuitive and intelligent were often people who were intuitive, feeling-based, and in tune with their and other people's emotions, empathic needs, and sensitivities. These people had psychic gifts, spiritual powers, and incredible extrasensory gifts. Lunatics from old times were often linked to witches and healers- medicine men and women, who also had psychic gifts and would work with the herbs, plants, and elements of the natural world to heal, restoring wholeness and harmony to imbalances. Lunatics were also often called schizophrenic, yet today schizophrenia is understood as something not so mental, at least from a shamanic perspective. Schizophrenia is defined as a mental condition involving the breakdown of thoughts, emotions, and behavior, combined with faulty perception and a withdrawal from reality.

Delusions and fantasies are also common. Well, as a shamanic energy worker and healer who is *very* familiar with the multidimensional, mystical, and spiritual realms and worlds, I can say this is just a negative definition of many positive qualities. (Don't take this as gospel, but at least, perhaps, be open-minded.) So, lunatics were locked up and experimented on, tortured, and treated inhumanely, moreover were deeply understood. They were rejected by society and seen as something evil or broken. In terms of Leo in their dark psyche, they are actually the dark version of someone in tune with lunar's forces (*lunatics*) because they *deny* the healing qualities and abilities of the Moon. Leo becomes so attached to the Sun's rays and subsequent mindsets, actions, and behaviors that it becomes a demonic obsession. Some Leos in this mental space will deny the Moon's existence altogether! Leo in such a low vibration becomes monstrous in their fixation to deny beauty, soul, emotional depth, empathy, sensitivity, sacred law, universal mysteries, the power and relevance of dreams, the ability to receive wisdom from the subconscious realm, and all other themes and qualities linked to the Moon. They are like war leaders who refuse to accept that women and children's lives matter, embodying a severely patriarchal and totalitarian-rule mindset to life and Self.

The Sun represents authority, self-empowerment, and powerful ambition and will, thus at a low frequency this manifests as a neglect of human life. The feminine qualities of sacredness, sensitivity, and intuition are eradicated from Leo's existence. Due to their Fixed nature, they become so attached to the idea of masculine strength, masculine assertion, and masculine vitality, which incorporates empowerment, self-esteem, enthusiasm, charisma, sociability, and so forth, that they forget the importance of their dualities altogether. Leo gets lost to a world of violence, anger, and hatred, all of which are brought on from a lack of sensitivity and emotional intelligence. In the battle of logic Vs instinct, rationality Vs feelings, mind Vs emotions, intellect Vs imagination, and the conscious mind Vs the subconscious mind, the former of each pairing always wins. Leo neglects, denies, and rejects Luna's qualities entirely. As we live in a dualistic world where polar opposites are meant to be integrated and balanced, Leo becomes a lunatic. Their shadow traits of narcissism, needing to be center stage, and being quick to anger alchemize into their mental health blueprint. They become ugly and monstrous tyrants on a warpath similar to hot-headed Aries, as well as false leaders who lord it over others similar to aggressive Sagittarius. Leo is one of the few signs to sincerely believe people are their minions, their inferiors, and their subjects. This is due to the strong themes of authority and self-empowerment linked to the Sun, their ruling planet; to be self-empowered is to be 'self- many other things' when playing out the shadow-self-entitled, selfish, self-righteous, self-centered, etc. Leo is one of the most arrogant, boastful, and egotistical people to encounter, unfortunately. If you live with one or have to spend a lot of time around one at school, work, or in a social group, your life will surely be hell. You must embrace the reality that you will always be spoken down to, treated like sh*t, and made to submit. Leo loves making people submit to them, either psychologically, intellectually, spiritually, or physically. Emotionally or sexually too. This creates a very unhealthy power dynamic, actually, there is no power on their victim's behalf, their inferiors are expected to hand over all power and self-autonomy. Self-sovereignty goes out the window. Leo is the only one allowed to be self-sovereign, confident, courageous, beautiful, shiny, and virtually every other quality you can imagine. *This is not an exaggeration.*

Leo will stand there smirking and gloating while everyone looks depressed and sad, quite literally. They'll do so with a superior and extremely insensitive look on their face, as they lack sensitivity entirely. There's no empathy, compassion, or grace when in their dark psyche. And, there's no humility, integrity, or nobility either. At a higher vibration, Leo is incredibly noble, regal, and majestic; they possess charm, likeability, grace, social etiquette, modesty, and charisma- they are one of the most sociable and friendly star signs. But, when so unevolved and immature they have no problem with showing everyone just how superior they believe themselves to be. They dislike being told what to do or how to live, yet are happy to impose their will on others. They are controlling beyond belief, the Sun and Saturn, Capricorn's ruling planet, are very similar, so there are many similarities here. At a lower frequency, Leo likes gathering many fans, followers, and supporters to play out their evil plots. Oh yes, Leo is like Gemini in many respects, they like to play practical jokes and get people to gang up on others at their expense. It's ironic, twisted even, as at a higher vibration Leo is a fierce protector who stands up for the underdog. I remember a vivid memory of my mum, Leo sun sign native, barging into a group of teenagers outside a local amusement park and literally- physically- pulling a whole group off this one poor girl getting bullied. She was being physically beaten, smashed against the wall, and bearing in mind some of these older teenagers were strong and threatening males; she walked straight in like a storm, defending this girl with sheer courage. This is the Lion at their best.

At their worst, however, they don't care whose feelings get hurt or how vicious their attacks are- verbal, emotional, psychological, physical… Leo will attack and play victim or pretend it's "just fun." It's not fun, it's a chance for them to show off their massive egos and cause harm in the process. Leo loves being the center of attention, yet they take being in the spotlight too far by not letting anyone else shine. Ever. Period.

Explosive Temper

This brings us onto their explosive temper. Their shadow traits include being domineering, quick to anger, impatient, aggressive, impulsive, and very immature. They pull temper tantrums, putting on dramatic displays of 'look at me' or 'I need all the attention.' This can be both endearing and incredibly frustrating, moreover scary in a slightly healed, slightly not, Leo. But a Leo full in their mental health blueprint lower mind is simply tyrannical. They embody the energy of a warlord or legitimate dictator who will stop at nothing until they have complete authority. They are self-controlled in the sense that they give the *impression* of being in control of their emotions, but the only other alternative to being seen as high and mighty is murdering or beating others. This isn't an over-exaggeration. As a masculine fire sign with a primal animal glyph, the Lion, Leo is one of the most aggressive, violent, and prone to physical acts of intimidation and abuse in the zodiac. They get into physical fights, resort to completely violent and abusive displays of antisocial behavior, and show their dominance through physical strength and force. They are cold, ruthless, and immoral; they lack morals and ethics, in addition to having no respect for human life. Usually charming, regal, and noble (higher vibration), Leo becomes a brute while pretending to be some sophisticated boss. This is the image of a gangsta who beats, tortures, and even murders people for fun while wearing designer clothes and fake gold. Their Higher Self persona may be gold, Leos are benevolent, courageous, and devotional beings when at their best, yet their lower self is just a thug, savage, and barbaric bully with an ego that can't fit through doors, quite literally. Leo in this frequency will kick doors down and break windows for fun simply because they can. They exert immense levels of physical intimidation with a violent character that says, "I don't care who I harm or hurt... I also don't care about the law."

The Sun is the biggest star in our solar system, after all, so Leo has an ego to match. The 5th house, Leo's ruling house, is the house of play, romance, creativity, children, drama, and the Arts. Thus, at a lower vibration and when unhealed, Leo becomes addicted to drama- chaos, fighting, aggressive displays of needing to show others who's boss, and mind-dulling banter. As an intellectual sign, the senses become dulled, which means they forget the importance of deeper connections, emotional bonding, sensuality, etc. Although very different by nature, Leo displays many of the characteristics of Gemini's mental health blueprint. They gossip, slander, and stir the pot to see how much destruction they can cause. They like seeing others suffer, struggle, and become embarrassed or low in self-worth in a social situation. They love the electric buzz and thrill they get off of being seen as superior. This is Leo's problem, they're so logical and psychologically-focused that their shadow traits transform into something ugly. In their insatiable need to be seen as high and mighty, the lord or lordess of virtually everyone, and the queen or king of the jungle, Leo is very happy to watch other people's light diminish into depression and despair, and they do so with a smug look on their face. If you can recall a time when you were younger and trying to find yourself… just venturing out into the world, becoming expressive and confident for possibly the first time in your life, and someone just started smirking in the most irksome, brutal, and soul nauseating of ways, while you were feeling shy, scared, or unseen; this was a Leo! Or they had some very strong Leo placement, surely. Leo in a lower vibration is so annoying and vicious in their power and self-authority that they can turn the most calm, peaceful, and centered of person vex. Disgusting is quite a strong word, as it separates us from purity, tolerance, and acceptance, however Leo is truly *disgusting*. They have zero empathy, kindness, or genuine love and time for others, and only care about being seen as the shiniest, most attractive, beautiful, successful, gorgeous, irresistible, victorious, and so on. Once again, everyone else are their *minions*. They smirk and snigger. They are the definition of a narcissist, a definition of which can be found in *Aries: The Psychopath*.

Because of their Fixed nature, this influence is even worse due to having impeccable staying power. They become committed to the idea and notion that it's ok to be seen as superior (and treat everyone else like utter sh*t), therefore they can hold a smug or smirk look forever. The result? People walk away with their self-esteem destroyed, absolutely shattered. Leo in this space leaves what should be their friends, lovers, and family devastated, distraught, and thinking there is no hope left in the world. Leo's intellectual superiority puts out faith. It dampens purity, authentic connections, kindness, heart, sensitivity, soul, harmony, diplomacy, and vulnerability. Someone being completely vulnerable and open-hearted for the first time can be set on a dark path that could last months to years, further even a decade, from the subtle abuse inflicted on them by domineering Leo. I know this because I am a Pisces with my Moon in Cancer, two very sensitive and moreover impressionable water placements. In the past, I have looked up to Leos due to their level of respect. This is their secret weapon in their narcissistic abuse; they are *very* respectful, but, unfortunately, when in a lower frequency they are delusional as to what it means to truly command respect. Leo believes they are commanding respect, they *fixate* on their superiority, and then they stay there regardless of who suffers. Lost and trusting, naive, or innocent souls who need guidance are played on- Leo makes a meal out of poor Fishes, Crabs, and Scorpions. It's a sad truth, but they get high off of more sensitive people being drawn into suicide and despair...

Leo plays on other people's need for connection, intimacy, and companionship. They may appear charming, confident, kind, approachable, sophisticated, or sweet, but, just like a true narcissist, it's all an act. There's no real affection or genuine emotions there. Leo in this mental space will sincerely see everyone as their servants, real-life servants, maids, and slaves, and they'll treat them as such. If such terrible behavior or their unwavering smug facial expressions and attitude are called out, the only way they can go is to turn violent. They *refuse* to release control, because it would make them appear as a narcissist. It's an extreme personality disorder that will produce two extreme outcomes (their victims depression or suicide or them being publically shamed, in which case they have to become physically violent to show their force). As the brutal and heartless thug of the zodiac, Leo will never let anyone question their authority. If they do, hell breaks loose and Leo makes it a personal life mission to make that person's life miserable and loveless.

A Complete Lack of Self-Control

For someone who projects the persona of an army sergeant, general, or boss, Leo totally lacks self-control. This is due to being a Fixed sign with an explosive temper. Shadow traits include being extremely quick to anger, impulsiveness, severe impatience, getting annoyed at anything and everything, and, at their lowest, pulling temper tantrums like a toddler or teeanger. True story. Emotional self-mastery is not their strength when in such a low vibration, nor is higher spiritual awareness or wisdom. Remember that we are holistic beings with emotional, spiritual, psychological/mental, and physical bodies. Just as water signs might be more emotionally serene, spiritually insightful, psychic, and imaginative, and earth signs more practical, emotionally intelligent, and instinctive, Leo is primarily intellectual, physically active, and cerebrally gifted. It's ironic, as they are deeply romantic and loving when on top form, but in their dark psyche they are disconnected from their emotional intelligence, moreover their sensitive and self-aware side. Emotional disharmony diminishes their life force, creative spark, and inner divine glow. When at a higher vibration, these qualities lead to being so loyal, affectionate, and romantic (their positive qualities). Without emotional depth, awareness, or sensitivity, Leo is a wild beast acting from primal instincts. They're cold, ruthless, and somewhat heartless, just like a lion craving flesh to sink its teeth into; they're animals after all, and survival comes first. In their pursuit of physical necessities, Leo turns to logic, mental analysis, and rationality birthed from the potent rays of the Sun, which represents the conscious mind. There's no depth or subtle awareness, so they bulldoze over their own feelings while further failing to honor their true essence. Nobility, grace, diplomacy, kindness, and morality go out the window.

Belittling, patronizing, and with a "no f*cks given" attitude, Leo strolls through life like they are the boss, emperor, and ruler of everyone. They give the impression of being in control through such evolved conscious and solar forces (the Sun), yet, underneath the mask, there is a *wounded inner child*. Leo is ruled by the 5th house, again, the house of children, drama, and creative expression, therefore in a lower vibration they are very childish in their behaviors, thoughts, and mannerisms. They have no self-control and say what they feel or think instantaneously. They speak over others. They shout, they act high and mighty to get attention, and they crave praise, external validation, and admiration at unsustainable levels. The entire human race is at Leo's feet like a mother or father is expected to respond to every demand made from their child. Yet, unlike with children, the world owes Leo nothing. At their best, Leo is a self-sovereign being with their crown firmly on their head, walking through life with integrity, modesty, and amazing creative life force… to inspire, uplift, and motivate others into action. At their worst, the inner child distorts and twists into something ugly, something monstrous with a completely self-serving and selfish mindset. They believe they are entitled to everything, all possessions owned by others, material assets, resources, shelter, food, money, security, talents, qualifications, professional recognition, prestige, love, admiration- you name it; if someone else has it, Leo wants it or believes it is theirs, simply through their existence. It's very delusional on par with fellow fire sign Sagittarius.

Leo in such a child-like and inner child wounded state will send back a slightly less than hot drink or meal in a restaurant, multiple times; they will claim credit for everything their staff do if they're a boss or manager in the workplace, and they exaggerate their achievements and qualifications to get ahead of the competition. Masculine energy is naturally competitive, as it inspires action and force, so like Aries ruled by Mars, Leo ruled by the Sun is highly energetic. They possess elevated energy, enthusiasm, and vitality levels that make them highly charged, always on the go, and very busy minded. They're extremely ambitious, and in a lower mental headspace this makes their worst qualities come out in full force (self-entitlement, believing their superior, lording it over others…). Leo's arrogance is infuriating and not matched by many. They will lie to climb the professional ladder and cheat to win or tell lies to get a job or lump sum of money. Usually noble and beautiful Leo becomes a selfish child who lives, acts, and breathes as if they are the center of the universe, just like a young infant who genuinely needs constant love, care, protection, and support. Leo isn't grateful, they're *not* gracious, and they certainly don't consider the needs or feelings of anyone else. Imagine how an out of control child is. Well, this is Leo. Further, Leo is similar to someone with an asbo or serious personality disorder when in their dark psyche. They cause harm and distress to anyone they encounter without conscience- there's no remorse, humility, or desires for peace, harmony, and unity either. Leo storms around on an invisible horse with an invisible golden crown, as well as an invisible cloak... Leo is also a master of schadenfreude, which is smiling inside when others are down on their luck. They suck the light, love, joy, and happiness, moreover the luck out of others with their smugness, childish antics, and fraudulent personality (narcissism).

Erratic and Foolish

One of Leo's worst shadow traits that devolves into their mental health blueprint is pride. This fiery and overly masculine sign takes being prideful to new levels. Bossy, egotistical beyond belief, and totally irrational, Leo is a nightmare. As we live in a dualistic world, all forces want to be integrated, and it's even worse for Leo in many respects because they are ruled by the Sun, the dominant life force and planet linked to the conscious mind. The Sun and Moon are two of our primary influences, therefore they have a tendency to fall into extreme psychosis coupled with other personality disorders more than many others. Vanity and self-absorption become their primary focus, every morning is a case of *"who's the finest of them all"* while looking into the mirror... and an hour later... and at night... And then again in the middle of REM sleep! Leo will never admit to being wrong and they're further incapable of apologizing. This sign becomes erratic and foolish in social situations, playing the fool in a way similar to compulsive lying-trickster Gemini. At home, Leo will stalk and give their affections to multiple, multiple people, playing with hearts and giving false hope. Leo makes promises, shares their "love," and essentially makes many people fall in love with them, with no intention to follow through; or while being unfaithful. Oh yes, this is one of the most adulterous signs- Leo loves to cheat. It boosts their ego and increases their illusory sense of authority and self-love. Leo is the sign who misconstrues the true meaning of self-love the most. Self-love is the ability to love oneself, from a space of inner beauty and some, at least, spiritual awareness combined with higher perspectives. Narcissism, the opposite of self-love, is vanity, pride, and ego disguised as love.

They have weak heart chakras when young, immature, and imbalanced, due to being the central sign; the corresponding physical area for Leo is the heart, while Leo is known as the heart of the zodiac. Thus, the dark psyche Leo lives with a complete absence of heart, kindness, empathy, morality, and so forth. A weak heart chakra manifests as inhumane thoughts and behavior, in addition to an inability to forgive. Self-forgiveness is important for Leo's evolution, however it is difficult if not impossible for them to admit defeat. They are not the center of the universe and every human is not their slave or servant, but their pride gets in the way of this truth. Self-acceptance, letting go, and living by faith and higher spiritual perspectives are not a part of low vibrational Leo's life. Leo creates chaos very much like hotheaded war planet-ruled Aries, yet they won't admit or even accept that they leave such a mess. At their best, they are high-flyers, high-achievers, and ambitious creators with potent life force, innovation, originality, charm, and wit. Yet in a lower frequency they use these qualities for selfish gain. Also, they make little to no time for self-reflection, always wanting to be sociable and seen in a positive public eye. This makes them fake, superficial, and, over time, delusional as to their own greatness or talents and gifts. NPD can equally develop if their mental health blueprint becomes a part of their future timeline self. Leo is the cruel and mean-spirited, bitter, 'little old cat lady' who everyone sees as kind-hearted for keeping so many cats, yet delusional, disconnected from family, and part of a wounded older generation. Not all people reach 60+ without having healed their wounds, yet this image of the wicked cat lady who has fostered her resentments and annoyances without healing or doing any shadow or trauma work is the Leo blueprint in its unhealed manifestation. Leo is bitter, excessively proud of the wrong things- or no things (made up things), and utterly erratic. They're foolish, treating people like slaves in the way an unhealed old lady looks down on teenagers while being cold and extremely rude to everyone she encounters.

From another perspective, Leo is also the crazy football hooligan who will beat an innocent bystander to a pulp because of pop or t.v. culture. Leo represents glamor and the Arts, so they take societal conditioning too far. We all know there is a huge level of conditioning and superficiality present in society- from billboards to advertisements and distorted concepts of beauty or competition, to a consumerist mindset. Well, Leo's love of drama and pleasure makes them monstrous and disillusioned. They are aware on some instinctive level that they're being negatively influenced, there are subliminal messages aiming to suppress the human spirit and disconnect them from beauty everywhere; there are signs of hostility, hatred, and prejudice all around, perpetually being etched into our subconscious minds… Yet, because Leo has a superficial personality coupled with minor-major narcissism (NPD), they don't care. They choose to hide behind the "powers that be," denying all responsibility and accountability as to their own choices and actions. Leo makes terrible choices, yet passes the blame. Like with all zodiac signs, their usually good qualities are twisted into something sinister, manifesting as the lower vibration of their Higher Self. Courage is replaced with cowardice, devotion is diminished by neglect, and a high level of responsibility is taken over by a *complete* lack of accountability. This will surely trigger them, but Leo becomes a coward. Leo's ego encourages them to promote and develop truly disgusting behavior, attitudes, and mindsets, which eventually become belief systems. Being Fixed signifies holding onto outdated and irrational, moreover utterly barbaric beliefs... Their shadow traits of aggression, being domineering, and bullying tie into this, making them a nightmare to deal with. They push their agenda on others and mistake self-leadership for being a mean-spirited tyrant! Inner beauty goes out the window and Leo begins to see lovely qualities like kindness, gentleness, and sensitivity as weaknesses. Usually benevolent, compassionate, and supremely generous Leo becomes a monster who loses touch with the godly aspects of life and Self, including a connection to the divine.

Like Narcissus, Leo disconnects from the beauty and depths of the soul to live life superficially, materialistically, and arrogantly. They live in their shadow and then force everyone else to remain in their shadow too. In their rejection or denial of the subconscious and its subsequent positive influences in life, Leo wishes to stay high and mighty, keep on pushing, and failing to work on their wounds. They then pick up on trauma that binds them to their lower mind, simultaneously failing to cleanse, soul-search, introspect, heal, and do the inner work. As such an energetic and sociable sign, moreover with an extroverted personality, gregarious Leo finds it impossible to slow down and go within. This keeps them entwined with an illusory reality where they sincerely believe they are the center of the world. Introspection, slowing down, and looking within on a real, deep, level are very hard for them. They would rather party, play, or travel and be adventurous. They prefer to keep light social connections that allow them to hide behind their shallow and superficial follies, further circulating toxic mindsets and behaviors. Like the football hooligan or bitter old cat lady, Leo is lonely inside while projecting their insecurities out into the world. And, if we observe their glyph, we will see why it's trickier for Leo than others to accept that they have insecurities. Do you really think the Lion would bend down and pay respects to an antelope or a zebra? No, of course not. They would roar and rise up in pride while putting on the most deafening displays of power and self-importance. They show their strength. They make their violent side known. This is Leo.

A Bully Without Conscience

At their utter worst, Leo is the bully of the zodiac, domineering, rude, arrogant as hell, superior, self-entitled, and mean-spirited. They will stomp on a snail or kill a passing butterfly just for the "fun" of it. Ruled by the 5th house, Leo confuses fun, pleasure, and joy for acts of evil. In other words, the positive characteristics of the 5th house are twisted into something dark and sinister. Leo is one of the signs most likely to be a sadist or succumb to a dom-sub relationship. When at the top of their game they are charismatic, fun-loving, and highly talented, they possess a number of imaginative and creative skills, and usually excel in an artistic outlet. But, when devolved they mistake "joy" for "sick and twisted barbarity"- there's no real fun or play in their life, just a monster who wants to cause harm and chaos. Leo is so tyrannical that they will bully their own children! A Leo parent, if still in their dark psyche, wants to steal the show from their kids, undermine, and actively criticize, insult, and slander them. There's no-one quite this self-centered, moreover unkind and belittling according to astrology, and I can personally share some stories to confirm this. Leo is relentless in their need to be the only one with talent, beauty, self-esteem, etc. They bulldoze over other people's feelings and snigger or smirk at their real world talents and qualifications or accomplishments. They're so in denial to their own lack of real prestige, fame, and social class or achievements that they appear like fools while thinking themselves to be on a higher level. At their lowest, Leo is the thug or chav who thinks they're a boss or CEO.

Leo steals the show in an unhealthy and overpowering way. They make everyone around them feel weak and depressed, all the while commanding and demanding without heart-centered guidance or higher reasoning. It's all about them. *My way or the highway. Me, me; me.* A constant need for attention and admiration coupled with an aggressive and emotionally imbalanced character puts usually loving and loyal Leo on a timeline of destruction. Their beautiful qualities go out the window, and they fall prey to their own traps, such as believing physical beauty and physical strength to be the only things worth fighting for. Leo forgets the importance of friendship, community, family, vulnerability, intimacy, and sensitivity- open-hearted and genuine relating, communication, bonding, etc. Leo is so self-centered that they neglect core parts of their character, like working on becoming more sensitive, vulnerable, sensual, emotionally transparent, and genuine. Furthermore, due to their romantic nature, Leo craves intimacy, but because their mind is distorted and confused they don't know how to get the intimacy and affection they so powerfully desire. The only way they think they can be, through their high vitality and evolved physical instincts, is to demand and bully people into succumbing to their will. Leo has immense willpower combined with ambition, however they are insensitive and unempathetic with zero compassion, tolerance, or integrity. Sociable, passionate, expressive, affectionate, faithful, romantic, warm-hearted, and benevolent with a wonderfully charismatic and upbeat personality, Leo has the heart of a murderer when deep in their dark psyche. Leo is the natural leader as well, therefore they have no shame or remorse in what they do. A lack of shame and remorse is what prevents grace, forgiveness, and true healing from occurring. Trauma bonding, a wounded inner child, and severe projection ensue… The only way to heal and evolve is to accept that they are not the only powerful or talented person in the world, and that softness does not equate with weakness. They can transform from the ego to the higher mind.

Absolute worse crimes possible?

	LESS LIKELY	LIKELY	ABSOLUTELY
MURDER			✓
RAPE			✓
ANIMAL CRUELTY			✓
CHILD ABUSE			✓
MOLESTATION	✓		
TORTURE		✓	
HUMAN TRAFFICKING	✓		
SLAVERY		✓	
BESTIALITY			✓
TERRORISM			✓
KIDNAPPING			✓
GENOCIDE			✓
NUCLEAR WAR DECIDER		✓	

CHAPTER 6: Virgo the Mentalist

House: The 6th house, the house of work, daily routines, health, cleanliness, and order.
Planet: Mercury, the planet of logic, intellect, analysis, and communication (positive), and intellectual superiority, delays, setbacks, and disappointments in travel, technology, and communication (negative).
Element and quality: Earth and Mutable.
Color: Brown, the color of grounding, dependability, practicality, and earthly wisdom; green, the color of the heart, empathy, kindness, and selflessness, and gray, the color of sophistication, logic/intellect, seriousness and sensibility, and professionalism.
Physical area: Intestines, abdomen, spleen, and pancreas (+ digestive system).
Dates: August 24th to September 23rd.

Virgo is a dark magician, an alchemist of intellect, logic, words, reasoning, and communication. Ruled by Mercury, they excel in the realm of the mind, from higher analysis to problem-solving and fine-tuned perception to intuition. But they are also an earth sign, which makes them magnetically influential. There is additionally the added element of being a Mutable sign, giving them advanced adaptability and flexibility in the realm of mind and psychological gifts. Put all of this together, and you will see how Virgo in their dark psyche becomes a dark witch. They are dark magicians, using such evolved psychological and intellectual gifts for wrongdoings. Virgos are the evil masterminds of the zodiac.

They will plot and scheme up wicked plots to influence or control others. Never taking accountability, they deny the need to control and manipulate and thus return to secrecy. This is even more dangerous in many ways than the signs who clearly show off their mental health blueprint, such as fire sign Aries who sets a clear warpath with others, or earth sign Taurus who is quite apparent in their out of control desires. The saying *it's the quiet ones you have to watch out for* applies here.

Let's look at the definition of a mentalist:

A dark magician who uses advanced mental, psychological, and cerebral powers to control, influence, and dominate others. This person is a mad wo/man who enjoys playing mind-games and then returning to secrecy or solitude.

Let's break this main definition down, shall we!

A Dark Magician

Virgo is a dark magician, a mentalist, and a mastermind. They thrive in the realm of intellect, logic, and higher reasoning, as they are ruled by Mercury. But they are also an earth sign, which makes them incredibly magnetic. People are magnetized to Virgo's apparent depth, sensitivity, and emotional intelligence, moreover their evolved mental powers and wit. Like with all other star signs, however, it's all a con; when in their mental health blueprint, they are not whole, healed, or balanced. They're not mentally well nor are they actually deep. A higher vibration Virgo is deep, sensitive, empathic, compassionate, and down-to-earth; sensual, soulfully grounded, and in tune with a unique type of emotional intelligence. Earth is yin and therefore feminine. But, in a low mental headspace, Virgo is the evil mastermind who dismisses the importance of their emotions and feelings entirely. They focus only on their wit, mental abilities, and cognitive gifts, and this creates a very cold and detached individual. Virgo becomes a walking robot, a lifeless and robotic holographic brain who sees all, yet has the emotional depth of a teaspoon (as the saying goes). Their positive gifts of rationality, logic, subtle perception, observation, analytical thinking, and wit are used to control and manipulate others. Their shadow traits include being critical and judgemental, so in their dark psyche these become monstrous and ugly personality deficits, whereby everyone around them feels constantly put down and judged. Virgo believes themselves to be psychologically and intellectually superior, and, on a level, they are. Mercury is *the* planet of communication and logic after all. Yet they also believe themselves to be emotionally superior without any emotional depth, sensitivity, or empathy. This creates a dangerous individual who is fuelled by a cold and calculated approach to life, self, and virtually all relationships. A human without heart is a danger to themselves and others- without heart, there is no space for tolerance, compassion, or healing to grow. All the characteristics that make Virgo beautiful and sincere when grown and matured are gone, they are a mere shell of their future gloriest self.

If we look at the Tarot, a powerful divinatory system that reflects the human journey, soul, and psyche, we can explore Virgo's dark psyche deeper. The Magician is the first card of the Major Arcana representing the number 1. In numerology, 1 is masculine, very mental and cerebral, and with the qualities of self-leadership, innovation, originality, intuition, discernment, inspired action, and self-autonomy. The Magician card symbolizes taking action and manifestation, in addition to personal power, resourcefulness, and extrasensory gifts. The Magician is a creator and manifester, but the energy is masculine-unlike the High Priestess who carries a feminine energy. In truth, Virgo is a mixture of both, embodying the darker energies of the Magician and his feminine counterpart (the

High Priestess). In reverse, the Magician represents manipulation, deception, and using spiritual forces for evil, wrongdoing, or darker motivations. Virgo's opposite sign is Pisces, the sign of soul alignment, spiritual enlightenment, and a number of psychic, divine, and mystical gifts. In astrology, it's taught that we're supposed to find harmony with our opposite sign, so when delving into the Virgo dark psyche we can see how badly Virgo messes up! Their attempt at power, control, and manifestation goes horribly wrong, distorting and twisting into some parallel universe reality whereby forces of good are replaced with forces of evil. Also, at their best Virgo is an impeccable planner, organizer, and structured being of order. They crave order, organization, and structure at all costs, choosing to live their life with a perfectionist attitude. The Magician in reverse is a symbol for poor planning, therefore Virgo's usually stellar intellectual and cerebral gifts are channeled into the wrong plans, manifestations, and dreams. Virgo has visions, they receive ideas and glimpses of beautiful future outcomes from their higher mind, but they are also ruled by the ego. Thus, their channel is faulty. This negative influence is amplified due to Virgo's glyph, the Maiden or Virgin. The Maiden/Virgin represents purity, Virgo is (higher vibration) the sign associated with purity, sacredness, and cleanliness- a clean mind, body, & spirit, divine order, knowledge of sacred laws, and so forth. You can only imagine what they're like in their dark psyche… The Virgo mental health blueprint creates a disillusioned and misguided individual who believes they are operating from a baseline of purity, when, in reality, are contributing to evil plots. Unkindness, a lack of harmony and teamwork, and the absence of authentic compassion, empathy, and sincerity take over Virgo's life.

Going back to number 1, a masculine number linked to logic and intellectualism, Virgo sees the world through mental analysis; they become wholly rational and analytical, of everything and everyone. There's no imagination. There's no holographic-quantum-multidimensional awareness. They become closed off to mysticism, spirituality, and holistic vision or sight. Virgo is like a tiny flashlight focused on one small area in a massive and enormous space. Their vision is limited, moreover repressed and blocked, Virgo has many blocks to true enlightenment, intelligence, and wisdom. They think they are omniscient, all knowing, and all seeing, and this is the problem. They're in denial as to their own intelligence, greatness, wit, life experience, and so on. Virgo believes themselves to be the most intelligent person in any room, as well as a successful business CEO or boss… without having got there yet. There's a major internal distortion, rooted in their 'strength-gone-wrong'- modesty. At their best, Virgo is the most modest, humble, and down-to-earth sign; their humility is unmatched by many others. Yet in their dark psyche, they think they're being humble, when in actuality they're coming across as arrogant and critical gits. Virgo is a cynical, judgmental, and smug git who sniggers and smirks in a way similar to Leo. They become incompetent while projecting the public persona of someone already established. One of Virgo's main driving forces in life is to be successful, financially stable, and materially abundant. They are very materialistic signs, so much so that a need for security and practical foundations define them. In their pursuit of such things, in their mental health blueprint, they are frustrating know-it-alls with a superior attitude! They are attuned to a future vision of themselves because they are instinctive, intuitive, and higher minded, however the way they present themselves is not, in any way, shape, or form, representative of their current self. They're delusional, and the problem is that people think they're cute. They come across as sweet, as, unlike more aggressive and "in your face" fire or air signs (masculine signs are 'yang,' which is extroverted and o.t.t.), there is always a level of reservation with Virgo. This reserved, somewhat shy, and modest persona is what makes people think they're simply cute and sweet or reserved and humble. And this is where the issues begin.

From this space of confusion and misdirection, Virgo is free to carry out their evil plots. Virgo is the only sign outside of the water signs who can blend into the background, going completely off everyone's radar. They cause mayhem and then return to secrecy. They plant bad seeds in people's conscious and subconscious minds, and then pretend to be innocent or even unintelligent. *"Who, me?"* This is Virgo. Silly, unpleasant, annoying, infuriatingly intellectually superior, and full of insecurities, Virgo is very pessimistic under an external layer of false pretense. Virgo has many, many insecurities coupled with low self-esteem and extreme self-doubt. Due to such an analytical and pessimistic mind, they are constantly criticizing themselves. Because they also criticize others, this amplifies negativity in their life; they are cynical and critical of many things, so the spiral of pessimism continues. Being so insecure signifies an ability to rise up from the depths of the shadow or the murky waters of self-doubt. Heart, empathy, and feelings are required for this, but in their mental health blueprint they're incapable of moving past their fixation on logic and intellect. They're a contradiction, in fact, as they're a Mutable sign, not a Fixed one, which should give them some level of flexibility. Firstly, you should know that Virgo is completely rigid, conservative and way too focused on order, structure, and planning. This sucks the life force and joy out of their life, which further contributes to such pessimistic thinking. Secondly, when they are in their dark psyche, they use their adaptability to continue to stir the pot, playing devil's advocate, and contributing to more mayhem and chaos. Mental confusion is the aim of the game. They get a mental buzz off of people believing them to be superior and more accomplished, all the while secretly knowing they're living in a 'visionary' stage. It's all a con, a cheat; a steal. Virgo is the dark fox when in such a low frequency…

Causes Mental Confusion

So, Virgo embodies the energy of the trickster. They become a dark fox, the fox spirit animal having symbolism including being cunning, jokerish, and deceitful, also an embodiment of the trickster. Unlike Gemini who clearly shows the world their devilish trickster side, Virgo hides. They play mind games, plant evil seeds in other people's consciousness, and make people feel inferior, not worthy, etc. Then, they return to secrecy, playing innocent and hiding behind other more bold and gregarious personalities. Virgo is the type of person, when in their dark psyche, who will stir the pot quite viciously and then pretend like they're nothing. Their version of 'vicious' is in fact subtle, hence how they get away with it; earth is subtle, magnetic, and passive, therefore Virgo is a *silent deadly type*. Envision the image of a ninja who kills people with utmost skill and then returns to traditional values of respect and humility. They create mental disparity and confusion through years of study, introverted activities, and self-mastery of their mind and intellect. Virgo loves to learn, gather information, and exercise their intelligence, further they usually become experts or masters in their chosen field of study. At a higher level, Virgo is the skilled perfectionist who excels, conquers, and achieves. They are masters of destroying other people's self-esteem because they are living a lie, they're living in an illusion. Virgo processes things mentally, you see, so when they receive instinctive and intuitive messages from external environments, they don't know how to process this properly. They rationalize and analyze everything, which inevitably means everythings gets lost in translation. Important higher perspectives, soul visions, and insights into their true path or purpose are lost (because they're only seeing rationally or logically… life involves a balance; we're *multidimensional* beings).

Then, Virgo sets on a path based on faulty perceptions and beliefs drawn from the conclusions their mind has formed. Over time, their self-esteem is destroyed and they live from the insecurities formed that have further refused to be looked at. Out of all the star signs, Virgo is the one with the lowest self-esteem, and this is because they're always criticizing themselves and others. They're *so* cynical too. And, they lack vision combined with big-picture thinking and seeing; Virgo is the perfectionist, the small-minded pedantic cynic at their worst. They are excessively concerned with minor details and rules, as well as analytical powers over feelings, empathy, and so forth. Overscrupulous, Virgo's shadow traits make them into a tyrant when they let themselves devolve into their mental health blueprint. As the cynical and small-minded trickster, Virgo is very influential, but due to their feminine-yin nature (earth sign) they never seem to seek the spotlight, at least not directly. This creates a dangerous personality. *It's the silent ones you have to watch out for* applies to Virgo. Virgo will never let on either, they prefer to be seen as helpful, kind, and service-oriented. This is due to their core frequency, being the helper and being of purity. Their glyph stands for purity while helpfulness is one of their strengths they take most pride in outside of their intellect and wit. So, when in their dark psyche they go about helping and being of service the wrong way, operating from distorted perceptions and faulty belief systems, which people take as truth.

I've had Virgo friends who have set me on the entire wrong course in love. An apparently simple "A doesn't love you but B does" can be taken as gospel from humble and supremely trustworthy (higher vibration) Virgo. That's the thing, Virgo is incredibly trustworthy due to their evolved levels of responsibility, duty, and self-discipline, therefore they are the sign most likely to be sought on for wise counsel, practical advice, and grounded guidance. This friend meant well, I'm sure, but she was misguided. Person A did, in fact, love me, and we could have shared a very magical and authentic true love connection with depth and longevity. Person B was, ironically, a Virgo who had failed to heal his shadow (to add to the plot twist, I saw him in the *highest* esteem… because he was a humble and noble Virgo!). Astrology creates a whirlwind of energies to navigate. My Virgo friend clearly attuned to a specific vibration that led her to give this arguably misdirected advice, and this made me miss out on true love for a long time… Years, a decade. This is the general rule with shadow astrology and the mental health blueprints of each star sign; a wrong decision or piece of advice can set others on a dark path for years to decades (to lifetimes). In Virgo's case, their glyph represents purity and sacred law and order on the highest of levels, so they are trusted and looked on for wise counsel. As Mercury is their ruling planet, their communication skills are great too. Underneath it all- the humility, the modesty, the clear intelligence and level-headed persona; Virgo is, in actuality, functioning from a deeply cynical and judgemental world view. There's little to no holistic sight, bigger picture vision, spiritual perspectives, or multidimensional awareness, and the result is missing out on key pieces of the puzzle.

In terms of the Magician tarot card, this faithful and sweet earth sign will see infinite potential realities and timelines and then convey the message intellectually. They have a cord to the divine, the cosmos, and all subtle and hidden energies and secrets, as their opposite sign is Pisces, yet they don't know how to be a proper channel. They then become the dark magician creating mental confusion, chaos, and disparity everywhere they go. This influence is made even worse if you're dealing with an ambitious Virgo, as they then become ruthless and business-like- even in family and friendship bonds. This sign will tell you black is white while white is black, all the while knowing the opposite is true. Virgo distorts truth, perhaps not in a gossipy way like fellow Mercury-ruled

Gemini; Virgo is too sophisticated and diplomatic for antisocial behavior, but they will make it clear that they *know-it-all* while others know nothing at all. Virgo believes they are omniscient while possessing the emotional depth and vulnerability of a teaspoon, once again.

Intellectually Superior Without Heart

This brings us onto their shadow that projects into their mental health blueprint. They are perfectionists to the point of self-sabotage and self-annihilation, quite literally. Empathy is a keyword for the Virgo life path. When older, matured, and balanced- whole within, Virgo is destined to be a teacher, lecturer, speaker, author, writer, successful business person, or, at the least, a materially abundant person who has made some key career achievements. Virgo is hard working without fault, they're determined, trustworthy, reliable, responsible, duty-bound, and very practical. Combined with the earth element's key set of characteristics linked to ambition and grounding, they are deeply sensitive, serene, peace-loving, compassionate, nurturing, and caring. Virgo is capable of sincere displays of empathy and kindness, more so than all other non-water signs, in fact (outside of Taurus who is ruled by Venus). They're generous, selfless, and utterly devoted to their friends and family when on top form, and as the being of service and helpfulness there is nothing too much for them. They live with compassion and emotional intelligence and apply that empathy to the advice and wisdom they offer. Yet, in their dark psyche, they possess no heart and no empathy. Virgo is a very troubled individual and, unfortunately, often goes unnoticed. They're overlooked, undermined, and undervalued. Even when they're trying to rise from the depths of their mental health issues and imbalances, they never-rarely receive the help they need. This is because they are known as the helpers, everyone knows that Virgo is of sound mind, moreover they are very strong. At least, that's the image they've projected for so long, right? Wrong.

Virgo is deeply sensitive and vulnerable. They put on an intellectually superior attitude because they are hurting deep down. They are genuine and sincere, they want to help others so desperately, so they are always the ones giving and not receiving. This creates a major imbalance- the universe asks us to give and receive in equal measure, as this is what allows for equilibrium and harmonious living. Well, Virgo forgets to receive help, guidance, and so forth, instead hiding behind false pretense coupled with a "know-it-all" attitude. Over time this creates a lot of problems, and, again, because they're so used to giving without receiving back, they are *incapable* of asking for help. The few times they do they seem to get shut down, bless their sweethearts. Sometimes they are a victim, they're not a cold or aggressive sign when in their authentic self, but other times they are not a victim- it's all their own doing (from their superior and bossy persona). When in their dark psyche, Virgo is a bossy cynic who thinks they're a boss. When they try to heal their wounds and shadows, people don't want to help them, also believing they've got it all figured out. In fact, there will have been many times Virgo has said with clarity and conviction "I've got this!" when behind the surface they are crumbling.

This brain-heart divide leads to their suffering, as well as their inability to heal and evolve. Either Virgo will get the help they need, receiving counseling, therapy, etc., or by finding people who truly see and support their strengths (kindness, generosity, selflessness…) or Virgo will go down the cold and callous route. Cruelty is Virgo at their worst. All sense of compassion, empathy, and kindness go out the window. Virgo becomes a remorseless shell fuelled by a need to show their intellectual superiority, at all costs. They haven't received the love and sensitivity they needed, right? Perhaps. In our mental health blueprints, we're all delusional and misinformed to some degree. But with Virgo, this need to prove themselves through being cold and heartless is taken to extremes... Mercury the messenger planet of logic and intellect sends them mixed signals that contradict their feminine-yin nature. At their worst, Virgo will pick wings off of butterflies and stand on snails. They'll drown small creatures for "fun" or laugh about babies, animals, and children suffering. Their mind becomes lifeless, inhumane, and immoral, the total opposite of their higher frequency self of the Maiden. The Maiden is pure, innocent, and genuinely concerned with the well-being of others…

Denies Accountability

In their lowest vibration, Virgo's usually positive qualities associated with the 6th house are expressed in reverse. The 6th house symbolizes work and daily routines, health, fitness, and lifestyle choices, and duties and responsibilities. Mundane jobs that pay the bills and keep things flowing from the ground up come into Virgo's domain, as do the small details that contribute to the whole; dental hygiene, domestic cleanliness, errand running, keeping on top of finances, making sure there are savings in the account for a rainy day, and other apparently trivial things like doctors, dentists, and healthcare subscriptions. Virgo is a perfectionist, who, once again, *loves* order and routine. Without these things, they fall apart- they actually feel like their life is meaningless. Usually highly responsible and accountable Virgo becomes totally irresponsible, ungrounded, and unaccountable. They lack vision, which disconnects them from their holistic self; they lack psychic instincts, subtle and spiritual perception, and imaginative powers of observation and persuasion. Any advice, counsel, or information given and offered is then reneged or denied when things go wrong, or when it's time to face the music. Any actions taken are also denied or seen as not real, i.e. not serious. The truth is, everything Virgo does is serious; it's thought-out, well planned, and intended with utmost sensibility and practicality. Yet if they make a mistake, are wrong, and so forth, god forbid anyone who questions them! They're not authoritative in a Leo or Aries type of way, however they do want to be known as bosses. Maybe not the only boss, this sign is not associated with tyranny or bullyish displays of power and self-autonomy, yet Virgo is very concerned with public image and social etiquette. Their strengths of order, organization, and structure signify that they refuse to be seen in a negative light. They equally refuse to accept accountability and take ownership for any of their "wise counsel" or "sage wisdom."

Mercury combined with the 6th house allows them to walk through life with a unique level of nobility, grace, and prestige, always remaining humble and diplomatic, so never taking the spotlight completely, but gaining a lot of respect and admiration in a healthy way. In their dark psyche, therefore, they want the respect and admiration without doing the work- without looking at themselves properly, in addition to never exploring (and healing) their wounds and shadows. Virgo is a master of self-denial, and to add to this they are one of the least spiritual signs around. So things like shadow work, trauma and wound healing, exploring karmic and universal themes and cycles, and authentic spiritual practices that could lead to new philosophies and enlightenment are not seen as serious. Virgo adopts a very 3-dimensional view of the world, becoming pedantic and narrow-minded at *extreme* levels. They close themselves off to healing and growth while putting everyone else down, the people who could help them and contribute to their self-evolution. Virgo blocks their own finances, professional development, and personal growth. They're so concerned with the small details and trivial mundane aspects of life that they prevent their own education, cultural, professional, spiritual, and holistic self-development. It's all about the here and now, from a ground level up focus, not from a top down. Small-minded and judgemental of virtually everyone else, Virgo believes they have all the answers without really knowing anything at all... Virgo in their dark psyche may have just started to explore certain topics or expert fields of knowledge, yet they act like they are a master. Also, the way they approach learning and knowledge acquisition is extremely limited, as they *only* connect to their left brain; logic, analytical thinking, and rational thought.

This creates a close-minded individual who is incapable of accepting ownership, additionally they fail to right their wrongs, say sorry, and "grow up." Virgo in this low frequency is incredibly infuriating due to the sheer level of hypocrisy, cynicism, and intolerance they give off. Usually down-to-earth and friend-in-need Virgo can make people very angry when in their mental health blueprint. Uncontrolled perfectionism takes over, only this perfectionism is a distortion of ultimate and higher truths. They think they're the only ones who know how to do things correctly or that there's only one version of 'correct.' Relationships break down, and at worst, people turn against Virgo which leads to further self-sabotage and isolation (due to them desperately needing love and support *while* giving off a superior vibe). Virgo will wash one plate three times, hoover the same small area for an hour, or align their tea bags while their lover, partner, or family member looks on at them like they're crazy. To add, their loved ones try to verbalize their disdain and Virgo acts oblivious- the "who me" energy takes over. Eventually people get sick and tired of their behavior. Virgo's daily routines and severe need for order and perfection literally makes people sick and tired. It's a paradox that pushes people away.

Hides in Solitude and Secrecy

Finally, after all of Virgo's imposed perfectionism and intellectual superiority, plots, schemes, and master plans to create dysfunctional relationships or break up amazing ones, they return to secrecy. This is a true dark magician, a powerful manifester and intellectual who returns to the solace of their own company after creating destruction in the world. Are their intentions pure? Who knows, *all* signs think they're acting justly when in their mental health blueprint. Virgo is introspective, introverted, and surprisingly artistic. They lack imagination and creative vision, at least in a Sagittarius or Pisces sense, but they do have a unique level of skilled mastery when it comes to their chosen craft. From science to business or art to music, Virgo will surely become prestigious and recognized through determination and hard-work. To get there, they must overcome their shadow traits and wounds, which inevitably lead to a lasting mental health blueprint if left unhealed. Virgo has a warped self-image and warped world view. They see things distorted and disoriented, and this is because they have conflicting primary influences. Mercury tells them to be analytical and rational, while their earthy nature asks them to be sensual, passive, and instinctive. At their best, Virgo is both logical *and* instinctive, analytical *and* emotionally intelligent, and intellectual *and* compassionate, nurturing, and empathic. They're very sweet, in addition to being devoted to not only their career and security but to their loved ones. A warped body image, for example, based on society's restrictions and ideas of beauty can leave an already sensitive Virgo very fragile and broken. They believe themselves to be inferior, ironically, once again having many, many insecurities. Virgo is full of self-doubt, and merged with low self-worth and self-esteem they become isolated and lonely.

Anything they do or say in a social setting is a front. They are not someone associated with narcissistic personality disorder, but they do put on a mask. They give themselves impossible tasks linked to beauty, perfection, work prestige, success, accomplishment, and creating financial and domestic bliss and security, that they fail to enjoy life. Virgo lacks fun, spontaneity, and adventure, so much so that they unconsciously or consciously suck the life out of others. They see themselves as isolated and imperfect while projecting the image of confidence and having their sh*t together. Virgo does not have their sh*t together, by any means, thus the result is alienating others combined with digging deeper holes. They refuse to ask for help nor will they admit they need to grow up, heal, or mature. They want to be in control so desperately. They also want to engage in self-care and self-love, as a feminine earth sign, however they don't know how to do this (due to Mercury). In a low vibration, Virgo becomes completely pessimistic, self-loathing, and in denial to their own beauty and greatness. Unfortunately for them, they project on others, making everyone else feel as low as them. It's a depressing cycle. Virgo gets overwhelmed to the point of self-sacrifice, they believe the only way they can escape is to sacrifice themselves for others, through charity, helpful service, and so on. Of course, this is the *wrong* way to go about things; what Virgo needs is to *refind* themselves, through *self*-love, *self*-care, and *self*-empowerment. Sacrifice is one of Virgo's worst qualities.

At their lowest, Virgo is the sign associated with neurological and digestive disorders. They are extremely anxious and nervous, developing minor to major forms of social anxiety, neurosis, and undiagnosed (unaccepted) depression. They experience burn-out regularly, yet won't seek help or admit they are in such a low mental space. They become irritable, annoyed at everything, and supremely touchy, further becoming hypochondriacs as well as "insert every possible neurological imbalance and condition here." Virgo is abnormal, irrational, and disconnected from their potent intuition, and they forget the importance and power of emotional intelligence combined with instinctual responses & clues from their environment. They think and analyze, pushing aside their and other's feelings; they push friends and family away and miss out on amazing opportunities… 'Less is more' isn't a possibility in their world, they further judge and put down others who may have some wisdom or common sense to bring to the table. In home, family, business, or social life, Virgo becomes a not-so-wise bossy-boots without actually being a boss, or if they are a boss they close themselves off to the help of others. Virgo is a *no* person (not a yes person!). They think they can do it all alone, they refuse to delegate, and key strengths like integrity, grace, and humility diminish in the name of trying to retain their independence. Virgo takes pride in their self-autonomy, and at a higher vibration they are deeply self-sovereign bosses in control of their own life. Yet in their dark psyche, they are merely wannabes with *some* level of intellectual superiority, but predominantly at a loss of self. They're disconnected and playing out childhood wounds and insecurities. Virgo is the case of being a workaholic without actually getting anything done… They drive themselves, and others, crazy, and work on a task relentlessly without contributing to a real end goal or vision.

Virgo becomes joyless, passionless, and judgemental of themselves and the world to the point of extreme pessimism and burn-out. Then, all the wonderful acts of charity and kindness they have done- their beautiful deeds- get forgotten. People overlook and undermine Virgo's strengths because they have started to focus on their modesty, but what are they being modest about? Their light side has been polluted by darkness, so any small moments of victory and greatness are overlooked. Virgo's shadow is strong, however unluckily for them their strength of humility prevents them from receiving the external help and support they need. The image to reflect on is a rabbit chasing a carrot on the end of the stick, with the mastermind (the person holding the carrot and stick) never having any intention of letting the rabbit eat the carrot. The poor rabbit could run for decades in the hope of receiving their just rewards, but their own stupidity and silliness prevents them from the 'win.' Virgo's lesson is to embrace their gentler feminine side, be more passive and receptive, and delegate. They need to be open to receive, as well as slow down, work on their shadow traits, and reverse the bad karma they've created. Their work ethic is too strong, so the work, rest, and play balance needed for true success blocks their own goals. Furthermore, Virgo is a hypocrite, someone who pretends to be some hard-working boss who behind-the scenes slacks, goofs around, and binge-watches t.v. This is when things get dangerous, as their cold and business-minded side comes out; they believe they're entitled to certain job positions, promotions, and rewards... Virgo becomes ruthless.

Yes, they're a symbol of fertility, but they can't get by on illusory notions of superiority alone. When things aren't going right, Virgo will resort to blaming those closest to them, those who have been their silent or apparent rock. Virgo treats their loved ones like dirt when they are, in fact, precious gems. Why do they do this? Because they deny the need for help for so long. Even when they do receive clear help, they fail to appreciate it and the people offering it, due to being undervalued and underappreciated in past times. Again, it's a cycle, and Virgo is the only one to blame. Self-blame, self-pity, and self-sabotage ensue, and the only way out is to turn to the one thing they judge the most: spirituality. Virgo's mental health blueprint can be overcome by seeing a shaman, reiki healer, or holistic therapist of any kind, or a counselor, life coach, and so forth. Spiritual and self-development workshops, courses, and events are very beneficial for the Virgo psyche, so take note, dear Virgins… You are *allowed* to receive help. You are not the only service-oriented being who believes in purity, sacredness, and divine order. Moreover, there are multiple aspects and manifestations of such things. At their worst, in the darkest and deepest places of the Virgo psyche, Virgo is a mental health patient who is more likely to be a serial killer than any other (so sorry, Virgo). This is the type of personality who would make a lowlife slasher movie using real characters, or kidnap, torture, or rape helpless victims because they believe it is their right; they are intellectually superior, so these *"peasants need to be taught a lesson…."* I, Virgo, am just *"putting them in their place…"* Sorry to be so crude. At their best, Virgo is the selfless and devoted artist, intellectual, and helper who lives by strong values of morals, ethics, and integrity. Shadow work coupled with embracing higher spiritual ideals and philosophies are essential to rise above the dark depths of their mental health blueprint.

Absolute worse crimes possible?

	LESS LIKELY	LIKELY	ABSOLUTELY
MURDER			✓
RAPE			✓
ANIMAL CRUELTY		✓	
CHILD ABUSE		✓	
MOLESTATION			✓
TORTURE			✓
HUMAN TRAFFICKING			✓
SLAVERY		✓	
BESTIALITY		✓	
TERRORISM			✓
KIDNAPPING			✓

GENOCIDE	✓		
NUCLEAR WAR DECIDER	✓		

CHAPTER 7: Libra the Sociopath

House: The 7th house, the house of intimate relationships, business partnerships, legal contracts, and marriage.

Planet: Venus, the planet of pleasure, beauty, sensuality, and romance (positive), and self-indulgence, hedonism, out-of-control eroticism, and perversion (negative).

Element and quality: Air and Cardinal.

Color: Orange, the color of sociability, companionship, joy, and warmth, and blue, the color of communication, intellect, self-expression, and the imagination.

Physical area: Lower back, kidneys, and bladder (+ endocrine system).

Dates: September 24th to October 23rd.

Libra is one of the most sociable star signs with key attributes including friendliness, sociability, and lots of mental and psychological gifts. Ruled by the glyph of the Scales, Libra is one of three signs of duality, which makes them alternate between extremes, highs and lows, and various opposite qualities and forces. At a higher vibration, Libra is a just and harmony promoting diplomat with strong levels of empathy, kindness, and gentleness. They're artists, intellectuals, and wonderful friends due to being so balanced, also having the perfect combination of left Vs right brain qualities. But, at a low vibration, Libra is a sociopathic monster who lacks all sense of social skills, charm, and etiquette. They lack morals, ethics, and human decency, as well as succumbing to the lower mind and ego.

Venus' influence also makes them extremely people-pleasing, indecisive, and pleasure-seeking; they have a lot of love to give, coupled with deep romantic longings. Yet they get lost to sociopathic tendencies that disconnect them from their deepest desires, truth, and soul longings. Libra turns into a cruel and aggressive, moreover manipulative version of their gloriest self.

Let's look at the definition of a sociopath:

A mentally ill person who alternates between extremes, has a difficult time functioning in reality, and possesses antisocial personality disorder. This person lacks control, accountability, and self-awareness, moreover conscious relating.

Let's break this main definition down, shall we!

Mentally Ill

Libra has a mental illness similar to Aries, Gemini, Leo, and Virgo, as well as the disillusioned aspects of Sagittarius and Aquarius. This is something more common in fire and air signs, because they lack depth and emotional sensitivity. Libra is the social butterfly of the zodiac with many friendship groups. They have many, many friends, admirers, and followers, and they are amazing listeners, speakers, and communicators. On top form, Libra is the excellent communicator and gifted intellectual- they're logical, analytical, intuitive, imaginative, and the most balanced sign in terms of left/right brain hemisphere qualities. They're also ruled by the Scales, one of three duality glyphs that makes them both live a life of extremes and seek unification. Put all of this together, moreover combined with them being an air sign, you will understand why Libra is one of the signs associated with mental illness. They are mentally imbalanced, distorted and fragmented in their perceptions and observations, which creates an ill individual. Libra's entire identity is rooted in the loving and authentic connections they keep, from business bonds to friendships and family to lovers. But, in their dark psyche, they play out their shadow traits at extreme measures. These include: superficiality, intellectual superiority, people-pleasing, self-sacrifice, and codependency. Libra is a bit of a contradiction because they have two very different foundational influences. Venus is the planet of love, beauty, sensuality, female energy, pleasure, and romance, which rules them, their personalities, and their desires in life. Yet, they are an air sign, and this makes them masculine, extroverted, and somewhat aggressive in their mannerisms. All yang signs tend to be aggressive and impulsive in some way, shape, or form. These two very different drives give Libra mixed signals, making them resort to sociopathy and amplified shadow traits when they feel confused, lost, or lonely. A dark psyche Libra gets pulled in multiple directions in a way similar to Pisces, as they are a dualistic sign; polar opposites rule their life… It's always an inner battle between logic Vs intuition, rationality Vs the imagination, intellect VS instincts, thinking Vs feeling, and so forth.

Libra has many different subtle forces and energies giving them mixed signals. Let's start with them being a masculine air sign. Air is masculine, making them extroverted, sociable, friendly, bright, witty, and very bubbly. At a higher vibration, Libra is the life and soul of the party, the social butterfly and chameleon, and the powerful friend, listener, and communicator. They make excellent artists, speakers, musicians, teachers, counselors, diplomats, and entertainers of all kinds. At a lower frequency, they impose their intellectual superiority on others, further becoming aggressive and supremely impatient when people don't listen to them. Libra wants to be heard and seen; on some level, their instincts tell them they have a unique set of skills to share with the world, which they do. But in their dark psyche they are still living in fantasy-land, in preparation stages. They're not "there" yet, however they act like they are. The type of delusional and aggressive behavior they display is similar to Sagittarius or the imposed level of false sophistication and superiority shown by Virgo. Libra thinks they're already at expert, master, or teacher and elder level, so they act in such a way. Yet, in truth, they are children- impulsive, impatient, and immature. All air signs are immature when unevolved, as air is very chaotic and impulsive. There's no structure- it just flows with the various impressions and currents. As an air sign. Libra is no different from Gemini or Aquarius, which gives them a mental disorder (imbalance). The only difference is that they have a feminine planet, *the* planet of female sexuality, sensuality, feminine wisdom, nurturance, empathy, subtle instincts, romance, feelings, and pleasure. This is one of the most deep, soulful, and femininely magnetic, and this is why Libra is known as the most diplomatic, balanced, and harmonious zodiac sign (higher vibration). But, when unhealed and immature, they become codependent, indecisive, and people-pleasing at extreme measures. Libra doesn't know which way is up or down, quite literally. They are fuelled by a need to be seen in a positive light, due to Venus representing beauty and tranquility on the highest of levels, yet they are incapable of achieving this positive public perception. Libra's problem is they want to be seen as good, pure, and noble by everyone. They give their energy, time, and love out to virtually everyone they encounter, so they become superficial and appeasing in the process. Their intentions are impossible to accomplish, but they fail to recognize the error of their ways due to being so intellectually and psychologically superior. Libra believes they need to give their time and love to everyone, or they will be a bad person. This is a faulty belief system birthed from their dualistic nature, and it eventually leads to a lasting mental health blueprint if left unchecked.

So, in their pursuit to be seen as positive and beautiful, shiny, attractive, intelligent, wise, helpful, etc. Libra becomes a doormat. They give a lot to others while being undervalued, underappreciated, and overlooked in the process. They become mega people-pleasers, which signifies pushing aside their own needs for the hope that people will love them. It's a form of narcissism, although the root of this instinctive desire is a lot more pure than others with NPD. Venus tells them to seek beauty, connection, and intimacy, therefore they try to do this to the best of their ability. Their desires for authentic emotional bonds, intimacy, and friendship, connection, or companionship are sincere, they're very genuine. However, it comes across as narcissism and even insincere because they are too cerebral, analytical, and intellectual. Where's the feeling and empathy?! Libra attempts a 'close bond' with multiple people, failing to secure even an authentic relationship or transparent connections with anyone. As the social butterfly, Libra has eggs in many, many baskets, and this only increases their toxic shadow traits (superficiality, people-pleasing, codependency…). At their worst, they are totally codependent on others through the love and attention they give. This energy may be brief or it may be built up over a long period of time; either way, Libra in their dark psyche always goes overlooked while giving a lot to others. Libra literally gives their whole Self, and this is because they're ruled by the 7th house of partnerships, marriage and romantic relationships, spouses, business bonds, and contracts between people. Opposite to Aries who rules the 1st house, the house of personal identity, primary personality, and the Self, Libra is at a complete loss of self from always giving away their energy, love, resources, time, devotion, and so forth. The 7th house symbolizes moving away from 'self' to 'other' and this is what Libra the Scales does...

They want balance, harmony, and compromise so desperately that they fall into their extreme follies: sacrifice. In their pursuit of happiness and peace, Libra sacrifices themselves. They sacrifice their sanity, money, ability to be professional or earn an income, security, shelter, savings, good looks, charm, health, well-being, and virtually anything else you can think of. If Libra wants you as an ally, friend, or lover, there is nothing too much- they are helpers and lovers at heart, so in a low frequency they have a hard time saying no. Actually, boundaries combined with saying no is impossible for selfless and devoted, friendly Libra. Characteristics of antisocial personality disorder include a complete lack of empathy and compassion for others, impulsive and aggressive behavior, manipulation and deception at extreme levels, attempting to control others for personal gain, using intelligence or charm and charisma to misguide, lying for selfish motivations, and physical intimidation, violence, and threats. These are all the opposite of high vibrational Libra, so it's clear that Libra in their dark psyche is a sociopath on a warpath with the world.

Distorted Belief Systems

Libra is the sort of person who will subtly neglect their children or animals and believe they're the "perfect parent" or "perfect pet owner." Libra abuses others, yet will never fully see the error of their ways. They don't believe they are in the wrong or are doing anything wrong, hence distorted and dangerous belief systems arise. Libra believes they are being helpful, kind, and sincere, moreover are offering wise counsel or sound advice. Yet they are operating from a major mental imbalance. They're functioning from the extremist people-pleasing and codependent behaviors outlined, thus their words and actions aren't actually helping anyone. They're causing harm and creating chaos and dysfunction all the while hiding behind a false mask; their charm and charisma are highly evolved when at their best, yet in their dark psyche they are fake. They're superficial, insincere, and incredibly manipulative- they're out for themselves, selfish, and self-centered. A Libra dark psyche individual will neglect their own children and then play the image of perfect mum or dad to the authorities. They're major con-artists! And this is because they're living from a distorted and inharmonious mind, they are fragmented internally, which extends out in the physical plane and world, as well as into their relationships. Libra is frantic, even fanatic, in their desire to be seen as beautiful, noble, and wonderful that they misconstrue and misdirect. Superificality is not a positive trait, moreover it makes people seriously dislike Libra. Libra gets caught out, yet because they refuse to accept accountability or own up to their follies and negligence they continue to play out their false stories. This is when narcissism does take over and, eventually, people lose all trust and faith in usually selfless and sincere Libra. In a low frequency, they become con-artists and master manipulators who operate from a vibration of greed, pleasure, and selfishness. Venus, their ruling planet, symbolizes hedonism (shadow), so Libra becomes a *hedonist*. They live to serve themselves, receiving mixed signals from the multiple avenues of wisdom and guidance flowing to them.

Air is flexible and fluid, it flows and adapts. Venus steers them towards love, intimacy, and deeper connection, but their ego doesn't know how to apply these subtle messages practically. They're not yet in a vibration of love, emotional depth, and higher self-awareness; they're living from their ego or lower mind, and not their higher mind. Libra receives glimpses of their beauty and greatness from their Higher Self, but the ego is still their driving force, as is raw emotions. Libra has powerful passions and desires that make them into egotistical and self-serving jerks when unhealed and unevolved. Hedonism is translated as pleasure-seeking, sensual self-indulgence, and a lack of self-restraint. Well, Libra has no self-restraint or control. They live, act, and speak from primal impulse. The Scales makes them alternate between logic and instincts, rationality and intuition, and intellect and imaginative thought on a daily basis, every few seconds to minutes. *This creates a fragmented mind.* Their inner moral compass becomes twisted as we explore below. Libra is also self-obsessed. As is the case with all yang signs, they have a narcissistic personality, just as the yin signs can be manipulative. They become self-obsessed to the point of developing faulty belief systems. They want to be adored, admired, and seen as the best, most talented, beautiful, and so forth. Libra is a narcissist with a superficial and superior personality, so they are always seeking the spotlight when their internal moral compass has become distorted. Libra becomes obsessed with how they look, the clothes they wear, what people think of them, and how many admirers they have.

Libra is the type of person who will break your heart, flirt with you at extreme levels while in a relationship, and enter into a new love affair while married or living with someone. They're obsessed with romance and beauty, but unlike Taurus who is also ruled by Venus, Libra is an extroverted and masculine yang sign. So it's more difficult for them to express their love of beauty and sensuality in a healthy and harmonious way. They find it very hard to come to terms with authentic notions of beauty. They're ungrounded, imbalanced, and very uninformed. They're phony and like having their intense levels of beauty and attraction reflected back at them. They're obsessed with everything to do with how they come across, how many people are attracted to them, and how much they can steal the show. It's in a way similar to the fire signs, but not as intense or grandiose. It's more flamboyant in an expressive way, like how an entertainer or musician shines on stage. Libra is a peacock who spreads their feathers commanding others to do their mating dance… even when they have a mate… or even when they're supposed to be professional! The problem is that they do this when they're not in their talent or gifted self, so it just becomes an ego display. This leads to relationship breakdowns as well as people disliking them. At a lower vibration, Venus is all about vanity, false pride and superficiality; pleasure, instant gratification, and a love of the limelight. The higher manifestations of Venus are obviously depth, soul, and authentic intimacy, so you can see the clear divide here. These dramatic ego displays lead to people realizing that Libra is a bit of a fraud and a con-artist, moreover not actually that peace-loving. It's a contradiction in character, as Libra is the sign of harmony and peace, but when they're displaying their ego without pure or good intentions they become manipulative. They work against teamwork and unity, instead contributing to a disconnected paradigm.

Like Leo they become serial cheaters or like Gemini pathological liars. Over time these contradictory actions lead to faulty belief systems that make them think such behavior is ok, as well as doing things for attention is acceptable. The long-term effect is that they start to do things for vanity and attention and then blame others when they don't see Libra as empathic and sophisticated people. Libra wants to be seen as non-superficial, empathic, kind, sincere, and genuine, as these are innate core strengths that allow them to be sociable and likable. However, the moments of extreme shadow ruin their reputation, and a tainted reputation is hard to undo. Similar to narcissistic Sagittarius, Libra's lesson is to accept that they may have picked up some bad karma, also needing to leave behind toxic social or friendship circles. It's hard because they have likely built a life around the friendships and contacts they've formed, yet they aren't real; they're not in alignment with their true soul's purpose or path. There are different timelines existing. In such a low vibration, Libra dislikes accepting accountability for their actions and would rather shift responsibility.

Anti-Social and Extremist; A Con-Artist

Their inner moral compass becomes twisted. At the highest vibration, Libra is a judge ruled by the need for evolved levels of fairness and harmony. They are just with a supreme moral compass, ethics, morality, and human kindness and decency are paramount to them. Diplomatic, extremely wise, perceptive, intuitive, and observant, Libras make excellent judges, counselors, coaches, diplomats, lectures, researchers, writers, analysts, artists, speakers, musicians, actors, and confident public personas who stand strong in a public eye. They love the spotlight, but they're not arrogant or egotistical; Libra possesses a healthy level of ego to get stuff done, make a change, etc. they're changemakers and visionaries when at their best. So, in their mental health blueprint they are the most condescending and superior, moreover *fake* people you will meet. They are con-artists, their inner world is twisted and distorted to extreme levels, thus they are incapable of ascertaining truth. If we look at a symbol of the Judge, we can see that judges are just, fair, and devoted to discovering truth. The Scales, Libra's glyph, equally symbolizes fairness and balance, which eventually become unity, solidarity, and oneness. Well, Libra doesn't understand these concepts, or if they think they do they are largely mistaken and then embark on a dark or wrong path. Libra will make wrong choice after wrong choice, take wrong turn after wrong turn... They will turn against faithful and loyal supporters, friends, and fans while giving their love and strength to horrible characters. Libra thinks aggressive sociopaths and bullies are "cool," yet empathic, kind, and morally aligned people are "nasty," "in the wrong," or "tyrants." Everything is a dark and foggy mirage, so reality itself is distorted. Similar to Aries, Sagittarius, and Aquarius, Libra creates a deeply misguided world view that leads to imprisonment, court orders, major money loss, missed opportunities, and their downfall.

Libra at their lowest is the type of person who is likely to become a skilled armed robber, con-artist, or fraud specialist. Their usually positive traits of potent wit and intelligence, logic, higher reasoning and analysis, amazing intuition, and elevated communication skills are used for manipulative and deceptive motives. Libra is incredibly manipulative, knowing how to deceive and con others for personal gain. A lot of what has been said for Gemini can be applied to Libra, in fact, minus the extreme "trickster" energy. ***Everything written with regards to Gemini being a compulsive liar, major gossiper, and***

truth-distorter can be consulted for Libra. With regards to manipulation, in an attempt to appease and be everyone's favorite person, Libra deceives others through the sole desire of being liked. They would never see themselves as a narcissist, and this is where imbalances arise. A mental health issue is an internal distortion that needs to be rectified. In Libra the Scales' case, they're always weighing up options, so although they may not comprehend that they're being manipulative, they are playing with people's lives. Through comparison coupled with extreme analysis, merged with the motivation of ascertaining the best mindset, emotion, or path of action for *their* sole benefit, Libra manipulates people. An example would be analyzing who's side to take so Libra can make use of their diplomatic or colorful gifts or be seen in a favorable light. This is superficial and manipulative behavior. In their best self, they act selflessly, genuinely devoted to helping and counseling or guiding others; but, in their lower dark psyche they're only concerned with public image. *How will I be seen? How many people will like me? Will I maintain the persona of being everyone's best friend?* These play on their mind like a poltergeist! They promote sh*tty behavior while preaching about being peace-loving and fair. They gossip, slander, and have fun at other people's expenses. They laugh at human or animal suffering and act *unmindfully*, the complete opposite of mindfulness and conscious communication. Libra acts like their all love and light while showing clear sociopathic traits, belief systems, and behaviors…

A Total Lack of Self-Awareness

And, this makes them lack self-awareness. They sincerely believe they are high and mighty, righteous, and pure. Their glyph is the Scales after all, the cosmic judge and balancer of all energies. Like the ancient Egyptian goddess Maat who balances, a powerful symbol of justice, truth, and cosmic harmony, Libra's path is entwined with the need to do the same in daily situations. From the mundane to more serious matters, Libra is a truth and justice bringer. But, in their dark psyche they are nothing more than a fraud, a charlatan. They have idealistic gifts, but this doesn't make them self-mastered. On the contrary, they are unaware and unconscious of their energy, shadow, and actions, moreover the distorted beliefs that are guiding them. While believing themselves to be prey (due to their just and harmony-loving nature), they actually become predators. They prey on the weak and vulnerable, as in their lower self they *are* the weak and vulnerable. They are codependent, needy, and sensitive, as well as people-pleasing. In their ego they get a kick and buzz off of the apparent excitement of seeing others down or in pain. It's twisted, of course, as is the case with all oppressive personalities in their dark psyche. The truth is, they are provocateurs edging people on to bully or belittle. In fact, as a master communicator, Libra is an excellent persuader and influencer. Although they're ruled by very different planetary influences, Libra is similar to Cancer in this respect; they can persuade and seduce others to do what they want. Venus is subtle, magnetic, and very seductive…

While Libra believes they are promoting peace, harmony, teamwork, cooperation, and so forth, they are actually pushing hidden agendas. They will either have unconsciously sided with bullies and oppressors, believing very destructive and evil antics are just "fun" or "play," in which case Libra continues their agenda- they are codependent, remember; weak and seen as prey to many too. Or Libra creates their own mean-spirited plots and schemes through self-righteousness coupled with a severe superiority complex. In either case, Libra becomes a persecutor while convincing themselves they're the justice-bringers of the group or social circle. *They deceive themselves.* Usually colorful, upbeat, charismatic, intelligent, and charming, dark psyche Libra is a vicious and vindictive bully who preys on others through past negative experiences. The innate characteristic of justice is alchemized into something ugly from memories of when they were sensitive and treated poorly. In their belief of interconnectedness combined with us all being one- oh yes, Libra is very open to metaphysical values and concepts; they take past negative experiences to appease their own behavior. They appease terrible behavior in the present so they don't have to look at their wounds and heal their trauma or shadow. Why do they do this? Because it would destroy their current world. It would break down their illusions and remind them that they're not in their best self, they're not self-mastered, and they have deep healing and soul-searching to do. It would further expose their narcissistic personality deficits, moreover the bad deeds they've been performing or supporting. Remember that Libra is one of the most social signs, thus their entire sense of joy, fun, and connection is tied into friendship and social groups. Accepting that they're both appeasing and deceiving themselves would be the first step to recognizing they're due for a *Tower* moment.

The Tower in the tarot symbolizes change, upheaval, and powerful awakening through faulty foundations crumbling down. Well, this is Libra in their mental health blueprint. Like many others, they built their life off of false, wrong, or misguided belief systems. As a sociable and cerebral air sign, Libra's persona is built around society's conditioning, so it's even worse for them in many cases. Usually charming and noble Libra believes they have to act, speak, and think a certain way to be liked and accepted. They're the perfect example of conformity, bless them. Yet all illusions must come tumbling down at some point, and when they do they start to see how virtually all (minus perhaps a few) connections in their life are fake. This is why they cling on to outdated and toxic ideas, mindsets, and relationships- the truth would cripple them. They're not a Fixed sign, so it's not impossible for them to break free from the chains that bind them, it's just difficult. As for conformity, Libra is someone who follows the status quo, hence why they lack total self-awareness. In their lower self, they follow. In their Higher Self, they are natural and amazing leaders, teachers, and communicators. Their Tower moment or moments are devastating because even when they are in their superficial and immature younger state, they are still fuelled by a need for authentic bonding and intimacy. Libra is deeply transparent. They're the *only* yang sign (fire and air) to be ruled by a feminine planet.

Sudden change and upheaval comes to them, and due to having shadow traits including extreme sensitivity, codependency, and the need to be loved and liked by everyone, this can break them on multiple levels. Fortunately, Libra always has inner strength as well as outside support to draw from. They are blessed with elders, teachers, and family who will offer them wise counsel in the perfect moments. Ruled by the 7th house of partnerships and relationships, intimacy defines their path, therefore they are never left totally in the dark. Unluckily, however, a Tower moment does bring all of their illusions regarding the false connections in their life tumbling to a pile of ash and dust. Libra tries to avert disaster through clinging on (codependency), reinforcing superficial friendships and conversations (narcissism), and pretending to be just, fair, and balanced (their superiority complex). They also fear change, which makes them act from the ego and lower mind or self even more. It's a vicious cycle that ends in catastrophe, whereby they leave environments, relationships, and social groups in an explosive way or are ousted out by the people they've been supporting and appeasing. Of course, Libra has destroyed themself in the process, they're not a victim. No-one is. In their mental health blueprint, they may believe themselves to be the victim, but they've unconsciously become a bully or persecutor- or bully's best friend- in the hope to fit in and be accepted. This contradicts their true character on every level. So, there are undoubtedly karmic repercussions. Libra's saving grace is that their intentions have always been to keep the peace and harmony, stay strong and social through playing devil's advocate, and not wander off in fear. So in a twisted way supporting tyrannical mean-spirited people has helped them escape their other shadow flaw: conflict avoidance. Sometimes.

Denies, Rejects, and Bypasses

At their worst, Libra avoids and runs away from confrontation and conflict. They're so ant-conflict and anti-confrontation that an argument scares them, this is why they make excellent judges, diplomats, and mediators when evolved and matured. In a lower vibration, Libra will deny, reject, and bypass at extreme levels. They take no accountability, refuse to work on their shadow follies, and pretend. They're pretenders. Libra is one of the few signs who will speak mistruth to your face while you're giving them the most selfless, angelic, or unconditionally accepting and compassionate space to be honest. It doesn't matter how pure or high your vibe is, Libra will not speak the truth if it interferes with their wrongdoings or BS. Unlike Maat, the cosmic balancer who weighs different things to determine an outcome, low frequency Libra plays devil's advocate. They stir the cosmic pot in a way very similar to Gemini and shapeshift based on other's reactions. They look for reactions and responses, they're master manipulators remember, moreover the qualities of potent observation, perception, and intellectual skills are used for wrongdoing. Libra will then become sneaky, callous, or subversive if they don't get their way or if people clearly see through their deceptions. As a major people-pleaser who both appeases and charms, Libra's dualistic nature makes them like a yo-yo of mind and emotions. They alternate between sweet talk and emotional manipulation to steer outcomes, communications, and agendas.

Even if their intentions are good, such as to maintain a friendship or begin an artistic project with lucrative prospects, they still reap bad karma… because they're playing on people's kindness. Libra knows people are open to their charm- they're highly intelligent and intuitive. As the balanced air sign, libra is highly evolved both rationally, logically, and cerebrally and intuitively, imaginatively, and instinctively. Thus, they're not stupid. They may play dumb, but they're tuned into multiple subtle frequencies of intelligence, including multidimensional perspectives. Libra is hyper-aware of people's needs, feelings, talents, and so forth, and they use a combination of instincts and higher analysis to sensitively guide people. People think they're just being charming and sweet, when, deep down, they're trying to attain some level of recognition, respect, prestige, professional upgrade, or monetary gain. In addition to all the bad consequences outlined so far, the result of this is Libra entering into the one thing they avoid at all cost… conflict. Inevitably, hidden sensations and motivations come bubbling up to a grand finale. Then, dark psyche Libra enters into flight or fight response. Libra will be ganged up on, alienated, or walk away like some vulnerable and love-struck puppy, quite literally. They deny all of their input and actions, and instead walk away. Everything they've created, the months to years of energy and time given to a place, person, or project; it all evaporates. Sometimes it can all be gone in under an hour. Libra lacks vitality and competition relating to standing their ground. They may be superficial and narcissistic, apparently confident and chatty; but they don't know how to stand up for themselves or their beliefs. They lack the key qualities of their opposite sign Aries.

So, Libra becomes the lost puppy, underdog, and loser all in one. They become weak and helpless, looking to others for support due to their codependency or turning towards passive aggressiveness. *Neither work*. People have finally found out that Libra may not be so perfect after all. It's a sad case of events, as Libra is sincere, sweet, and devoted to their friends and projects, even when in their lower mind. They're one of the few signs who truly adore the people in their world, yes, *even when* they are still dealing with shadow self setbacks. But, Libra has to face the music, and due to denying accountability coupled with walking away from a fight- withdrawing completely like some coward, actually, people no longer trust Libra. They don't trust them, their character, or anything they have to say. They're artificially sweet despite some good intentions for teamwork or innovative solutions. If you think about some of the other zodiac signs and their glyphs, like the Lion, Goat, Centaur, Ram, Bull, or Scorpion, a *fake smile* would be taken as a threat. They wouldn't see it as a business offering or lucrative opportunity, it would, quite literally, be taken as a threat to their security and family or kin. This is how Libra comes across. Their fake charm, smiles, and flattery are not received well by many signs, it would actually look more like a menacing grin and sign of attack in the animal world! Thus, Libra thinks they're providing opportunities and blessing, when, in reality, they're showing signs of threats. Why is Libra so misguided? Well, they've denied their shadow for so long, moreover have digressed deep into their polarity; being anti-conflict and anti-diversity ultimately creates a polarity within. Life is about balance, which is more true for Libra the Scales, one of only three duality signs, than it is for most others.

In their attempt to continue their self-denial they create the catalyst that leads to their deepest healing. This is *rejection*, being seen as going on the offense, or starting conflict with the people they're trying to collaborate with. In the end, their shadow sparks their path to self-mastery and self-evolution… because being pushed out of a phony social circle or business bonds built off of deception is exactly what they need to heal. It's a beautiful irony, so you can thank Venus, the planet of love and beauty, for this harsh wake up call, Libra! It's painful, it's traumatizing, and it can lead to potentially years of solitude and soul-searching. However, it's necessary to escape the chains of their mental health blueprint. Life shows them that they can't bypass forever. To add, Libra is a Cardinal sign, so there will always-usually be an element of aggression even when they're believing themselves to be keeping the peace. Another key theme linked here is the distinction between their public and private face. They are two-faced characters when in their dark psyche, which only adds to the theme of self-denial combined with rejecting healing and soul growth more. I'm sorry to share, Libra has secret lives linked to sociopathy many people will be shocked to discover. Like a superior judge who is self-righteous and the "most noble person in the room" (assuming this judge *isn't* a real-life saint or angel…), Libra puts on a social mask and facade that they refuse to let people uncover. We all have secrets, yet this blocks them from the thing they crave the most: authentic and deep bonds. Their need for intimacy, depth, and soul bonding strives them towards secrecy- they believe people will reject them if certain truths are uncovered. Of course, the opposite is true; people look to Libra of all people to tell the truth. This paradox leads to depression, further manipulative and narcissistic tendencies, and a totally codependent mindset. Many issues ensue from here. The price of denial? Their life. Libra ruins their social, love, financial, professional, or family and home life. They destroy their own opportunities and create major roadblocks in their path to true happiness and prosperity. Libra's key lesson is to tell the truth, to find balance and harmony on an authentic level, and to understand that they have a dual side to them. In addition to being a logical and analytical air sign, they're also ruled by the most empathic and sensual planet of them all (Venus). Turning towards natural and organic beauty, sensuality, feminine wisdom, and themes and energies where their ruling planet is exalted, 'Old Soul' *Pisces*, can help them drastically.

Libra needs to come to terms with the fact that they can't do things the way others do. Some people are suited to being glamorous, flamboyant, and utterly sensational in a fiery and extroverted way; this isn't Libra's core strength. Libra is empathic, sensitive, cooperative, compromisable, compassionate, and selfless when on top form. The symbol of the peacock is soul-deep beauty- the beauty of Spirit, sensuality, and self-expression of the soul, not glamor, glitz, and physical notions of beauty. And, being an artist, actor, entertainer, musician, speaker, leader, or teacher is not all about standing in the spotlight in an egotistical or 'look at me way.' Again, this may suit some, but Libra's highest expression is being an advocate for beauty, grace, and integrity. They are humble and graceful when at their best, there's a powerful level of gentleness and sophistication too, not aggression or dominant force. We're all different. In their attempt to conform, fit in, and be like everyone else- or be liked, Libra decreases in integrity and authenticity. So, to rise from the depths of their mental health blueprint they must accept, embrace, and heal. As a dual sign, they have many, many strengths and gifts to draw from. Vulnerability is beautiful. Sensitivity equates with soul to this Venus-ruled passionate yet modest sign too. Seeking pleasure, luxury, abundance, beauty, and intimacy (Venus themes) should not be equated with attention or spotlight seeking, gathering followers, fans, or admirers, or showcasing their talents just for admiration. This is counterproductive to their evolution while completely degrading to their life purpose. Another thing, *self-indulgence* is symbolic of the Libra in the dark psyche, similar to Taurus. Also, repressing their darkness leads to more darkness, amplified shadow traits… Libra must accept that they are unique, even if it makes them less liked, more feminine, and so forth. Society tries to contort Libra like a puppet on a string, and it succeeds for a while. But as the social butterfly of the zodiac, they will eventually see sense, regain full consciousness, and adjust to their higher selves. When they do, it will certainly bring one or more Tower moments, which is the beginning of their journey out of their sociopathic cocoon and into the light. Go with grace, Libra.

Absolute worse crimes possible?

	LESS LIKELY	LIKELY	ABSOLUTELY
MURDER			✓
RAPE			✓
ANIMAL CRUELTY	✓		
CHILD ABUSE		✓	
MOLESTATION			✓
TORTURE	✓		
HUMAN TRAFFICKING			✓
SLAVERY		✓	
BESTIALITY	✓		
TERRORISM		✓	
KIDNAPPING	✓		
GENOCIDE		✓	
NUCLEAR WAR DECIDER		✓	

CHAPTER 8: Scorpio the Doomed

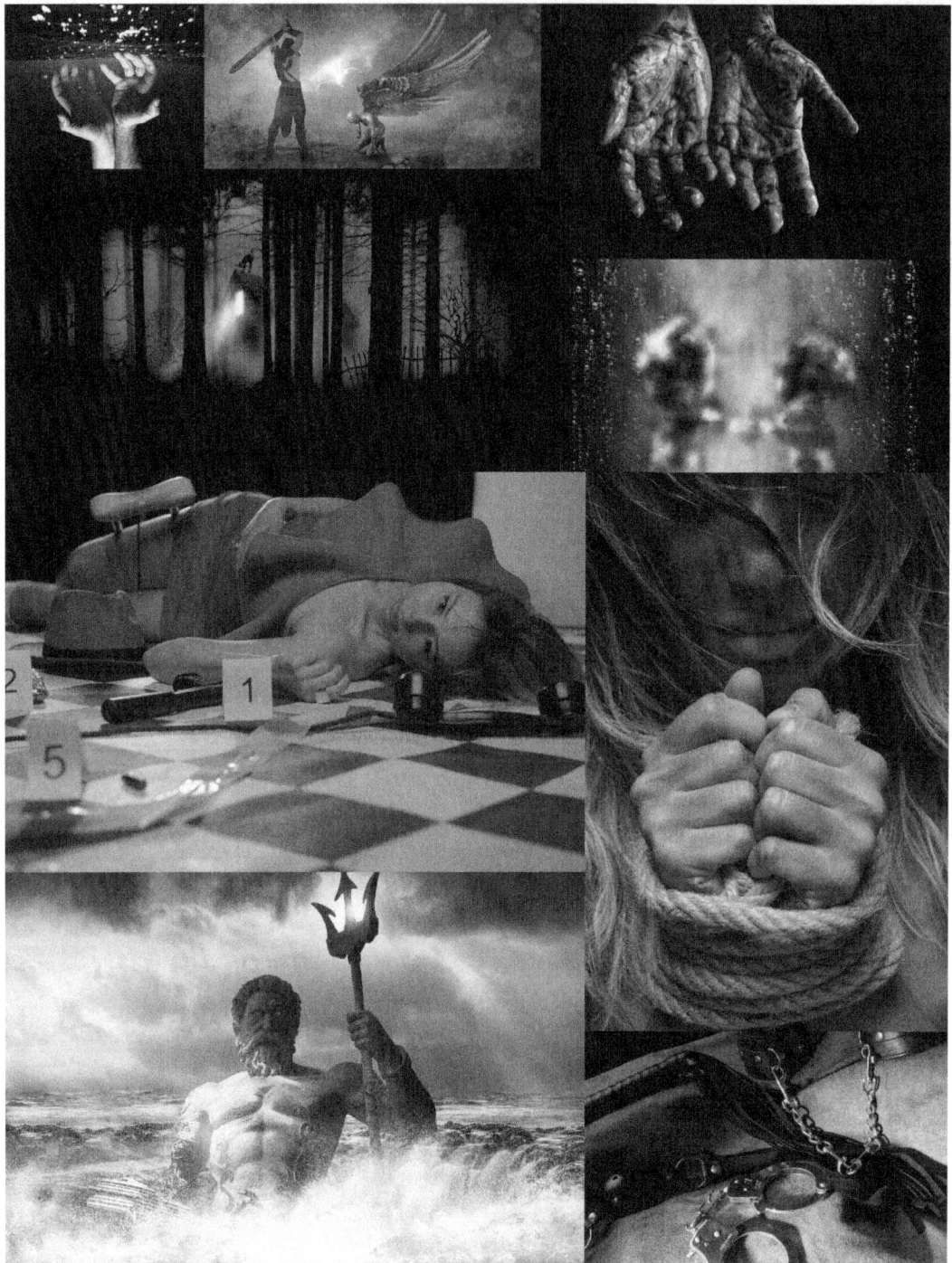

House: The 8th house, the house of sex, death, alchemy, transitions, inheritances, and other people's money.

Planet: Pluto, the planet of rebirth, transformation, emotional depth and intelligence, and mysterious powers (positive), and destruction, the underworld, wrong use of power, and control (negative).

Element and quality: Water and Fixed.

Color: Red, the color of passion, sexual power, and all matters of security, survival, and self-preservation, and aquamarine, the color of tranquility, the imagination, angelic and divine contact, and prophecy.

Physical area: Genitals and reproductive system.

Dates: October 24th to November 22nd.

Scorpio is the depressive doomed isolator with extreme lone wolf syndrome. They keep to themselves, distance themselves from close friends and family, and put themselves in a bubble of introspection. Their need to detach and distance themselves from social scenarios is extreme, and it leads to both amplified shadow traits and a deeply pessimistic outlook on Self and life. As they're ruled by the house of death and transitions, coupled with Pluto's primary influence of a deep inner pull towards personal transformation and awakening, Scorpio runs the risk of falling into the infinite vastness of the sea. As a water sign, they are emotionally intelligent, wise, empathic, and incredibly intuitive, but they're also prone to dark energies linked to the shadow realms. As a natural shaman, seer, and shapeshifter, or, at the very least, with powerful intuitive, psychic, and instinctive gifts; Scorpio enters into the darkest spaces of the spirit world.

Scorpio is the extreme pessimist who won't accept that not everyone wants to listen to their ideas, viewpoints, or intuitive perspectives. They spend copious amounts of time in isolation and then come out like some mighty warrior, imposing their beliefs and knowledge on the world. The secret is: they are highly sensitive, also intensely loyal and devoted to those they love... Yet they are so private and secretive that they are misunderstood. Not everyone is psychic either.

Let's look at the definition of a doomed person:

A person living in constant despair, hopelessness, and desperation, also believing that their life and the universe is doomed; depressed, melancholic, and helpless with a complete loss of inspiration, creative life force, and joy.

Let's break this main definition down, shall we!

Perpetual Despair and Depression

Scorpio lives in constant depression and despair. They see everything as dark, doomed, and gloomy, and this is because they are ruled by Pluto and the 8th house. This is the house of death, rebirth, sex, shared resources and finances, transformation, and the occult. Scorpio is deeply spiritual, moreover are natural shamans, so they have a strong connection to the shadow realms and self. In fact, shadow work, healing, and exploration is integral to Scorpio, whether they're conscious of it or not. They are deeply introspective, introverted, and artistic with a real love of deep study, soul-searching, and delving into metaphysics and the occult. They are natural shapeshifters too- incredibly intuitive, psychics, and instinctive people with evolved senses and instincts. When in a low mental headspace, they are extremely depressed, in a constant state of despair, and pessimistic. They see life, Self, and the universe as dark and gloomy, a world disenchanted. They get lost in their own suffering and darkness, as well as the shadows of others. Scorpio sees shadows everywhere, they refuse to accept the light and love in others, and they fall into an isolated space of disconnection. As the natural shaman and shapeshifter at a higher vibration, Scorpio becomes disconnected from people, joy, and creative avenues. Scorpio is a highly imaginative and musical person, who when in such a depressed state all inspiration is sucked out of their life. This creates a negative spiral. Toxicity becomes their daily reality, yet they don't see themselves as toxic. They see others as toxic, and this leads to a lot of problems, moreover perpetual depression.

Scorpio believes all is doomed, taking on a type of dystopian view of life. Scorpio will enter dark spirals of consciousness, going down dark rabbit holes that lead to further despair; there's no hope, no joy, and no way out. Scorpio will see glimmers of hope, as they are incredibly intuitive- even when in their mental health blueprint. But, these psychic visions and instinctive responses often lead them further into doom and gloom. Darkness breeds more darkness; negative thinking and daily patterns give birth to more negativity and pessimistic thinking. Pluto's influence makes them think about life cycles of death and rebirth often, perhaps even daily. Scorpio is very knowledgeable of natural cycles, mysticism, metaphysics, spiritual concepts and ideals, and universal themes of healing, natural law, and so forth, in both their light and shadow. In their dark psyche, however, they still see spirits, in addition to having access to psychic-mediumships and potent intuitive gifts. Unfortunately for them, they may start to see dark spirits or believe in dark entities. I personally don't advocate this, as a shamanic energy worker who has had many Dark Nights of the Soul. Yes, there may be "evil" spirits on the invisible planes, but there are "evil" people in this earth plane, so why connect to them? Opening oneself to dark forces is common in a dark psyche Scorpio. This is the sign most likely to do a ouija board, sit in darkness and think about their death or evil acts of the world, and contemplate suicide or a dramatic ending.

The Dark Night of the Soul is integral to Scorpio's journey. At a higher vibration and later in life after many trials and lessons, Scorpio has mastered the quantum and spiritual planes. They've mastered many levels of healing, self-knowledge, and lessons pertaining to ancient wisdom. Also, they've become experts in the Dark Night of Soul, which is linked to positive magic, the astral realms, and cycles of time. Ruled by the 8th house, Scorpio has innate knowledge of past lives, universal cycles, and sacred and ancient laws. They are deeply knowledgeable, in fact, of psychic and spiritual phenomena, past and future lives, ancient memories and wisdom connected to humanity's history, and themes some people think are merely fantasy. Soul contracts, soulmates, and karma come into Scorpio's domain as well. Thus, at a low vibration, Scorpio explores these themes, consciously or unconsciously, yet they see *only* the dark. They are deep in the tunnel, and they believe there is no light at the end; or they see the light as a faint and distant glimmer believing there's no way to reach it. They lose faith combined with trust in themselves and the universe. Usually psychic and spiritually powerful Scorpio enters a period of spiritual desolation, emptiness, and apathy. They became separate from the Divine, the place that is usually the source of their extrasensory gifts and self-knowledge. Divine wisdom and healing energies that are readily available to them diminish, as they start to see from pessimistic eyes. Loss and melancholy fills their lives.

Inner darkness and turmoil come to the forefront, which affects all aspects of Scorpio's life, which we explore in the next point. They fall into a self-created pit whilst perpetuating self-created prophecies. This essentially means being so negative that they "predict" future negative outcomes; through their advanced vision, intuition, and spiritual powers they distort and twist the gift of prophecy. Scorpio is prophetic at their best, yet in such a low headspace they create a bad future for themselves, and potentially others. Scorpio gets lost down the rabbit hole, falls into dark and deep holes, and enters an inescapable void... They start to feel like everyone as well as life itself is against them- they unconsciously give themselves endless setbacks, challenges, and hardships. It all starts with the mind, you see. With two planetary rulers, Pluto the modern-day ruler and Mars their ancient ruler, Scorpio is very powerful. They're resourceful, ambitious, independent, competitive, passionate, full of energy and vitality, spiritually perceptive, and gifted with many additional Plutonian qualities. But Mars makes them intense with high life force. So, when at the top of their game they are one of the most resourceful and independent people around, but when in a lower vibration they are still powerful. Their power is, however, used to create harm, separation, or self-sabotage. With regard to the Dark Night of the Soul specifically, a Scorpion specialty, this signifies deep and profound spiritual and karmic lessons, coupled with breaking through illusions, ego, and fear. Scorpio begins to see through key illusions and fears, moreover ignorances linked to the lower mind and ego, yet, because they are still young and unevolved, playing out their mental health blueprint, a lot of the information is lost in translation. It's not received properly. They may receive snippets in the way it was intended to be channeled to them, but there are still distortions and illusions.

Scorpio starts to project their shadows and the collective or individual shadows they pick up on. Don't get it twisted, Scorpio is incredibly psychic, even at a low vibration. But these psychic downloads, messages, and glimpses come to them through distorted channels, as has previously been mentioned. They aren't able to make sense of such potent visions or higher insight perspectives because they are not yet fully aligned to their Higher Self. They become pessimistic and live to spread mistruths, false or dark belief systems, and negative world views. Being so in tune with the collective consciousness energy field, combined with their evolved level of intensity and spiritual depth, makes them advocates for the current state of affairs, as well as global consciousness. Pluto and Mars give this seductive and spiritually evolved sign intense power, but how do they use this when in their dark psyche? Well, it may be interesting to know that Bill Gates is a Scorpio native. I've personally explored his natal/birth chart, *in depth*, and can humbly say his intentions are not pure or righteous. If he were to give away 110 of his *111 billion dollars* to actually make this world into the beautiful, unified, and divine earthly realm it was intended to be, then one could change my mind. But he has used his gifts of ambition, determination, passion, and potent intuition to create money for himself, create a massive divide in humankind, and live selfishly. In doing so, he's unconsciously or consciously created a dark timeline and fate for the rest of the world. No one human should have the largest percentage of wealth while 99.9% are stuck in poverty, entrapment, slavery, abuse, and a pathway to death from malnutrition, poor shelter, etc. Bill Gates is the perfect example of a dark psyche Scorpio who has failed to clear their karma, heal their traumas, and moreover move into adulthood in their dark psyche. Thus, Scorpios in their dark psyche take all the pain, trauma, and darkness they feel and live to serve a timeline of darkness. Sometimes they are victims, other times they play the victim through failing to take responsibility. From a higher and cosmic perspective, no-one is ever truly a victim, therefore Scorpio has total power over their fates.

Outside of the "victim-martyr-persecutor/savior" triangle shared by sister sign Pisces, Scorpio plays victim. They fail to work on their shadow on a deep and authentic level, and further play into wounds and insecurities. *"Everyone else is being a sh*t person, why should I be the only one making a change?"* This is Scorpio's daily mantra when in such a low mental headspace. They attune to a higher frequency and consciousness through intense soul-searching, introspection, and astral and dream work, and then choose to enter the darkest places of the soul. They recognize, through powerful gifts of intuition and extrasensory perception, that the world truly is f*cked; there is a lot of darkness, despair, and suffering. Yet, instead of taking ownership for their current life situation- the depression, melancholy, and lack of self-empowerment, they contribute to the suffering and trauma further. The irony is that Scorpio is one of the most powerful star signs. They have considerable life force, determination, and tenacity, in addition to being extremely resourceful, to create their ultimate life. There is always light at the end of the tunnel, but, like Bill Gates, a dark psyche Scorip will use their god-given gifts for selfish and demonic means. Scorpio in this space might become the ruthless and hothead business leader or head of a corporation that steals from others, pollutes the earth, or hides behind terms like 'charity' or 'nonprofit,' all the while making millions. Scorpio money-laundering, commits benefit or tax fraud, lies to others to increase their chi levels, or forgets to be compassionate and heart-centered altogether. They become selfish, self-entitled, and arrogant, qualities of which stem from their ancient ruler, Mars. A lot of what has been shared for Aries applies to Scorpio, however in a diluted form (Mars is Scorpio's ancient ruler, not current one).

Projection and Shadows

Scorpio is one of the worst projectors, which is due to Pluto's dark and murky influence. At a higher vibration, Pluto may be a master alchemist, amazingly spiritual, wise, perceptive, soulful, and multidimensionally gifted, but, at a lower vibration, Pluto is intense, immersed in darkness, and linked to death. Scorpio gathers infinite channels of information from their environment and then projects it back out into the world, and into the people they encounter. They lack all essential characteristics necessary for sound action and thought, like the left brain/hemisphere qualities, logic, higher mental analysis, reasoning, problem-solving, and intellect, and the right brain/hemisphere qualities, like imagination, intuition, spatial awareness, and holographic multidimensional perception. These are skills that are usually integrated and shown at a high level in a whole and healed Scorpio, but are completely absent when in their mental health blueprint. Like warrior Aries, Scorpio has a strong karmic path that is usually rooted in the ability to bring great change and inspiration to the world. They do this through music, art, inspiring visionary works, books, teaching, speaking, writing, counseling, healing, or being a wayshower through any service or profession they've mastered. Scorpio is the sign of self-mastery, so when unhealed and in despair they project everything going on inside into the outside world. As above so below, as within so without. Scorpio is destined to heal, educate, uplift, or inspire in some way, or at least achieve a sufficient level of success, prestige, and professional accomplishment without sacrificing their beautiful gifts. In addition to being ambitious and resourceful, they are kind, empathic, compassionate, nurturing, sweet, caring, and sensitive with a powerful level of soul and sensitivity.

While other signs might enter a Dark Night of the Soul once or twice, and rise out and through, Scorpio stays there for years on end. A Scorpio dark psyche depression can last a decade or even more if they refuse to work on their shadows and wounds. They get lost in the shadow lands and start to believe that life is a reflection of their inner world, which is gloomy and pessimistic beyond belief. Scorpio refuses to break away from the ego and the illusions that accompany; they succumb to the abyss due to the positive promise associated with the Unknown. The unknown is a mystical and inspirational place infused with wisdom, important lessons, and potent streams of consciousness. But Scorpio goes too far into the great abyss, forgetting to return to the light, to the Source of creation, and to their center. The Unknown draws them in like a moth to a light because it's where the answers to secret knowledge and hidden wisdom can be found. Again, being ruled by the 8th house signifies that they are fascinated by the occult, metaphysics, and mysticism and spirituality, therefore they feel most at home here, even when it's dark and gloomy. Being ruled by the 8th house signifies that they have powerful inner drives of companionship and intimacy, moreover sacred union. Scorpio craves deep connection, love, sex, and so forth, so in a low vibration they are ruled by projection. They begin to see demons everywhere, in their own reflection, in others, in movies and music... Unfortunately, Scorpio is one of the most likely to rape or become a sadist. A merging of ancient ruler Mars and the murky depths of Pluto create a demonic individual, one ruled by instinctive and lusty primal desires. And, Mars' influence makes them incredibly dominant, but unlike Aries who has the element of fire, Scorpio's emotional and soul-penetrating nature makes them believe they own others, or have a right to other people's bodies.

Scorpio will go through repeated difficult periods that shouldn't last as long as they do. From toxic relationships to collaborative and partnership breakdowns, family issues to creative blocks, and new friendship circles formed only to evaporate weeks- months later, Scorpio has the "repeat" button super glued down. Scorpio seems to experience mishaps and disappointments more than any other, and this is due to being so dark and gloomy. They have moments of shininess- they come out in the light sporadically or in a powerful way that lets their gifts be known, but they then return to darkness. Like a Scorpion, Scorpio likes to be left alone, or so it would seem, however, behind the surface they are craving to be understood. They are not the victim, like all signs, they create this internal battle. Luckily, such hardships create a powerful, determined, and resourceful individual later in life, but they have a lot of shadow blocks to deal with first. Ruled by the 8th house, Scorpio is the most likely according to astrology to experience death of loved ones, life-threatening illnesses of Self or others, and divorces of parents. If they don't experience these directly, they will certainly explore these through self-reflection and introspection, and then "take on" the despair associated as if it were their job to heal it. They are partly right, as, as the sign associated the Shadow Self and Shamanism, it could very well be part of their destiny to heal collective wounds. In fact, working to transcend collective and planetary karma through their own personal evolution is core to this telepathic and spiritual sign. So, Scorpio gives themselves impossible tasks and tests to complete that aim to heal and transcend individual and planetary karma. Unfortunately, despite having a rare level of spiritual awareness combined with psychic gifts and instincts, Scorpio is *not* an experienced professional. They're still in the self-learning stage themselves, so they become the perfect example of the baby trying to run before they can even crawl! This created an internal battle that leaves them feeling lost, lonely and disconnected from everyone around them… which only amplifies their depression.

A Loss of Joy, Love, and Intimacy

Scorpio's life becomes meaningless. They become demoralized at extreme levels. There is no joy or purpose- at a higher vibration, Scorpio is full of passion and purpose, moreover they are aware of what their soul's plan and path is. In such a low mental headspace, they have no idea who they should be meeting, what changes they should be making, and where they should go. Scorpio forgets the ancient cord and knowledge connecting them to the Divine, to Source, and to God or the Universe. If they do receive clues from the outside world or their subconscious mind or Higher Self, they overlook them. They instead turn to the dread and despair they've become too familiar with. It sort of becomes a safety blanket, and this is true for all water signs. Just like Cancer and Pisces, Scorpio is hyper-emotional and super-sensitive; the only difference is that they try to hide it more. Unlike the Crab and Fish, the Scorpion can be deadly, so this symbol provides further wisdom. The Scorpion can defend itself much better than the other water signs, and in some cases they have lethal power (for defense and self-protection). But,

Scorpio hides behind a hard and even cold and callous front. There is the aspect of having Mars as an ancient ruler, which makes them just as competitive, passionate, and strong-willed as Aries. It also makes them ambitious and, in some cases, ruthless beyond belief. However, Scorpio will always predominantly be a water sign, therefore they are sensitive, sweet, and in deep need of nurturing and loving bonds.

Any hardness or coldness Scorpio puts on is an act because deep down they are supremely affectionate and loyal beings. They live for intimacy, whether it be platonic or romantic, and have sincere hearts and spirits. This "front" then creates a cold-hearted individual who pushes everyone away or contributes to the negativity of the world. Inside, they may have amazing intuitive revelations and psychic messages or wisdom to share, but they just appear pessimistic, moody, and cold. No-one wants to go near them let alone listen to what they have to say. Scorpio so desperately wants to share wisdom, inspiration, and what their intuition tells them will lift the group up, yet they become the lone wolf and black sheep. Scorpio is the black sheep of the zodiac alongside mystical and spiritually evolved Pisces. The three things they desire the most, joy and deeper connection, intimacy, and love, are eradicated from their world, and it's their own doing. Ok, sometimes Scorpio may be fearless and brave and come out of their shell, showing the world their true heart and soul- only to be turned down or ridiculed; but, primarily, they are not victims. At a higher frequency, Scorpio is the wise wo/man who lives with heart and soul, showing people the true meaning of depth, emotional wisdom, and sensitivity. They're not wishy-washy, but command utmost power and respect, because, unlike some other signs, they are fueled by a sincere need for emotional depth and intimacy. Spiritual depth and intimacy too. This gives them a certain level of power. In their dark psyche, they lose all sense of hope, joy, faith, love, and opportunities for connection. Even when an opportunity to open up and receive the love they desire so deeply is staring them right in the face, they project their shadows or unhealed wounds, or choose only to see the negative. In their mental health blueprint, Scorpio is a lost cause.

Meaningless, hopelessness, and a disenchanted world view fills their life. They become vindictive and mean-spirited towards friends and family, or even towards powerful creative and business collaborators who could help them. Oh yes, Scorpio will turn revengeful towards others with success, power, prestige, love, or happiness in their lives. The Scorpio personality is complex while simultaneously being a blend of varying qualities and characteristics. This is because they have two planetary rulers from two different elements, fire and water. Fire and water create steam! The visual to see here is new and higher consciousness arising from the material realm. Or, in other cases, fire and water mixed together create destructive explosions... More on this in the final topic of exploration. Due to their potent link to higher realization, universal truths, and consciousness. Scorpio starts to predict their own or others' dark fates. The term "self-perpetuating prophecy" applies here. At their best, Scorpio is a master of extrasensory, psychic, and intuitive perception. They are natural seers, shamans, counselors, soul guides, teachers or wayshowers of esoteric knowledge, and experts in the realm of mediumship, metaphysics, and the occult. They genuinely have access to the hidden and invisible realms, transcendental states, and so forth. And, they are very prophetically gifted. Thus, in their dark psyche, they start to "predict" and "prophesize," but from a very dark and diabolical perspective. Their modes of perception and observation are distorted, faulty even. They become the *dark shaman*, the prophet and seer who will only see individual and collective dark fates. This is something shared by Sagittarius the delusional who also has a link to celestial and higher consciousness energies.

At their worst, Scorpio is a dangerous individual, because people believe them. People can sense on some instinctive and intuitive level that they are wise, intuitive, and straight-out psychic, so people believe their dark prophecies. Scorpio delves into the Occult, yet because they're misinformed and misguided they give out *wrong* advice. The impact of this can be disastrous. To add, Scorpio is a natural master of lucid dreaming, astral travel, and receiving advanced wisdom from dream states, so they seem to be looked on for wise counsel and guidance in these areas. Yet, once again, they have undertaken no real course of study, professional self-development, or grounded pathways to give out such advice. Scorpio in theri mental health blueprint is the Hierophant in reverse. Upright, the Hierophant major arcana tarot card represents spiritual wisdom, traditional institutions, and religious beliefs, which gives them real prestige coupled with a legitimate basis to teach and lead from. In reverse, however, the Hierophant symbolizes personal beliefs, freedom, and challenging the status quo... Freedom when acting from ego or distorted belief systems (and not the Higher Self) can be catastrophic, as personal beliefs and ideologies are injected into their "teachings." Personal opinions replace high perspectives, bad past experiences diminish truth, and Scorpio lives, thinks, and acts from a need to prove themselves or disprove others. Everything becomes backwards. Illusion, pain, and false truths become normal in their world and the worlds of people they're connected to. It's always masked in a false spirituality or truth though, thus downward spirals begin.

Extreme Isolation and Solitude

Low self-worth and self-esteem ensue. Self-pity fills Scorpio's life, while slitting wrists, attempted suicides, and the most extreme displays of self-harm and warnings to friends and family become a regular daily feature. These are part of the Scorpio dark psyche. They enter into excessively long periods of isolation brought on by a loss of Self; the ego has taken over, in addition to the lower self ruling them as opposed to the Higher Self. Scorpio is the lone wolf and when in such a low vibration, this is taken to new heights (or lows) of solitude. Scorpio lives in introspection mode, believing the only way they can escape the self-pity they've created is to learn, study, and master. They are the sign of self-mastery, but they don't know how to achieve this properly. Wisdom and knowledge acquisition becomes their daily quest, and although they do learn a lot in these years-long periods, it ultimately disconnects them. Scorpio become incredibly unsociable, so much so that they don't know how to interact with others. They are incapable of basic social skills and become abnormally shy, reserved, and awkward. In social scenarios, they are the most awkward and melancholic star sign. Ever. Addictions, substances abuse, and suicidal thoughts or attempts take over. They turn towards drugs or spiritual activities that are on par with taking drugs; Scorpio is able to enter transcendental and mystical states without substance, so the feelings of sublimity and euphoria become a type of drug. They get naturally high off of the mystical energies, a unique gift associated with Old Soul Pisces (and trust me, I can confirm this is true…). But in a low frequency this is not a gift, it's a curse. Scorpio may be an excellent next level artist, seer, psychic, clairvoyant, prophet, or healer, but they need to actually interact with other humans to be able to fulfill this mission.

If we look at the *Wolf spirit animal symbolism*, we can see how instinctive, intuitive, and protective over friends and family Scorpio is (higher vibration). Yet, in their mental health blueprint they are misguided to the point of using their instincts to cause harm; there's a reason why instincts are often called killer instincts! Scorpio can cause serious harm or even death through the false guidance they give. And, as the lone wolf of the zodiac, they fail to heal their wounds and right their wrongs, choosing to stay attached to the comfort of the darkness they've gotten so used to. *They find solace in their shadows.* Trauma bonding as well as unhealthy attachment is associated with Scorpio. They become lonely while projecting the image of being 'all one.' They believe in interconnectedness and community, on a deep, deep level, yet they don't have the skills, wisdom, or life experience to implement it in a grounded way. A lot of what they do and feel exists in the ether or subtle realms of consciousness, so it's difficult to exist in the real world. They enter into extreme periods of isolation that separate them from their higher mind, from Source, and from the true seat of knowledge and power that makes Scorpio who they are when in a higher vibration. Scorpio believes they're some magical shaman or spiritual master when, in actuality, they're a pessimistic prick. Sorry to be so blunt. Scorpio believes themselves to be spiritually superior in a way Virgo and Libra think they're intellectually superior, as, when at their best, they are.

They become judgmental, arrogant, and condescending, thinking they're the only ones who have metaphysical or secret wisdom, moreover a link to the occult or divine. When they finally leave their bubble of solitude and isolation, they *explode* their months- years of knowledge acquisition in a deeply "not-the-right-way-to-go-about-things" way. Usually empathic and caring Scorpio becomes an arrogant jerk, only concerned with how they appear in a public light, not the actual impact they're leaving on others. This is due to Aries ruling the 1st house of personal identity and the Self- public appearance, superficial concepts of beauty, and so forth. Remember that Mars is Scorpio's ancient ruler, therefore they are still influenced by them (Mars, Aries, and the 1st house). Actually, the Aries personality is a second dimension to Scorpio's true character, only a little more watered-down. This makes Scorpio aggressive, self-entitled, and egotistical in their delivery of wisdom and intuitive guidance. Yes, Scorpio is very wise and self-aware, yet their approach is completely wrong. Imagine not seeing your friend or loved one for 3 months and then in one chance encounter they unload everything they've been learning on you, as if you're inferior and know nothing? No-one would be best pleased. Further, people see a Scorpio who has finally left their isolated cocoon as extremely strange, as well as *untrustworthy*. At a higher vibration, Scorpio is responsible, ambitious, and faithful, thus people tend to trust them. In their dark psyche, people don't trust the information they're giving at all, and it eventually pushes Scorpio back into their solitude. It's a vicious cycle. Scorpio's life purpose is to heal their wounds and work on their toxic shadow traits for good, so they don't project on others.

Deep-Seated Manipulation, Jealousy, and Vindictiveness

This leads us onto the final theme of the Scorpio dark psyche, extreme manipulation, jealousy, and a need for revenge. Scorpio will plot their revenge for years to decades, quite literally. Their sign is associated with the shadow self, shamanism, karma, and healing ancestral wounds and energies. Scorpio knows how to do deep trauma and wound work at a higher vibration, so in a low frequency this makes them very susceptible to dark forces, like deep-seated jealousy and possessiveness. Scorpio is one of the most possessive star signs. They are Fixed, therefore they are extremely possessive, and when hurt or betrayed, *vindictive*. Scorpio will embark on a revenge warpath for years to decades… to centuries. This deep pain will last for eternities and lifetimes if Scorpio fails to heal their wounds. The issue is, they're not always betrayed, they just think they are. Scorpio in love or attached to a person or relationship will take a brief moment of soulmate connection or chemistry as a betrayal. Like the Scorpion who attacks when they feel threatened, they have an explosive side. They will defend and protect themselves because they secretly have very fragile and sensitive hearts. Scorpio mistakes passing attractions, light-hearted flirting, and innocent connection as something serious and relationship threatening. In love, they are so jealous and possessive that they will end a 5 year relationship over a trivial occurrence! Scorpio is a deep, deep sign, you see, so while they may be empathic, loyal, kind, sweet, and caring, they also lack the light-heartedness and upbeat persona needed to find balance in life. In romantic and sexual relationships, they arise like the *kraken* from the deep waters if they sense any sign of unfaithfulness or disloyalty. They are a bit hypocritical, however, as in youth they are very frivolous- they are one of the most likely to cheat, moreover they have many sexual partners. Scorpio is the most sexually active and liberated sign alongside Mars-ruled Aries.

So, this hypocrisy creates unresolved pain and trauma over time, in addition to an inability to let go and forgive. They lack self-forgiveness for the unconscious hurt they've caused others; they were just being free and young, exploring their sexuality, right? Well, un-self-forgiveness translates into a lack of forgiveness for others over time. They find it impossible to forgive imaginary, real, or perceived betrayal and infidelity. When they love, they love with their entire souls; Pluto makes them deep, passionate, and intense. They are supremely sexy, according to astrology they're the most seductive and sexually magnetic around. Thus, in their dark psyche they become vindictive and jealous beyond belief. They want revenge, even if their need for revenge is rooted in some illusory vision of what their lover has done. If it's real or merely a fantasy birthed from deep and passionate love & attachment, Scorpio begins a path of revenge, needing to "ruin" their lover's life. If they split, Scorpio will make their life hell, sending them *'psychic attack'* so they feel worthless and unlovable. Scorpio is fully capable of ruining another's self-esteem based on how much power they have. As a spiritually evolved sign ruled by a watery planet, Scorpio is fully capable of psychic attack. They are psychic, magnetic, and instinctive beyond belief, so they know how to manipulate and control energy. More on this in a moment. If they stay together, Scorpio will still make their lover's life hell by ruining romantic dinner dates, nights in, and almost-magical moments. Their lover will show them their heart or open up fully, and Scorpio will unleash the jealous monster inside. Their shadow self includes being vindictive and spiteful at extreme levels so in their mental health blueprint there is no self-control whatsoever. In a higher vibration, this sensitive and spiritual sign is incredibly self-mastered, however in their dark psyche they only care about getting justice or revenge. They don't care about how they come across either, public opinion coupled with superficial things don't interest them. Therefore, they will make their jealousies and spite known. This drives their lover away or, at the worst, leads to passion crimes, sexual violence, and potentially dangerous situations.

As for no self-control, Scorpio is ruled by murky and deep waters. They're hyper-emotional and super-sensitive, and they have a hard time controlling their desires. In youth this can be as innocent as being flirty and hyersexual, wanting to play the field and experiment sexually in as many ways as possible. Later in life, this can manifest as something more serious, like passion crimes, which signifies sexually assaulting, raping, or even murdering their lover in a fit of rage. Scorpio is intensely passionate, and like the waves of the oceans they can be unpredictable. In a higher frequency they may be devoted, loving, and self-mastered, but in their mental health blueprint there's no sense of self-control or emotional and physical boundaries at all. Mars' influence makes them violent and quick to temper, as well as full of lust, passion, and energy. Pluto makes them link sex and intimacy with darker themes, and when in their dark psyche this gives rise to dark fantasies, dom-sub unhealthy dynamics, and dangerous eroticism similar to Taurus. Scorpio is the sign most likely to become sadistic, wanting to control their lover through an insatiable sexual appetite. They're certainly skilled, so combined with their powerful emotional intensity, sex appeal, and charisma they can bind someone to them in a deeply unhealthy way. The dom-sub dynamic is very real and destructive in this sign; think whips and chains, obsessive behaviors in love, and excessive love-making and kinky sex sessions, but constantly, and at expense to other key aspects of life. Scorpio goes o.t.t., they take love, romance, and intimacy too far. Scorpio's magnetism, charisma, emotional intelligence, empathy, and nurturing yet equally powerful and presence-commanding nature makes them irresistible… Yet, in sexual partnerships, they become overly concerned with power and winning their lover over. Due to their intensity and jealous-possessive streak they can turn nasty in a heat of a moment.

One moment, it will apparently be cool, and, the next, it will be a tsunami or hurricane of emotions and projection. Scorpio has an inner rage and jealousy that matches Aries' need for war and conflict. Their rage is emotional, stirred up from the instinctive need for loving bond, companionship, and intimacy. Like with Taurus, Scorpio's opposite sign, Scorpio becomes a vengeful and volatile psychopath who will stop at nothing to show their lover just how much they love them, and just how far they're willing to go to prove their loyalty.

Scorpio equates spite and jealous outbursts in relationships with love and devotion; they're devotional and loyal when maturer and more evolved, but in their lower self they are overly concerned with dramatic displays of showing their love. The irony is, Scorpio is secretly shy, reserved, and scared to be left alone, they crave companionship and love above all else. This is due to being ruled by the 8th house, symbolizing partnerships, sex, death, and karmic contracts. A Scorpio worst nightmare is being rejected or failing to secure true love. To add to this, they are aware of karmic engagements like relationships that are built off of toxicity and trauma bonding, and further know the difference between these types of relationships and true love or higher soulmate relationships, but they are so *possessive* that they don't have the willpower to let go. In other words, they hold on for much longer than they should. As a Fixed sign, they cling to the idea that true love is forever, even when there are clear signs it's not a true love relationship. Scorpio wants so desperately to have that idealized romantic love, yet they fail to listen to the red flags. A complete contradiction in character due to being so intuitive and instinctive, Scorpio will be oblivious or in denial as to how bad a relationship is going. Either things will reach a violent head with daily explosive arguments and heated passionate make-up sex, which leads to further emotional disconnection (amplifying their inner darkness, inevitably), or they will cling on for an eternity. In the latter case, this usually resourceful and ambitious sign misses out on a world of opportunities, from professional and creative partnerships to educational and cultural doorways. Abundance, prosperity, and friendships suffer. Family and home life suffers, while all sense of inspiration, joy, and zest disappears from their life. Scorpio is in love feeling good feelings momentarily, while being unhappy inside.

This is because they've given off so much negative energy, making their lover or partner feel bad and guilty for having friends or brief moments of chemistry, etc. Scorpio creates a vicious cycle of denial, hatred, and betrayal all the while convincing themselves they're innocent, or their vindictive and evil ways are just. Being mean and heartless to someone who is trying to show you the utmost care, affection, and respect is *not* just. But, they act from their intense desires and emotions, which steers them of course; they're not aligned to their Higher Self in this energetic space. Thus, karmic consequences ensue, and as Scorpio's entire identity is rooted around love and intimacy this sets them on a downward spiral. They fail to see the lesson or spiritual meaning, moreover the opportunity for self-evolution in the experience, and instead attach to the toxic aspects. Karmic contracts and sexual agreements entered into are ruled by the 8th house, Scorpio's ruling house. Scorpio becomes mistaken and deluded as to what true love is. They believe they're in a soulmate connection when, in actuality, they're in a toxic-karmic entanglement! Due to ruling the 8th house, Scorpio's life path involves transcending the trials and tribulations as well as the false love stories and timelines, to find their great soul mission or purpose. Scorpio's true path and destiny is almost always discovered at the end of coming out of one or a few long-term and key karmic relationships. At a higher vibration, they are the sign of alchemy, rebirth, and transformation… on the deepest of levels. In their dark psyche, they are the opposite, therefore love, sex, and marriage potential or partnerships feature strongly in their life. Scorpio's mistake is idealizing, succumbing to possessiveness, and then turning vindictive and revengeful when things finally run their course.

It doesn't matter whose fault it was or even how, why, and how mutually agreeable the separation was; in their mental health blueprint, Scorpio will never see it as a blessing or opportunity for self-evolution. The 8th house is *the* house of marriage, sex, death, transitions, and love contracts, after all. Their lower self acts out against the highest potential manifestation of all of these things. As for karma, this intensely sexy and seductive sign accumulates a lot of bad karma. If it weren't bad enough that their shadow traits coupled with their elevated sex appeal and promiscuity result in negative repercussions, they're also ruled by Mars, which makes them even more karma-prone. Debts must be paid. They can't sit in secrecy and solitude sending negative energy or harmful intentions to past lovers or third parties who were slightly involved in a betrayal, and then expect to find a happy connection or true soulmate bond. Life doesn't work like this. Scorpio's years of self-neglect, building spite, and depression make them into a sh*t magnet when they finally come out of their dark slumber. Everyone picks up on Scorpio's judgements and misinformed beliefs one way or another. No-one is happy with them, moreover many people feel it's their duty to call them out. In a higher frequency, Scorpio is a wise wo/man, a psychic and powerfully intuitive soul-warrior with good intentions for their personal power and magnetism. But in a lower vibration, they are simply arrogant and spiritually superior, in addition to, of course, being full of projection. Their lessons are to heal their own wounds and trauma or pain before trying to unleash their elevated spiritual powers of perception and ancient knowledge on the world. From within to without and as above so below, Scorpio must focus on their own path and purpose.

Absolute worse crimes possible?

	LESS LIKELY	LIKELY	ABSOLUTELY
MURDER			✓
RAPE			✓

ANIMAL CRUELTY	✓		
CHILD ABUSE		✓	
MOLESTATION			✓
TORTURE			✓
HUMAN TRAFFICKING		✓	
SLAVERY	✓		
BESTIALITY		✓	
TERRORISM		✓	
KIDNAPPING			✓
GENOCIDE		✓	
NUCLEAR WAR DECIDER			✓

CHAPTER 9: Sagittarius the Delusional

House: The 9th house, the house of morals/ethics, philosophy, higher learning, and spiritual & cultural ideals.

Planet: Jupiter, the planet of luck, expansion, travel, and abundance (positive), and blind faith, ungrounded vision, immorality, and reckless behavior (negative).

Element and quality: Fire and Mutable.

Color: Orange, the color of passion/joy, intimacy, friendship, and sexuality; yellow, the color of confidence, ambition, optimism, and self-empowerment, and purple, the color of ancient wisdom, intuition, higher truth, and self-knowledge.

Physical area: Hips, thighs, and legs (+ pituitary gland).

Dates: November 23rd to December 21st.

Sagittarius is ruled by Jupiter, the 9th house, and the glyph of both the Archer and Centaur. This represents a perfect balance or unification between the lower and higher selves. Sagittarius is both primal and spiritual, liberated and ambitious, and instinctive and concerned with higher things. They're truth seekers passionate about justice, morality, and higher spiritual, educational, and cultural ideals. But, because of their impulsive and flighty, moreover impatient, aggressive, and highly physical/sexual nature, they can devolve into the lower self. When they do and they start to get too attached to the people, places, and things that have only served their devilish side, their life begins to spiral out of control. They mistake good for evil and right for wrong, and vice versa. Being so immersed in their shadow traits, which bring them sheer joy and fun when younger combined with being more immature and unevolved, as we will be exploring; makes them susceptible to darker forces, or they're the ones instigating harm and foul-play.

Sagittarius is ultimately a very physical and energetic sign, so coupled with being so impulsive and spotlight-seeking, i.e. loving attention and admiration for being seen in a positive light, they get lost pretty quickly to negative currents. Due to their self-righteousness, arrogance, and superior nature, it can then be impossible to leave behind the chapters they've gotten so used to...

Let's look at the definition of a delusional person:

A highly judgmental person who has notions of grandiose, superiority, and self-importance while believing everyone to be beneath them; paranoid, mistaken, and misinformed with extremely faulty belief systems.

Let's break this main definition down, shall we!

Highly Judgemental With A Superiority Complex

The usually fun-loving and optimistic Archer is highly judgemental and delusional when in their dark psyche. They believe themself to be better and judge everyone, and I mean everyone. They have notions of grandiose and a real narcissistic personality, so much so that many Sagittariuses, like fellow fire signs Aries and Leo, are diagnosed with Narcissistic Personality Disorder (NPD). You can read the description of Narcissus in Aries' chapter to understand this sign's mental health blueprint better; they are a spitting image of it. Everyone is beneath them. They are egotistical, self-righteous to the max, and blunt to the point of abusing others. They think they're being shiny, but, in reality, they are bullying others through their preconceived ideas of self-importance. They believe themselves to be intellectually, spiritually, creatively, artistically, and logically superior. Sagittarius is a highly intuitive individual, however when in their totally self-righteous headspace they misuse their intellectual and intuitive power. In fact, they become very dark and dangerous to others, using mental confusion to instill fear and false information in their victims. Sagittarius is very similar to Gemini and Virgo in this respect, the two signs ruled by Mercury. This is because Sagittarius is ruled by Jupiter, a planet similar to Mercury although a lot larger.

Jupiter symbolizes higher ideals, learning, educational, philosophy, spiritual concepts and studies, cultural activities, and travel. Everything related to the higher mind and intuition, spiritual ideals, and philosophy come under Jupiter's realm, so the shadow side of this is seen in Sagittarius when devolved. When unevolved and at a lower frequency, they become irrational and concerned with power. The ego comes out in full force, as the ego is a lower manifestation of the higher mind and Higher Self. Egotistical, self-serving, and self-righteous tendencies are part of the Sagittarius shadow, but when taken to extremes they become monstrous in their mannerisms. There's no such thing as respect or social etiquette and charm, which is what a higher vibrational Sagittarius embodies. If they do display charm, it's the fake charm shown by narcissists. They wear a social mask, it's all a facade; they crave followers and fans above all else. Being so delusional birthed from such extreme self-importance and self-righteousness turns them into a mean-spirited tyrant. But because they have such a big personality coupled with the fact that they're usually seen, or already known as, sunny, positive, and optimistic, they seem to get away with it. In fact, Sagittarius gets away with their shadow more than all other signs. And this is because they are ruled by the planet everyone loves, the planet of luck, expansion, and travel itself. Jupiter is arguably one of the more superior, and with such a bubbly and optimistic personality who gives love and light to people when they need- Sagittarius when at the top of their game, it's no wonder that this jovial sign gets away with murder. Unfortunately, this saying can become a harsh reality, as a physical "prone-to-aggression and violence" fire sign (more on this in the final section).

A superiority complex that pushes others down while intimidating them is Sagittarius at their worst. Sagittarius is a bully and ugly spirit who bulldozes over everyone. They lack sensitivity, empathy, and kindness, and the usual honest and joyous personality everyone loves becomes a monster, quite literally. They walk around on their high horse and walk away from social settings like some massive walking ego. That is, if they've been called out publicly and haven't been able to admit defeat, find some grace, and accept the enormous size of their ego. There's no hope for them at this stage, so they will either resort to physical violence and aggression to intimate others into silence, or walk off like some weirdo. Sagittarius' ego becomes bruised and then they don't care about what they look like. They are a contradiction, and there's a lot of different information to present here. On the one hand, their NPD (extreme narcissism) makes them crave admirers and followers at all costs; their social facade and mask is fully on, and they are clearly selfish and self-serving in their mannerisms. There's nothing kind, compromising, or sweet and selfless about them. Keeping their mask firmly on is their primary intention. But and on the other hand, when they have had enough of all their inferiors and, again, won't admit to their wrongs, they storm off like some pr*ck. Or become violent and abusive if alcohol, drugs, or other substances are involved… or if they also have antisocial personality disorder.

Sagittarius refuses to change when deep in their mental health blueprint. This empowered yet overpowering fire sign sees everyone as their subjects, their minions, and their inferiors. Everyone is meant to be submissive to them, and if they aren't they will seek to destroy them. Oh yes, happy and jovial Sagittarius is a destroyer of souls. Jupiter's influence makes them soulful, majestic, and noble, but it can also create a devilish person who needs to be seen as the sole king or queen; the sole heir to virtually every kingdom or queendom. It's a sad truth because Sagittarius has so many wonderful traits. They sit on their high horse with their ethereal crown firmly on their head, without realizing that their crown has become full of dust and dirt. Moreover, the gold and celestial shine has diminished and faded... This is the best imagery for Sagittarius in a low mental headspace. As the sign associated with the shaman and cosmic shapeshifter, Sagittarius is also a dark magician. They use their magical, charismatic, and innovative powers to cause harm, misleading and manipulating others. Sagittarius, manipulative? I know, this may be the first time you've heard this. Sagittarius' manipulation is not like a Cancerian's; it's more aligned to intentionally distorting and twisting the truth. To be blunt, Sagittarius is so fanatic and self-righteous, moreover ruled by the planet of higher truth, learning, and philosophy, that they are very wise. They are so wise, intuitive, and bright, in fact, that when they are seeking power, money, or fame, they really don't care who they cause harm to. Sagittarius embodies the energy of a dragon, and although you might misinterpret dragons as cute and cuddly, dragons unleash monstrous consequences through their out-of-control fire. Combined with this is the fact that Sagittarius is a natural born leader, so when you put all of this together you may understand why they are so deceptive. They BS others. They play games. They see vulnerable and naive characters and think it would be fun to unleash some terror and cruelty on them. Just like a dragon who looks down on an entire city as if it's the city's (and all its inhabitants) overlord, Sagittarius will play with people's lives for instant gratification. This is one of the most immature, irresponsible, and reckless personalities when in their mental health blueprint.

Utterly Delusional

So, Sagittarius is delusional. In a social setting they are the only ones who are allowed to be confident, expressive, and amazing. They need admiration and attention, as well as being in the spotlight virtually all the time. They don't let others talk and they can't handle that other people may have gifts, talents, or beautiful qualities. There's nothing wrong with being a wonderful person or wanting to be seen in a positive light, yet sagittarius is the *only one*. If they are around others like them then they bounce off them, and this paves the way for gang culture. Sagittarius is one of the more likely to be involved in a bullying gang or criminal gang when older. They thrive off of the attention and fake power. At home in a domestic environment, Sagittarius requires their minions to be submissive and silent. They are honest and blunt, so when in such a low vibration these qualities are transformed into something truly horrific. They become "honest" to the point of abuse, becoming psychologically, emotionally, or physically abusive and/or violent. They are delusional in the fact that they think it is ok, that this behavior is right and acceptable. It's not, by any standards. They silence others, expect them to refrain from speaking or having opinions. They become intolerant, impatient, and undisciplined in their words and actions, moreover they disallow others from having a voice. Sagittarius becomes like a drill sergeant or army officer, but a corrupt one who cares little for human life.

Other people's opinions, feelings, and wills don't matter; insensitivity coupled with a lack of empathy are taken to extremes. Overall, they impose their will on others whilst simultaneously blocking other people from shining, sharing their gifts, perspectives, and opinions or wisdom, and using their voice entirely. All sense of respect and mutual harmony goes out the window. *It's my way or the highway.* Solely on the delusional factor, they genuinely believe that they are better in every way. *How could anyone else possibly be confident or expressive? How could anyone be as or more talented than me? How can anyone have any gifts whatsoever?!* These are the questions they tell themselves, eventually convincing themselves they're the truth. On this note, it's important to know that as the truth-seeking sign who strives for universal and higher truths, in addition to spiritual ideals, Sagittarius in a low frequency plays out the polar opposite side of this need. The desire for truth, justice, and social cohesion distorts and twists into a sociopathic, narcissistic, and demonic need for oblivion. In other words, if they can't be seen as the best or come out on top, no-one else can. Sagittarius will destroy another person's character, identity, and self-esteem, making them unbelievably low and worthless. And, unfortunately, they get a kick off of others' suffering, they find joy and pleasure in other people feeing worthless or even become depressed or suicidal. Similar to fellow masculine signs (air and fire), Sagittarius smiles at people being utterly submissive, yet equally sad and hurt, to them. Feelings don't matter, the heart goes out the window, and all sense of soul and nobility are lost to their ego's will. This dirty character is the type of person who will make someone fall in love with them or become a real follower and fan, like Narcissus, and then stomp over them.

Asd the sign of adventure and travel, Sagittarius takes a love of freedom and fun too far. In their mental health blueprint, they will get up and leave home without a suitcase or even wallet. They take on the world head-on, with a youthfulness and sense of trust that can be seen as inspirational. But, in their dark psyche this makes them totally reckless and frivolous. The lower vibration manifestations of being carefree and travel-loving come out in full force; instead of traveling for culture, new educational opportunities, or spiritual and personal growth and self-development, Sagittarius will destroy all the things that should be bringing them pleasure. Polluting our earth and seas, choosing holiday destinations or travel experiences that are as anti-environmentalism or ecologically mindful as possible, and drinking themselves into oblivion. Oh yes, Sagittarius is the party-animal, a real social drinker and fornicator. They're promiscuous while being full of wanderlust. At their worst, this is the sign who will be found in a pit, murdered as a foreigner, or raped through extreme intoxication. Their mental health blueprint is defined as being completely reckless, shallow, impractical, childish, and immature, as well not caring about the earth that sustains them. The 9th house rules travel and cultural experiences, so at a lower vibration Sagittarius is the unconscious traveler, the wild party-animal with a "no f*cks given" attitude that can be infuriating to more grounded and emotionally mature types. They lack all sense of sensibility and ethics. If this spirals into something long-term, Sagittarius will lose all sense of higher intuitive guidance regarding their life path and purpose, thus drinking or intoxicating themselves to an early death. Liver failure, serious digestive issues, and diabetes are associated with this sign ruling the hips and thighs.

Paranoid and Psychotic

Sagittarius makes people submit to them either emotionally, psychologically, spiritually-with their entire soul, physically, or in some cases sexually. They are dominant, assertive, and confident individuals with a powerful pull towards independence and freedom. But they don't give the same level of respect or freedom back, at least not when in their lower self. People become their doormats, they treat people like crap, and feed them scraps. What do I mean by this? They will give one smile after months of abuse, one bit of love or affection after treating their admirer, friend, or lover like dirt, or a small serving of food after eating like a king or queen for a long time. Sagittarius expects the world while giving *nothing* in return. They are takers, not givers or lovers at heart. Sagittarius is more compatible both sexually and platonically with other dominant signs, according to astrology. They fair well with Aries, Gemini , Leo, Libra, Sagittarius, and Aquarius, so they don't share the same gentle or yielding nature of the earth and water signs. Sagittarius likes to make people feel small and worthless, actively and with full intention destroying their worth; they lack humility and their best self, being noble, diplomatic, and full of integrity, diminishes. Thus, people become their doormats and personal property, they have to beg for a tiny bit of love, attention, kindness, sincerity, heart, soul, friendliness, and so forth. While Sagittarius is receiving copious amounts, they give nothing in return. This sign becomes brutal and heartless, in all honesty, and the "delusional to their own self-righteousness combined with the narcissistic side" doesn't help. So, after weeks, months, years, or decades of using others, taking advantage of their kindness, and seeing everyone as inferior, Sagittarius eventually becomes psychotic. They turn paranoid, believing the world and everyone in it to be against them. This may be true or it may not be- what is truth when you're so lost in self-denial and delusion?! If it is true, people have finally woken up to optimistic and sunny-natured Sagittarius' evil ways. This means Sag has also had a rude awakening.

At their worst, before they are healed and whole within (free of their mental health blueprint), they will be completely paranoid verging on schizophrenic. They see monsters everywhere, only seeing the bad in others, and failing to recognize the heart and empathy in humankind. They become paranoid to the world around them, and may even develop *agoraphobia*, the fear of leaving home, or *anthropophobia*, the fear of other people. They think everyone is out to get them, and this is because they have spent months to years immersed in master plots to destroy another person's character. This may have been someone who stood up for an underdog or someone they were targeting or bullying; or simply someone who saw through their BS. If you're someone who figured out that Sagittarius *isn't* the only star sign without a shadow side, and you chose to speak up, you may have been on the receiving end of defamation of character. Sag may have embarked on a dark path making the decision to destroy you, on multiple planes… Physically, they may have chosen violence or resorted to suing, filing false reports, or making your life hell in social circles or online. Emotionally, psychologically, or spiritually, they may have become violent and determined in their desire to belittle you. Thus, if you spoke up against their narcissism or other sociopathic-delusional tendencies, you became their toy. They drag people in with their false charm and big persona, and then they spit them back out. True story. They make people believe they're their friends, then they turn against them for petty and trivial reasons, such as asking for balance and harmony either directly or indirectly. Anyone who asks for respect and some empathy, i.e. for Sagittarius not to be a raging narcissist who has no care or compassion for others, is met with *venom*.

Once they've been exposed in any way big or small they become paranoid that others are out for blood. Again, this may be the case, but it likely isn't; there are a lot of gentle, understanding, and kind-hearted people in this world. Not everyone is fuelled by a need for justice or vengeance either. Positively, the reason why Sagittarius becomes paranoid is because of their noble and soulful nature. When at their best they are warm-hearted and kind friends who speak mindfully, further with a conscious and just approach. Key Sagittarius qualities include being diplomatic, honest, truth-seeking, wise, discerning, intelligent, logical, intuitive, and imaginative. Also, optimistic, bright, innovative, charismatic, fun-loving, adventurous, generous, jovial, warm-hearted, big spirited, idealistic, a visionary, and energetic, with high vitality and life force. Therefore, Jupiter's influence creates an honest and justice-seeking individual who understands the laws of karma. This includes wanting to heal and change, as well as hold yourself accountable to right your wrongs (Sagittarius in a higher vibration). Karmic law is something level-headed and morally just Sagittarius is deeply concerned with, so the paranoia may lead to explosive and destructive tendencies, but it's also rooted in a need for self-evolution. Such severe paranoia is make or break for honest yet equally egotistical Sag, bless their sweethearts. They can either rise up out of their mental health issues, realizing they've created a lot of bad karma through their words and actions, or inactions, and thus become the mighty strong and noble truth-speaker they were born to be… Or they can let their emotions get the better of them, succumbing to demonic forces and entities that want to mess with their psyche. If, in fact, no-one is out to get them and it's all in their head, they still have to deal with their mental health blueprint just like all the other signs. It's apparently harder for Sagittarius more than any other, apart from perhaps war-ruled Aries, king/queen of the jungle Leo, or 'the Devil himself' Capricorn.

Regardless of whether people have finally had enough and turned against them or whether they just wanted to restore some harmony and balance, perhaps only bringing into awareness their out-of-control shadow, Sagittarius has to inevitably face the music. They are *not* the only noble and royal people around, and many other people have gifts, talents, and wisdom that can inspire others. Being so unreasonable, obsessively anxious, and suspicious- the characteristics of delusional paranoia, make them *mistrustful*. And, once again, because we live in a dualistic world that asks for balance and harmony on all levels, the lack of synergy in previous years makes Sag fall into their extreme: social anxiety. They are no longer happy, upbeat, and positive, nor are they confident with highly evolved self-worth. *Their karma comes around.* What they've dished out is served right back to them, and this only enhances and perpetuates the cycle of paranoia. It's a vicious cycle.

Misinformed With Faulty Beliefs

Such obsessive, anxious, and unreasonably mistrusting energy and mindsets make them incredibly misinformed. They start to develop faulty belief systems, convincing themselves that white is black or black is white. They misperceive reality itself and become delusional to how things really are in the world. They put themselves in *psychosis*. Such faulty belief systems disrupt their family and home life, finances, luck, prosperity levels, and ability to form and keep authentic partnerships. At the highest level, Sagittarius is a teacher and wayshower who gathers life experience, wisdom, and lessons learned to inspire, lead, and teach. They're extremely inspirational, courageous, and disciplined due to Jupiter's idealistic influence. Yet, when in their lower vibration they perpetuate faulty belief systems keeping them trapped in toxic or unhealthy karmic cycles. Lust, one of their other worst shadow traits alongside aggression, narcissism, and self-centeredness, is one of their greatest downfalls, which keeps them stuck and trapped. They become blocked from healthy connections, ancient wisdom, and amazing community, business, and kindred spirit connections that can serve their soul. Evolved Sagittarius adores creative partnerships as well as colorful, spirited, and philosophical people, but to get there they must make peace with their pasts. This involves healing their shadow personality traits, the less desirable qualities that can manifest as a lasting mental health issue if unchecked for a while.

Jupiter is one of the biggest planets, which gives this passionate fire sign equal doses of ego *and* luck, self-centeredness *and* creative vision, and arrogance *and* freedom. They are fearless truth speakers and warriors for ideals, they see the big picture and have immense creative life force and spirit. But, when not at the top of their game they succumb to arrogance combined with a need to exert their dominance on others, simply because they're not happy. Other areas of their life, outside of their confidence and ability to be seen, are in demise. So, not knowing how to cope with not being the center of attention, they start to find solace in their place in a social or friendship circle or community. This is *not* sustainable, however, as it creates the dom/sub and egotistical false leader/doormat & subject dynamic explained earlier. It may seem ok for a little while, but it will undoubtedly not last forever; unless Sag wants to drive all their friends and followers into suicide. No, I don't think so! There needs to be fairness, balance, and harmony, moreover a release of power and control if social bonds wish to evolve into something more professional. Thus, Sagittarius' delusions make them misinformed, misguided, and continuously playing repetitive karmic cycles. In the words of one of my personal greatest inspirations, jazz bassist and artist extraordinaire, *Esperanza Spalding*, ironically who's music was introduced to me by a Sagittarius musician and old friend, "We could change the whole story of love, same old play I'm getting tired of... No more acting these predictable roles, just us living unconditional love..." (*Unconditional Love*.) At the highest vibration, Sagittarius is a tantric guru, a sexually sovereign and liberated soul speaker who is mastered in evolved forms of love and intimacy, like tantra. Also, they are obviously the only sign currently ruled by Jupiter who brings high levels of freedom, independence, and adventure into their lives, their professional, platonic, and love lives. This makes them sought after, soulful, and majestic, in addition to sexually experienced.

Faulty belief systems change realities, alter timelines, and can put Sag and anyone they're connected to on a timeline of darkness and destruction. Sagittarius' mental health blueprint can make them think good people are bad for them while bad people are good for them. They cling onto current or past versions of themselves, all the while missing out on future timelines and amazing opportunities. Through continued anti-social behavior masked as confidence, self-esteem, and standing in the spotlight (remember, at the expense of others, and without any balance or fairness), they tie themselves to unsavory characters or even *criminals*. Criminal behavior becomes normalized, extremely abusive and socially unacceptable ways are seen as 'business-as-usual,' and boring acts repeated daily are misperceived as exciting or fun. This signifies drama, gossip, and immature or reckless activities that are more often than not tied into addictions, excessive partying, fun at others' expenses and without morality or conscience, etc. Sag become immature, foolish, and reckless, as well as extremely blocked from their Higher Self. Ultimately, they got lost in a spiral of drama and false stories birthed from their own and other people's delusions. They've misinformed others for so long that they start to get misinformed, and, as they are so attached and addicted to the *false* joy and high of being admired, loved, and liked (minor to major narcissism), they are happy for any continued adoration they receive.

In a twisted sense, Sagittarius' victims serve them their karma. Because when they are finally free to heal and change, mature, and evolve through and past the toxic cycles they've played out, the people they've outshone and spoken down to reinforce their negativity. Their "minions" and "followers" become their karma. The result is that Sagittarius either has to cut ties with everyone, leaving the past completely in the past, or slowly reverse their karma. It is, unfortunately, very hard for this sign to apologize, however, due to such a righteous and arrogant personality. Unless Sag works on their shadow traits on a real level, this is the type of personality to become a lonely old arrogant man or bitter old lonely woman. Sagittarius is incapable of apologizing because it could break down their reputation. This is a real issue to their self-evolution. From one perspective, do they even have that good a reputation anyway? Isn't it all a facade, an illusion…? From another perspective, if they do actually have a good reputation, righting their wrongs could mean people turn against them and withdraw their support. Sagittarius may appear strong without question, but, deep down, this is a sensitive and emotional character who relies on companionship and social bonds. Sag puts on a front that says "I'm supremely independent, I don't need anyone else!" Yet, inside their skin, they are softies with their own insecurities and vulnerabilities. So, coming clean combined with admitting to their wrongdoings and bad ways is a big risk. As the sign associated with both courage and narcissism, bravery and arrogance, and higher ideals and independence, which way Sagittarius goes all depends on their fate. My advice to Sag is to learn that not everyone is evil or hateful, some people are genuinely empathic, kind, and forgiving…

In addition, with regards to delusions, they mistake idealism and vision for reality. Their glyph is the Centaur, half man and half horse, so very instinctive, primal, and energetic with immense physical vitality. Their planetary ruler is Jupiter, the planet of higher ideals, higher wisdom, spirituality, and philosophy. This makes them confused in many ways, as their mind thinks they are a seer or prophet while their physical reality proves different. A key example of Sagittarius in their dark psyche is drinking alcohol every day, polluting their divine physical vessel and disconnecting them from purity and sacredness, while believing themselves to be a saint. They will literally drink beer after beer or bottle after bottle, repetitively, all the while participating in toxic cycles that only serve their lower self; but talk as if they are a teacher or a prophet! It's incredibly infuriating to those who may actually be making change around them. This arrogant yet idealistic fire sign is a clear example of *not* walking the talk, in addition to preaching in an immature and unhealthy way. Sagittarius poisons themselves, fails to honor their Higher Self and the divine, and then talks for hours on end about how they're legit. At a higher vibration, they are destined to be a spiritual teacher, religious guide, shaman, seer, prophet, or leader of some kind, yet they must actually do the (inner) work to get there. They can't just sit in a social circle pretending, preaching, and winding everyone up while people clearly see through their BS. They can, but it will decrease their followers and reputation dramatically. Eventually, people get tired of even jovial and sunny Sagittarius through their severe delusions coupled with their mind-blowing sense of grandiose. I'm sorry to say, no real shaman or prophet drinks themselves to mild alcohol poisoning and lusts after "solely physically attractive bodies" while neglecting their divine, godly, or soulful nature in the process. As a primal animal sign, Sagittarius tends to combine partying with lust, alcoholism or drug abuse with porn or sex addiction, and self-righteousness with promiscuity and frivolity… unfaithfulness too. Similar to Leo, Sagittarius is one of the most likely to be a master adulterer. I've known many Sagittarius' who have had more than one "lover" on the go, but, of course, they deny it. This sign *hates* being questioned, their authority is paramount, after all. Combined with their need to be dominant and make others submit, all of this leads to the other manifestation of their dark psyche… Violence.

Abusive and Physically Volatile

Highly charged, quick to anger, and incredibly energetic, Sagittarius strengths include high vitality, energy, and motivation levels. Their glyph is the Centaur, the half horse and half man creature who represents the perfect balance between the lower self and higher self. Sagittarius is a primal and very, very sexual sign. They love love-making, physical intimacy, and affection, moreover companionship. But they also love lusty displays of sex and pleasure. Lust is a lower manifestation of their higher need for intimacy and connection, which is Sagittarius all over. The Centaur glyph (astrological symbol) represents fertility, movement, travel, freedom, primal instincts, vitality, and a need for both physical pleasure and higher spiritual, philosophical, and intellectual ideals. Their life force is misused when in their lower vibration or frequency, making them into sex-crazed monsters who look at everyone in an extremely shallow and superficial way. It's all about looks, physical attributes, and false flattery; porn star energy coupled with the desire for pornstar-style sex fills their minds and life. It's less about intimacy, romance, feelings, true love, and soul connection, and more about getting a quick fix… combined with what's immediately appealing to the eyes. Instant gratification and shallow beliefs, in short. This highly lustful influence has two possible negative impacts. One, it can make them play out further delusions, circulating the cycle of *narcissism*, aggression, and arrogance even more, in which case, Sagittarius never heals and stays stuck in their spiral of low self-esteem (masked as confidence in the public eye). Or they can become sincerely abusive and even violent. Aggression, intimidation, slander, verbal or emotional abuse, and physical fights can be initiated. Sagittarius is one of the most prone to entering into fights and knife, gun, or gang-culture crime. They are a fire sign ruled by a very physically vital glyph, after all. Jupiter is also expansive, which hinders their growth and self-evolution when already in such a low mental headspace; their ruling planet's influence "expands" what they're receiving most joy from.

Of course, this is a sick and twisted type of joy, because they're happiness is born from delusion, moreover is *not* supporting their Higher Self. Sagittarius may appear bubbly, sociable, and happy with a sunny and humorous disposition, but there are a lot of darker forces at play behind the scenes. In romantic and domestic relationships, Sagittarius can turn violent in an attempt to show off their dominance or power. Sagittarius loves being seen as dominant regardless of their gender. This expressive and extroverted sign needs people to admire them, worshiping the ground they walk on. They crave the spotlight and need "all eyes on them." If their lover isn't devoted to them in the way they want (even if Sag is not giving the same level of loyalty or love back) they may turn physically violent. Astrologically, Sagittarius is one of the most likely signs to beat on their spouse. Finally, satanic worship and other immoral, ungodly, and criminal activities occur when Sagittarius has gone too far into their delusions. They may feel the only way out of the hell they've created is to consult darker forces, not godly ones, all due to the potent religious and spiritual influence in their life. At their best and most evolved, Sagittarius makes the perfect priest, religious leader, spiritual teacher, shaman, guru, or prophetic guide. Thus, you can only imagine what they turn to when they've lost all sense of hope and grounding... They may mistake lighter spiritual forces for darker ones, and vice versa. Ultimate confusion and mental disparity arises that leaves usually soulful, majestic, and higher minded Sagittarius entwining with the wrong people, places, and things. Their destiny becomes misconstrued. Consulting ouija boards or making a deal with the devil himself through severe manifestations of harm called to animals, children, or adults are common with an out-of-control Sagittarius.

In terms of popular celebrity and Hollywood culture, Sagittarius is one of the most likely to perform Satanic rituals to give them success, fame, or wealth, I'm sorry to say. Remember that this is the sign with one of the biggest egos; fame, fortune, and glamor influence them more than most. At their best they are enlightened and inspiring wayshowers who motivate others, connecting to higher ideals and visions to empower. Religious and spiritual themes are part of an evolved and healed Sagittarius' life path. Also, their job is to recognize that their youth is, generally speaking, symbolic of their lower self- their primal self and needs, while their future is representative of the journey one takes to reach their higher selves. From Root to Crown, Sagittarius the Archer/Centaur is here to create a legacy. Greater humility and sensitivity combined with emotional depth, vulnerability, and empathy are called for to rise up into their Higher Self, the better part of their glyph. They must accept that their core personality is tied into narcissism, an overpowering ego, as well as other shadow traits like lust, aggression, and reckless-impulsive behavior. Only then will they be the soul-shaman, wayshower, or successful leader they were born to be.

Absolute worse crimes possible?

	LESS LIKELY	LIKELY	ABSOLUTELY
MURDER			✓
RAPE			✓
ANIMAL CRUELTY		✓	
CHILD ABUSE	✓		
MOLESTATION	✓		
TORTURE			✓
HUMAN TRAFFICKING			✓
SLAVERY		✓	
BESTIALITY			✓
TERRORISM			✓

KIDNAPPING		✓	
GENOCIDE		✓	
NUCLEAR WAR DECIDER			✓

CHAPTER 10: Capricorn the Control-Freak

House: The 10th house, the house of social status, legacy, career, fame, and prestige.
Planet: Saturn, the planet of discipline, structure, authority, and responsibility (positive), and over or mis-use of authority, patriarchal rule, restrictions, and oppressive regimes (negative).
Element and quality: Earth and Cardinal.
Color: Brown, the color of earthing/grounding, practicalities, sensuality, and being down-to-earth and dependable, and gray, the color of sophistication, logic and intellect, seriousness and sensibility, and professionalism and serenity.
Physical area: Bones, teeth, and joints.
Dates: December 22nd to January 20th.

Capricorn is the 10th sign ruled by the 10th house and high-flying and high-achieving Saturn. But, as much as Saturn symbolizes structure, responsibilities, legacy, and climbing the social ladder, this patriarchal planet also represents restrictions, boundaries, and the karmic laws of time and patience. This is one of the most slow-moving planets and its effects hit Capricorn, bringing up their shadow for healing. As you might already be aware of from the previous chapters, shadow traits left unchecked can lead to mental health issues. At their best, Capricorn is a tenacious and highly disciplined person who lives life with utmost integrity, honesty, and self-accountability, moreover determination to succeed and achieve. At their lowest, they are utter control freaks who will stop at nothing to impose their will on everyone and anyone. They become relentless in their need for respect, admiration, and recognition, and their usually sensual and generous nature gets lost to the darkness of their wounds.

When in their dark psyche, Capricorn is one of the worst people to be around, as you literally become their property. They believe that they own you, they feel superior on multiple planes, and they treat you like you're their inferior. They become your boss, even if you're their child, lover, partner, family member, or housemate.

Let's look at the definition of a control-freak:

A completely obsessive and compulsive person who seeks control over everything and everyone; gives constant commands while needing immense levels of respect, recognition, and accepted superior status.

Let's break this main definition down, shall we!

Obsessive and Compulsive

Capricorn is one of the most obsessive and compulsive people to come across. If you are dealing with a Capricorn in their dark psyche, they are obsessive and compulsive with whatever they have their focus on. At a higher vibration they are disciplined, devoted, and supremely determined beings; they're hard-working, tenacious, persevering, powerful, and motivated. When they are in their dark psyche, these qualities are transformed into something sinister, they are used to seeking complete control over others. Capricorn is the power-driven and hungry boss, drill sergeant, and influencer who takes command of a situation. They are relentless, totally unstoppable. So this makes them deeply concerned with public image, social status, and superficial things; how things appear to others, like class, clothes, race, cultural background, fashion, material items, qualifications, degree, job status, and so forth. I am not saying these things aren't important, but Capricorn takes them too far. They will shape their entire identity and lifestyle around the pursuit of these things, and at high, excessive, levels. They're materialistic, overly concerned with status and image, and aggressively forceful in their pursuit of money, wealth, success, promotions, prestige, fame, and anything else that gives them an elevated status. They're aggression is not like the fire signs who are actually aggressive- it's more of a magnetic force, but even magnetism can be destructive. As an earth sign, Capricorn is usually sensual, down-to-earth, and gentle. They're feminine and passive, although are more dominant than the other signs due to Saturn. In saying this, Capricorn is very forceful when in their unevolved or lower self, because they are playing out their will. Their ascended level of ambition, resourcefulness, and tenacity are unnegotiable. They are like a wrecking ball, tornado, and tsunami all in one… god bless the person or entity who tries to get in their way of success or accomplishment! Seriously, you don't want to mess with a Capricorn who has found their sense of purpose or life path.

Their passion may be subtle, yin, and more magnetic and gentle than some others, but they are a pure force of nature. Capricorn's mental health blueprint is built off of both their shadow and their shine, their dark and light side. It's a combination of both like with many others. For them, they alchemize their good qualities into something dark, making resourcefulness, perseverance, confidence, etc. into negative traits used to dominate others. Capricorn the Goat is also one of two signs associated with the devil himself, alongside Aries the Ram. Both the Ram and Goat are believed to be symbolic of the devil due to their horns. In Tarot, the *Devil* card is actually represented by Capricorn, and this signifies temptations, sexuality, and the physical world of pleasure. The Devil tarot card itself is symbolized by Pan, a half-man and half-goat demonic looking creature that is believed to depict Satan or a satanic energy. Well, Capricorn always strives for more and always wants to be the best in a way similar to Aries, another sign who shares the physical instincts, vitality, and passion of being an animal with horns. They may not be as competitive or war-driven as Aries, but they are the most ambitious, headstrong, and unwavering in their desires for professional and worldly victory. The 10th house sits right at the top of the zodiac wheel and represents social status, prestige, career success, fame, public recognition, achievements, and a high level of excellence and mastery. At the top of their game, Capricorns become experts and teachers in their chosen field of study or special skill. So, when they are in their dark psyche all of these inner motivations are distorted, moreover twisted. The script is flipped, and similar to Ram Aries they enter into a psychosis. Like Taurus the bull, they can become hedonistic and pleasure-seeking too, so it's worth familiarizing yourself with Taurus' mental health blueprint for an extra dimension of wisdom. This earth sign's problem is they are never satisfied with what they have, whether it be money, clients, cars, or followers and supporters. Outside of being a control-freak, they need to prove themselves to others through public image and persona, which is why they become so obsessive in their desires and pursuits. They are obsessive to the point of *fixation*, and this can cause havoc at home, in their family, or in social settings and groups.

Merging the most ambitious and willful personality with a compulsively-obsessive persona is clearly dangerous. Capricorn takes on elements of all the most extreme personality imbalances of all the other signs, quite literally. Notably, psychotic, sociopathic, and manic tendencies. Not narcissistic or interested in despair or hopelessness (sorry Scorpio, Sag, and Aquarius) Capricorn is a beast with a satanic character, which is worse in many ways. This means they are a negative influencer, using a combination of intelligence, logic, higher reasoning, intuition, and emotional intelligence to con, steer, impact, convince, or push others. At their lowest, they are cunning and callous beyond belief, so although a maturer and balanced Capricorn may be ambitious and tenacious to create fortune and abundance for family and protection, create legacy that can inspire or help others, or become successful for humanitarian, selfless, or compassionate motivations, a dark Capricorn will use their force for disconnection. Instead of wanting money, success, etc. to unify others, heal planet earth or our environment, raise consciousness, create a legacy for future generations, and so forth, they act from a primitive need for control. There's no light in their intentions. All they want is power over others and the world at large. This is the type of character who will hit the nuclear war button without second thought just to gain respect over, well, every human alive... Of course, this is not really respect, but forced coercion. They are delusional in a way similar to Sagittarius in that they think they have a right to do such things. Evil and good and wrong and right become interchangeable through misconception and misperception. Their superiority takes over and makes them believe they have more of a right to exist in this world, in addition to mistaking themselves to be intellectually, emotionally, physically, spiritually, artistically, and '_insert every possible quality here_' superior, than everybody else.

Referring back to the Devil card, this card represents being trapped, stuck, and blocked from both spiritual energies and your Higher Self. There are chains holding two lovers back, but the chains are loose, which shows that they could leave if they really wanted to. This image in itself tells a clear story into Capricorn's dark psyche. Firstly, the lovers represent a mixture of things, from opposite sets of qualities like logic Vs imagination and intellect Vs emotions to actual lovers, business partners, or lifelong friends. This shows how much of Capricorn's identity is tied into intimate relationships. As much as they think they can do it alone, they can't. They are bound to others in the same way others are bound to them, and especially considering they wish to achieve such a high level of prestige, fame, and accomplishment. The 10th house, their ruling house, is right at the top of the zodiac wheel representing social status and hierarchy; well, you can't expect an elevated social or public position without forming, and keeping, authentic connections. *No man is an island.* The devil binding two individuals to him is a message to Capricorn that they need to come to terms with their controlling side, further that they can't keep using ambition or strong will as an excuse for intimidating and suppressing others. Capricorn is the stubborn earth Goat who suppresses their emotions… more on this in the next point.

As natural managers, accountants, and entrepreneurs, Capricorn the Goat is the most likely, alongside ambitious Ram Aries, to cheat to win, alter numbers, and adopt a callous approach in business. Fair play goes out the window, there's no honor or integrity either. This is the type of person, when in their dark psyche, who will rise to the top becoming mega-successful, while behind-the-scenes committing tax, benefit, or business fraud on ungodly levels. The love of money drives Capricorn no matter how rich or accomplished they become. Picture a millionaire with an unhealthy and obsessive amount of cars, holiday homes, and bonds or investments. There's no cut off point or boundary. They wish to climb the social or corporate ladder so much that they cheat to get ahead, use dirty tactics, or become utterly obsessed with material things. At their lowest, Capricorn is materialistic and greedy, perhaps not as much as fellow earth sign Taurus due to Tauurs being Fixed (Capricorn is Cardinal), but they are certainly extremely materially-driven. Their love of money, luxury, and the finer things in life run deep. Their core character is defined by the need to accumulate, as it brings them their sense of belonging coupled with being seen. In terms of the social ladder, the 10th house sits right at the top of the chart, so this is the most prestigious placement. As they are natural managers, moreover experts of finances, money, and business matters, Capricorn is usually put in control of finances. This is a terrible idea! In their mental health blueprint, before rising into integrity, nobility, and modesty, this is the energy of the con-artist; the deceptive and dirty CEO, politician, or leader of a charity or non-profit who steals from the people they're supposed to help.

Moreover, because they're one of the most trustworthy star signs, people trust them, even when they're in their dark psyche, Capricorn gets away with a lot of things others don't. People know that they're responsible, practical, viciously hard-working, and so forth, so there's an innate level of trust and dependability. This is dangerous because their sober attitude and outlook on life is a mask to hidden deceptions and manipulations. All earth signs are manipulative to some extent- earth is feminine quality, and the earth emits a subtle and sensational, unique type of seduction. It pulls us in with its warmth and fertility in a way similar to how the oceans captivate us with their depth. It would be biased to not say that earth is manipulative, fire and air signs will always have some level of narcissism inherent within their psyche, after all. Thus, Capricorn is magnetic and passive, as well as receptive, yielding to some degree, and manipulative. They draw you in, sell you a dream or a vision, and convince you to turn their ideas into reality. At the highest vibration, Cancer is a master manifester who commands attention. They get people to do what they want, implement plans of action, and control people in a healthy way- through a real vision. They have excellent organizational, managerial, and orderly qualities. In their dark psyche, they are still influenced by the same subtle forces, but their intentions are *not* pure. They're not operating from a godly or righteous space. The infamous 'Red Wedding' scene from the *Game of Thrones* would arguably be created by a Capricorn. They carry an endless "Winter is Coming" energy, in addition to a dark and pessimistic outlook on life. But, they hide behind a charming and charismatic, moreover level-headed disposition. Capricorn season is synonymous with Winter season, therefore you can see why they will always be cold and distant, even when in their Higher Self.

Suppressive and Oppressive

The second meaning of the Devil tarot card is that the chains are actually loose, which signifies Capricorn always has a chance to break free and forge a new path. At the highest vibration, they are fearless and devoted business people, bosses, and CEOs who have spent years to a lifetime mastering their trade or skill. They are destined for success, abundance, prestige, or a lot of wealth and financial victory. So when they get lost to a path of darkness or internal chaos and disparity they see the world through faulty lenses. They mistake assertiveness for control, dominance for restrictions, and ambition for a dictatorial type of rule. At their lowest frequency, they are dictators and bullies who wish to obliterate anyone who does not comply with their will. This is due to them being so stubborn and fixated on the end goal that they suppress their emotions, which means they inevitably start to repress others. Through suppressing their own emotions, feelings, and inner needs for so long, they become lost to the world of believing it's ok to oppress others. This starts a downward spiral whereby they're not in tune with their authentic selves and thus make others feel it's not ok to be their authentic selves. It can be conscious or unconscious. As can be seen in the tarot card that symbolizes 'dark psyche Capricorn,' the devil prevents the two lovers from breaking free, so this signifies that Capricorn starts to do the same to others. They either embody the energy of the devil, making others submit to them in a totally immoral and satanic way (control, oppression, despair, suicidal thoughts, loss of hope, complete helplessness, etc.), or they become absorbed in their own self-control.

The negative attributes of Saturn, their ruling planet, includes restrictions, misuse of power, and over-exertion of authority. At their utter lowest, they impose irrational, ludicrous, and unbelievably outrageous restrictions on others, such as not allowing others to breathe! Oh yes, you heard this correctly. When in their dominant control-freak self they will "disallow" others from breathing. Or from eating, sleeping, resting, meditating, choosing self-care, cooking, cleaning, or any other activity when, where, and how they want. Capricorn dictates another being's entire life. Normal daily activities are demonized because they themselves have demonized their own emotions and self-care needs. They impose such strict and insane limitations and restrictions on themselves that they delude themselves into thinking no-one else is allowed freedom. The same is true vice versa. Saturn's influence when in their dark psyche blocks pathways to healing, freedom, and liberation. They prevent freedom, adventure, fun, joy, harmony, self-care, avenues to self-love, and more expansive spiritual ideals and philosophies from flowing. Saturn is known as the *Father of Time* and *Lord of Karma*, therefore there are some serious limitations in play. Restrictions combined with blockages define a Capricorn in their dark psyche; there's no room for creativity, freedom, travel, or play that elevates the soul and aligns you with the Higher Self or mind. It's all about perpetuating toxic cycles bound to restrictions. *Suppression, suppression; suppression…* Of Self and others. As can be seen in the Devil card, there's no chance of escape, at least not immediately or in the foreseeable future, so Capricorn must work through their blocks, moreover their faulty belief systems to refind their authentic voice and self.

They may be self-mastered bosses with natural levels of authority and personal power later in life, but only after they have matured, had sufficient life experiences combined with lessons for growth, and found wholeness and balance within. As the 'Father of Time' and 'Lord of Karma' Saturn demands, there's no easy or quick fix route; they must work through their internal blocks and distortions to rise to the top. Further, Capricorn is a scrooge, the grinch, and a ghoulish character when at their worst. Linked to Winter, Capricorn represents a season where we naturally feel repressed and suppressed. Winter is a time of survival, where we draw immense strength up from our Root chakras to survive. We're concerned with security, survival, and rising up out of depression, despair, and hopelessness. This is why Capricorn's shadow includes being pessimistic. Although the Dark Night of the Soul is spiritually and energetically associated with Scorpio, astrologically it's also connected to Capricorn. Capricorn therefore loses faith, choosing to only see the bad and ugly in Self and others. Everything becomes dark and gloomy for a while at significant stages of this earth sign's life. In a low mental headspace, this manifests as suppressing others through their own self-imposed suppression. They have a very difficult time experiencing joy, or perhaps only receive temporary instant gratification through food, alcohol, and entertainment (they are a sensual earth sign). Capricorn has a tendency to fall into extremes such as excessive food, alcohol, and drug consumption, binge-watching in a way similar to Taurus, and getting lost in a cocoon of pleasure and sensual delights. Relationships suffer as a result, while self-esteem and self-worth gets drastically lowered.

Capricorn denies themselves basic pleasures, usually. The comforts of home and private life, as are seen in their opposite sign Cancer, are repressed. They deny themselves basic living joys, comforts, and pleasures, so over time they start to take out their frustrations on others. They're so emotionally repressed and blocked that intimacy is a real problem for this usually down-to-earth and generous earth sign. In their dark psyche, they're a tyrant who fails to acknowledge the simple things in life, like laughing to a film after a long day's work, putting on their favorite music and dancing, or reading a book to unwind in the evening. They are chronic suppressors. They treat themselves as an after-thought, yet this only brings out their worst traits after they've got their temporary fix.

Controlling Beyond Coping Mechanisms

Thus, Capricorn controls others beyond normal or expected coping mechanisms. There's no such thing as room for change, space to breathe, or even minor allowances for self-love and self-respect. No-one is allowed to take back their power. In a way similar to Sagittarius, Capricorn may give out scraps of freedom or illusionary space and respect, but this is the catch- it's all an illusion. They have no intention of letting their captives or slaves be free. The illusion is that they appear to be loving, generous, and harmonious (when in their dark psyche), when in reality they are *only* about control. If you're their lover, housemate, friend, colleague, employee, family member, or child, your life is hell. Sorry to be so blunt, but it's the truth. Everyday feels like a prison cell, like you are their captive, and, in a way, you are. As a feminine earth sign, Capricorn has evolved levels of emotional intelligence, wisdom, empathy, and personal magnetism. They are incredibly magnetic yet equally dominant with Saturn as a planetary ruler. So, when they're at such a low and unevolved energetic frequency, this personal power and magnetism is used for "evil," for darker and demonic forces. Control at such an intense and unbreakable level is synonymous with the devil himself, hence why Capricorn is depicted on the Devil major arcana tarot card. Therefore, Capricorn will control, dominate, and dictate to the point of binding others to them in an unhealthy and toxic way. Once a cord is created, it can take months to years to unbreak. Attachment is one of the lowest manifestations of low vibrational Capricorn.

Also, trauma bonding is associated with this grounded earth sign. At their best, they are grounded, dependable, trustworthy, hard-working, persevering, and tenacious, so when these qualities are put to negative use it creates a powerful energy current of destruction and chaos. Capricorn binds others to their trauma, their unhealed wounds, and their toxic-shadow ways. They are incapable of accepting accountability for their energy or actions, and they further dislike, no sorry, *despise* being told they need to change. Any tiny notion or word of change, healing, or righting their wrongs is met with a warpath similar to Aries (the Ram). Yet, because Capricorn is a magnetic and submissive earth sign, not a masculine-electric fire or air sign, this pull is like a hurricane. They tornado their way through their own and others feelings and emotions. There's no room for sensitivity, empathy, or compassion, qualities evolved Capricorn possesses. They become an ugly tyrant glued to the idea that they *must* retain control, at all costs. Losing control or even releasing it would be a total devastation; it would make their whole world crumble and turn upside down. They cling onto the idea that being in control is the only way to success, accomplishment, and an elevated social or public status. (Or to keep their lover.) Remember that Saturn represents career success and legacy while the 10th house represents prestige, fame, and achievements at the highest level. Their end game combined with their long-term vision is to be a master, elder, and expert in their profession or vocation. It's all about service, but to get there they have some serious shadow traits, like everyone else, to overcome. If they can't transcend and heal, embracing change- something that is harder for them than most other signs, they get lost down the rabbit hole of their mental health blueprint.

Capricorns in such a low mental headspace will dictate how everyone should live, speak, behave, eat, dress, and think to the point of depression or severe mental health issues. They impose their will in a defensive way, as a feminine and passive earth sign, so they make others out to be the bullies and oppressors. They play the victim. They may not ever say the words 'I am a victim,' their superficial side wouldn't allow for that, as it would make them appear weak and inferior… and that would be the end of their world. No, they will act like the victim if a new person or someone with superior rank figures them out. They snap, turn, and become cold and callous, further making everyone else out to be bullies or control freaks. It's a type of psychological warfare similar to the way Gemini operates, i.e. making everyone submit to you for so long and then twisting perception in the final moments. Everyone becomes a problem except them. There's no accountability, self-honesty, and self-responsibility- the traits usually stellar in reputation grown-up Capricorn shows. They become delusional and disillusioned to their own mental health issues, as well as their internal emotional and psychological chaos. They dislike other people with personal power, self-authority, or any level of boss-status in a venomous way. Teamwork, cooperation, and harmony go out of the window. A need for extreme order and tradition replace all sense of warmth and relatability; Capricorn becomes ungrounded and irrational in a need to maintain or implement order, structure, etc. Such a rigid and conservative mindset squishes originality, creative vision, imagination, and innovative solutions. They may be masters of practical solutions, but they are one of the least imaginative star signs. This influence then amplifies the need to control others, as they see everyone else having fun or making use of artistic talents and gifts, and they get annoyed or envious. Capricorn would, quite literally, create a make-shift prison cell in their home to lock away their loved ones if they were getting too unruly, i.e. living their life by normal standards!

Commands and Demands Respect

Very different to commanding respect through natural energy, kindness, sensitivity, empathy, and so forth, Capricorn commands and demands respect in a completely inharmonious way. They become attached to ideas and realities that aren't real or that have been constructed by the illusions of their imagination. Capricorn is not very imaginative, actually one of the least out of all 12 zodiac signs due to being ruled by Saturn. This signifies that they essentially live in a world of make-believe brought by a lack of vision coupled with an ability to see through a spiritual lens. Of all the planets, Saturn and Neptune are the two that clash the most (alongside Venus and Mars who are absolute opposites). Well, Neptune rules Pisces and symbolizes psychic instincts, visions, astral and dream encounters, the multidimensional planes, mysticism, spirituality, healing, fantasy, and illusions. This is the most ethereal and spiritually illuminating planet, and it clashes with Saturn in a major way. This means that Capricorn finds it very difficult if not impossible to let loose, moreover open themselves up to a world of subtle and spiritual energy. They see the world through restricted lenses, tangible and concrete things, and a predominantly material viewpoint. They are more concerned with boundaries and rules while Neptune brings a message of holistic vision and idealism, which allows for freedom and soul growth in a way similar to Jupiter. So, ambitious and high-flying Capricorn treats everyone as their personal minions, even before they've reached boss-status. Without the relevant life experience, qualifications, victories, or even maturity and emotional intelligence levels, Capricorn acts like the CEO or owner. But what is there to own, this is people's lives we're talking about…

People aren't companies or robots, they're human beings with hearts, feelings, and desires, and this is what highly strung Capricorn fails to acknowledge. Such an extreme level of oppressive control only manifests after shadow traits have failed to be recognized and worked on, or in youth before they're made known. Traditions, societal law and order, regimes, police, authorities, restrictions on national and international levels, responsibilities, and obligations influence Capricorn on a daily level, and, later in life, if their mental health issues have built up, they can become real life monsters. Drill sergeants, war leaders, nuclear bombists, immoral corporton leaders and CEOs, corrupt police or prison officers, and evil managers or superiors in establishments where innocents require protection manifest. Capricorn is the most likely to misuse their power and authority to cause harm to others. Perhaps physical harm, and if not certainly psychological and emotional harm.

The ironic thing is many people look up to Capricorn due to such an evolved level of self-authority, even when they're in their lower frequency and vibration. They do command respect, although it can be immoral and unjust. However, people are innocent and try to see the best in this usually generous and sensitive earth sign; they don't possess the clear and extroverted aggression or force of, say, Aries, Leo, or Sagittarius, for instance. Thus, people intuitively recognize that although Capricorn may be acting unjustly or superiorly or being much too authoritarian, there is a unique level of sensitivity behind the will. This is *dangerous*, because no-one functions from a dark-psyche mentally-imbalanced space in their right mind. The result? People give their blind trust and faith, and this leads to physical harm, psychosis, or, in worst case scenarios, death. The illusion is that Capricorn is in control when they are, in fact, not. They have lost all sense of real control and power, hence why they have to cling so desperately to the notion that they are in control. Unlike Cancer, their opposite sign, who embodies a strong sense of sacred wisdom and knowledge, intuition, instincts to nurture and protect through home, family, and domestic routes to deeper connection, and unconditional compassion, Capricorn places conditions on the level of empathy and compassion they show. They are compassionate and sympathetic, but they lack virtually all the qualities of Cancer. It's all about structure, order, and authority, so there's no opportunity for depth, intimacy, and authentic bonding. This is the type of person who would rather make a living to provide for their family financially, yet experience no love, romance, or even communication in some cases. They just want to work, support materially, and provide for their "loved ones," but is this really love? Is there really love?! Capricorn misconstrues the true meaning of providing and protecting due to Saturn's extremely strict influence.

A Lethal Superiority Complex

Finally, Capricorn has a major superiority complex to the point of murder, violence, and corruption in positions of authority. As the sign most likely to become a real boss, business owner, or CEO, or equally an army officer, war leader, police or prison officer, barrister, cout official, politician, etc., Capricorn is bound to end up on a position of authority and command at some stage in life. If they do, let me tell you: if they're still in their dark psyche, this is the person who will torture, rape, or murder, I am sorry to say. They misuse their power and treat innocents who are supposed to be under their protection in the most heinous of ways. If they don't, then they resort to a murderous antisocial personality disorder. They believe its ok to torture, rape, and kill or steal, con, and cheat on a lower level of immorality and crime. Like Aries the Ram, Capricorn the Goat with the devil horns becomes a criminal with satanic forces guiding their way. They become so addicted to the control and power that they forget the necessity of human life, moreover ethics, morals, integrity, purity, benevolence, compassion, charity, good deeds, and nobility. All sense of integrity and modesty combined with respect, which are some of sane Capricorn's best qualities, diminish entirely. Capricorn in their dark psyche is a hurricane and tsunami, a force of nature, for sure, but on a negative path of destruction. They don't care who they intimate or bulldoze over to get to where they want to go. They have no empathy or respect for the pain and trauma they cause from being so callous, cold, and cunning. A dark fox, Capricorn embodies the spirit of a poltergeist who uses sharp wit, potent intellect, and a combination of advanced logical and intuitive gifts to lord it over others. What's the end goal? Ultimate authority.

A higher vibrational Capricorn might integrate their light attributes to achieve, create, and manifest in harmony with a greater life purpose, vision, or mission; their legacy or destiny. But, a lower frequency Capricorn is only concerned with how they look, including how much respect and authority they command. They are the definition of someone with a superiority complex, falsely mighty and highly strung, combined with a complete lack of care, compromise, and consideration. This usually sweet, nurturing, compassionate, gentle, and generous sign becomes a beast ruled by demonic forces on a mission to tempt, torture, and spellbind. All sense of legacy and professional prestige is lost, they have become so disassociated in their mindsets and belief systems, as well as the cycles that they think are normal or cool, that twisted distortion occurs. Any authentic intentions for fame, achievements, financial security, material abundance, the best partner, the ideal career, a loving family, and domestic and professional bliss are lost to their extreme stubbornness... the need for total oblivion through control. When feelings, emotions, and human decency go out the window, all else is lost. Logic has replaced instincts, a cunning mind has taken over feelings and emotions, and irrationality overpowers soul purpose or destiny; there's nothing left but the oppressive regime they have ruled with. (At home, within the family, with peers and friends, or on a larger scale in career service.) Capricorn then no longer has respect nor self-control, but a very destructive and dark rule of terror and abuse built off of a bad seed. This seed should have been pulled out and disregarded a long time ago, however they neglected their inner world for too long. The outer world took over and began to influence them in a negative way. *This is also why the Devil in tarot is known as the negative influencer.* He fills your mind with ideas and then you become bound to them through repetitive action. It's a horrific cycle to enter and further believe is your life path or soul's mission.

Like Virgo, Capricorn is incredibly cynical, judgemental, and critical. They look down on others, snigger and sneer through their advanced levels of ambition, and think they're superior while having the emotional depth of a teaspoon. They're so out of tune with their feelings that they become pretentious and pedantic, also succumbing to social anxiety coupled with nervous tension. As for a real spiritual disconnection, Capricorn has a difficult time accepting multidimensional, philosophical, and spiritual viewpoints and beliefs. They lose touch with the holistic nature of reality, which is a contradiction in character because in an elevated vibration this sign is suited to becoming a physiotherapist, personal trainer, yoga instructor, holistic massage therapist, or even complementary therapist. As a sensual earth sign, they are suited to working with the body, and this involves integrated emotional depth, wisdom, and sensitivity. Thus, Capricorn's job is to recognize that they developed some faulty belief systems, as well as created bad karmic repercussions. Acceptance is the first step to change, healing, and freedom, but, of course, this is more difficult for them than for others signs. There *is* light at the end of the tunnel, and this signifies that all sweet and humble Capricorn has to do is detach from the stories they've been telling themselves. Fortunately, physical reality is an illusion, we create it through our internal thoughts, feelings, and perceptions. Their life purpose can be aligned with once again while their legacy can be refound.

Absolute worse crimes possible?

	LESS LIKELY	LIKELY	ABSOLUTELY
MURDER			✓
RAPE		✓	
ANIMAL CRUELTY			✓
CHILD ABUSE		✓	
MOLESTATION	✓		
TORTURE		✓	
HUMAN TRAFFICKING		✓	
SLAVERY			✓
BESTIALITY			✓
TERRORISM			✓
KIDNAPPING		✓	
GENOCIDE			✓
NUCLEAR WAR DECIDER	✓		

CHAPTER 11: Aquarius the Disillusioned

House: The 11th house, the house of community, groups, social circles, and societal organizations.

Planet: Uranus, the planet of change, technology, innovation, and conscious revolution (positive), and rebellion, irresponsibility, dystopia, and sudden shocks/rude awakenings (negative).

Element and quality: Air and Fixed.

Color: Blue, the color of communication, intellect, self-expression, and the imagination, and white, the color of faith, virtue, tranquility, and self-realization.

Physical area: Calves and veins/blood (circulatory system).

Dates: January 21st to February 19th.

Aquarius is the Water-Bearer ruled by Uranus, the planet of change, innovation, technology, and revolution. This makes Aquarius very disillusioned when in their mental health blueprint, because they lose all sense of hope and faith in the world. They attach to pragmatic and futuristic timelines and views of humanity, believing that there is not enough progress. They convince themselves that there will never be change, as they can't see results *now*. The shadow traits of impatience, aggression, and being a rebel without cause transform into a darker version of themselves, thus, they stop having faith in humankind as well as our planetary shift in consciousness, which defines their sense of joy and passion. At a lower frequency, Aquarius is a rebel on a path of self-destruction who sees everyone who, apparently, hinders their progress as an enemy. They become supremely childish, impatient, and angry, moreover reckless and immature.

Usually innovative, original, and bright-minded, they devolve into a pessimistic and unkind person who cares little for human decency or emotion. Emotions are eradicated and they think, analyze, and rationalize themselves and others into obliteration. They become distorted and at a loss with themselves, misperceiving information and therefore disconnecting from the possibilities and potential of truth; higher and universal truth, and self-knowledge.

Let's look at the definition of a disillusioned person:

A perpetually disappointed and disenchanted person who discovered that life, Self, or belief systems are less good than were originally believed; a loss of faith, positive expectations, and trust in the validity and truth of things.

Let's break this main definition down, shall we!

Disenchanted and Disappointed

Aquarius is perpetually disappointed, disillusioned to the point of depression or isolation. Aquarius is a bit of an enigma in that they are both solitude-loving and social. They need social company just as much as they need to be in introspection and isolation to examine, evaluate, and study the world and its philosophies. Aquarius is a dreamer with a powerful altruistic and humanitarian side, moreover they are visionaries and idealists who have many mental gifts. They're innovative, inquisitive, highly intelligent and perceptive, colorful, imaginative, intuitive, original, idealistic, bright, witty, independent and excellent problem-solvers. They're sociable, intellectual, unique, and open-minded, with amazing logical and analytical skills. When in their lower self they are on a path of self-destruction and annihilation, attached to the idea of anarchy, change and revolution at all costs, and rebellion without just will or cause. Their Higher Selves might be powerful revolutionaries and changemakers with ideas of conscious rebellion in their mind, to initiate change and peace, bringing the world together in unity and harmony; but, their lower minds make them act from impulsive, immature and childish reckless behavior, and aggression. This star sign is one of the most angry and antisocial when in their dark psyche. They become paranoid in the belief that the world is disenchanted, that there's no magic or fun or joy. They start to see everyone is their shadow, a big flaw with the Aquarian dark psyche personality.

This means they project, projection being one of the most destructive personality deficits. It may not be as physically destructive as Aries' psychopathic displays of attempted control and power, nor as dangerous as Pisces' manic depression. But, low vibrational Aquarius is deep into the wrong belief system that everyone is toxic. We all have a light side and a shadow, this much is clear, however when we start to see others only in their shadow, it makes everyone doubt Aquarius' true intentions. Aquarius is incredibly irresponsible. Also, it makes people alienate them, believe they don't have any gifts or talents, and outcast them from social circles. This is all Aquarius' doing of course; we may all have a shine and shadow, yet not everyone is existing in their negative side. Projection is the act of unconsciously mirroring our bad qualities, thus Aquarius becomes attached to a disenchanted view of the world. Over time, as we're all interconnected, they begin to have their worst traits reflected back to them. People are so used to them being negative, mean, or gloomy that even when they rise out of their melancholy or hatred, everyone is sick and tired of them. *Treat others how you wish to be treated* is the best saying to apply here, but magnified. Aquarius doesn't treat people very well. It may be conscious or unconscious or a mixture of both, the sad truth is that Aquarius is so unhappy with everything not being as idealistic that they had hoped that they project their insecurities, fears, and doubts, as well as their own shadow, into the world around them. People get really p*ssed off with this sign! No-one can really verbalize their frustrations, however, and this is due to their shadow. Aquarius is one of the most emotionally aloof and avoidant- they're emotionally detached, distant, and ignorant to their own feelings.

They deny, reject, and avoid their inner world sensations at *extreme levels*. The only sign who is as bad as them is Gemini the pathological liar. This makes it impossible for people to speak their mind, express certain truths, or even engage in healthy and mindful communication. When at the top of their game, Aquarius is an extraordinary communicator, amazingly mindful and gifted. Yet, in their mental health blueprint they are terrible combined with possessing no empathy, honesty, or integrity whatsoever. Their usually evolved qualities of integrity, nobility, charisma, intelligence, wit, originality, and intuition are diminished and eradicated. The ego takes over. Unlike a Leo or Sagittarius who becomes narcissistic, Aquarius' ego is more rooted in the need to make everyone feel their mood, even if it's horrifically low. If they're sad, they want everyone else to be sad. If they're dissatisfied, they need everyone to be just as dissatisfied if not more than them. This is due to their glyph, the Water-Bearer, who is a visionary and changemaker with potent humanitarian and altruistic vision. They genuinely want to make the world a better place, so when in their low mental headspace they see it as their obligation to bring it back to their perceived belief of solidarity. But making others feel like cr*p is not solidarity, nor is it unity, teamwork, or togetherness. This is a major issue for Aquarius; they mistake oneness and interconnectedness with refusing to change, heal, and grow. If you're sad, you should try to look to others for support to bring some joy back into your life, or heal yourself through self-care, therapy, and so forth. This cerebral and over-analytical air sign doesn't understand this.

They rationalize their feelings out of existence, becoming set on an overuse of analysis and mental reasoning, all the while forgetting the importance (let alone the existence) of feelings, emotions, and empathy. They become obsessed, as a Fixed sign, with the belief system that because we're "all one" we should match each other's energy in a very black and white way. In a higher vibration they are teachers, wayshowers, and inspirationally optimistic and wise, with the capacity for high levels of learning, teamwork, and harmony. But, at a low vibration they deny the fact that we're also individuals, many drops amongst the waves and ocean… They find it impossible to accept that they may be the unhappy ones or that they may be in the wrong. Equally, they can't accept that others are inspirational and wise with lots of guidance and counsel to share. Aquarius always wants to be the wisdom bringer, moreover the intellectual one who uplifts others. Thus, they are disillusioned as to the fact that they are the ones in an unhappy and imbalanced state. From this space they become completely desperate, disconnected from their heart's desires, and sad verging on depressed. They see the world in a very delusional way and further get lost in fantasy, similar to final sign Pisces. Aquarius the Water-Bearer gets absorbed in the world of fiction, illusion, and fantasy brought by deep desires for community, connection, and heightened consciousness. They forget that they are a part of a community and put themselves in a type of isolated bubble, even in social situations. They cling onto the idea of complete independence and self-autonomy within social situations and circles without realizing that they need help and support. They close themselves off to others in a totally *disenchanted* way that alienates them, pushing them further into self-denial and self-pity. Aquarius thinks they can go it alone while making everyone strongly dislike, hate, or even despise them. If this negative cycle lasts a long time, it can lead to complete isolation and, eventually, misalignment with their soul's plan, path, and purpose.

Aquarius is arguably the alien of the zodiac, the one star sign who genuinely believes they are aliens in an "out-there" type of way, such as from spaceship landing to earth millions of years ago and our DNA being of alien origin. Other signs who hold this belief quite strongly are Sagittarius and Pisces, but Aquarius takes this to new levels. In their disenchanted world view, they believe we're reptilian. Oh yes, you must have heard of the reptilian alien-race theory. My belief and acquired wisdom is that there is some truth in this; our DNA holds multiple star races and therefore different alien species origins, from darker reptilians to lemurians, sirians, and so on. But, unlike some of us who may resonate more with the "light" alien races, Aquarius in their dark psyche believes we're all inherently evil. They think that our world is being ruled by a Reptilian Overlord Race who are controlling us through banks, politicians, media, etc. There is some truth in this, yet it's partial truth, moreover why tune into this? Darkness is one part of life, there is also the light. We may have evil reptilian DNA within us, but it's also part of the soul's journey to evolve and find enlightenment, thus aligning with our higher starseeded consciousness selves. This is what Pisces, the final sign, teaches; Aquarius is one sign below Pisces in the evolutionary scale, so it's understandable why they are "not quite there yet." No, Aquarius doesn't resonate with their positive and beautiful star seed qualities such as those from Lemuria, Sirius, or Pleiades. They instead choose to attune to the evil acts on a global scale merged with the evil parts inside us individually. This paves the way for a dystopian belief system that just enhances the cycle of pessimism and hopelessness.

Aquarius genuinely believes we will be wiped out by an alien race, that dark politicians and bankers or media moguls have control over us, and that an apocalypse is coming! They lose touch with the true essence of our souls, our organic origins, which signifies freedom. No-one has control over us. This is Uranus' influence at a lower level, where they believe that we have no freedom, self-sovereignty, or power to make change and initiate conscious rebellion or revolution. Everything is seen through a murky and polluted lens. I am sorry to say, but Aquarius does hold power, and if 1 billion people (as an example) are constantly projecting the thoughts of "there will be an apocalypse" or "an alien invasion is a real possibility in the near future" it only increases its chances. This is the irony… For anyone who understands consciousness and this human experiment, as I do, you will know that these *are* the intentions of the darker forces in play. They want us to believe there is no hope, that we are slaves to a system, and that our fates are doomed. This is the paradox. Through such repetitive and extreme negative thinking when combined with belief, we increase its chance of happening. It's a sort of self-fulfilling prophecy, but a dark one. In Aquarius' stubborn and uncompromising need for Utopia, they create dystopia. They create the polarity of the beautiful world they envision through the shadow traits of impatience and impulsiveness. They have no patience, so in their rush they only reinforce negative and destructive belief systems. I am not saying an alien invasion or apocalypse will happen in this material realm, however on an energetic level they are contributing to darker timelines. Uranus is all about potential, the future, and both evolution and revolution. Thus, Aquarius succumbs to an AI, robot, or apocalyptic reality, which on some level does influence the world around. Thought, beliefs, and emotions are powerful, and Aquarius has little to no control through such intense pessimism and impatience.

Deep Loss of Faith, Hope, and Joy

Thus, they start to experience a deep loss of faith, hope, joy, intimacy, optimism, and all loving connections in their life. They see the world from an utterly pessimistic view, believing there is only darkness, loss, and shadows to be found. This is an illusion, of course. At their best, they are some of the most bright, optimistic, and sociable creatures around; fun-loving, open-minded, and high spirited with a lot of positive energy to bring. But when in their low mental headspace they enter into a primitive mindset similar to a lowly mythological creature. Because they are so imaginative as well as connected to the ethereal, spiritual, and multidimensional realms, they see the world as if it's some sort of play or fantasy novel. They take any insights and visions they've received in dreams, on an ethereal and astral level, literally. They misconfuse reality in a way similar to

Sagittarius and Pisces. Aquarius is ruled by Uranus, so their identity is fuelled by the need for evolution of Self and others, in addition to implementing changes themselves, like through inventiveness, creativity, and intellectualism. They want to study, learn, and evolve, moreover heal themselves on all levels so they can "be the change they wish to see." From this space, they can contribute to some technological, scientific, spiritual, environmental, or alternative healing vision. Remember that they are the humanitarians and altruists of the zodiac. Everything turns dark for Aquarius when they fail to accept joy, love, or connection from others, further, when they impose their mood on others. They reject intimacy and friendship. They say no to business and educational opportunities, either directly or unconsciously. They put themselves in an extreme bubble of isolation and solitude to the point of not wanting to be social at all; a complete contradiction to their true nature. Their authentic self thrives off of social and friendship bonds- community is their life. They are deeply loving, affectionate, and extroverted when not choosing to be lone wolves.

That's another thing: Aquarius becomes an extreme lone wolf, only wanting to spend time in their own company because they believe everyone else's company to be diabolical. "No-one can be as positive, colorful, or joyous as me…" they tell themselves. Unfortunately, they are *not* upbeat or positive company in the slightest, they are moody and depressive weirdos. As the unique, quirky, and enthusiastic changemakers and visionaries (higher vibration) Aquarius becomes a real loner and weirdo in their mental health blueprint. If they've been working on amazing passions behind-the-scenes, like art, creativity, self-study, cultural and educational expansion, gathering knowledge, healing themselves, and so forth, they certainly don't show it in a social situation. In fact, they display the opposite. Aquarius will work themselves up for hours to days when they're "ready" to leave their bubble and cocoon, yet, when they finally reach their intended destination (gathering, social event, friend's house, etc.) their mood shifts. Drastically. They enter on an apparent high with some optimistic joy and life force, and after just a few moments- seconds to minutes- they change. They become the antichrist, someone so committed to seeing the worst in humankind. Uranus is the planet of change and revolution, so one tiny or minor negative vibration picked up on sets Aquarius off. Instead of recognizing that there are *multiple* energies, currents, and emotions swimming around, they instantaneously attach to the negative. This is largely due to their shadow traits of being totally impatient and impulsive. They're impatient to the extreme, incapable of slowing down and evaluating and reflecting in a social situation. This is, once again, a contradiction in character, as when alone in solitude they are fully capable of reflecting, examining, and observing with full awareness and intelligence. But, around others they flip like a yo-yo. Why? Well, Aquarius is an idealist committed to change on an individual and planetary-global level. They're so attached to the idea of utopia or idealism that they forget there are energies, experiences, and events that need to be journeyed through to get there. They want to go straight from age 1 to 100 in a flash…

Their planetary ruler, Uranus, makes them see the world as a game, complete with levels to swim through and master. But, in their dark psyche they want to cheat, continue to use cheat codes, and rush to the final level. In their darkest, Aquarius is the evil mastermind and joker similar to Gemini, moreover, they possess no empathy or sensitivity. This creates a dangerous mind considering their shadow traits; emotional aloofness, detachment, and disconnection. No emotions, empathy, or feelings and we essentially become robots. So, they analyze and rationalize whilst denying all feelings, emotions, and internal world sensations. Aquarius acts robotic and lifeless in thoughts and mannerisms, believing themselves to be of superior intellectual and even emotional status, without any emotional depth or sensitivity whatsoever. They become disillusioned to their own denial accompanied by a deep-seated apathy and indifference to the suffering, ill-health, and pain of others. Usually altruistic and open-minded Aquarius closes themselves off to their own empathic and generous, selfless, and humanitarian nature. At a higher vibration, Aquarius is selfless, noble, and deeply concerned with respect. This can be respect for mother earth, for humankind, for animals, and for traditions and rules; they respect others. Idealistic and planetary-minded, they put themselves out there with passion, charisma, and a range of mental gifts that can inspire and educate. They're genuinely concerned with unity, teamwork, and cooperative pathways to community and deeper connection. So, in such a low mental headspace, these gifts are alchemized into something negative, or eradicated altogether. There's no room for emotions. They become insensitive to the point of mean-spirited and brutal-unkind, uncaring, and totally selfish. Aquarius becomes self-serving and arrogant, masking their indifference combined with their lack of emotional maturity and intelligence with a false narrative. They project the image of being generous, charismatic, and helpful while being the only person *not* on a real wavelength.

At their worst, they are arrogant, aggressive, selfish, quite narcissistic, and threatening. They project their insecurities onto the world around them. Their inner world is in a state of disparity, disconnection, and apathy, and this radiates out into their perspectives and opinions. They still believe themselves to be superior though, and this is where conflict and even physical fights arise. They lack interest, concern, and enthusiasm for everything while convincing themselves they are the only visionary, idealistic, and humanitarianly-minded ones. They distort reality through their faulty perceptions, as most signs do when in their low mental health state. Further, they close themselves off to new opportunities and connections because they've etched into their minds that there's no joy or light to be found. They start to see shadows and monsters everywhere, unaware that they are not, in fact, living in their light; they're living in a fantasy-world with extremist visions of utopia. The realities Aquarius dreams of are only possible in movies, or hundreds of years into the future! But they see it is very possible. Like Pisces, the manic depressive who gets lost in fantasy-land, they live in their own cut-off bubble, believing things that aren't real and disconnected from a higher truth, as well as the truth of their souls. They start to lose trust in people, institutions, family, their muses, and even belief systems themselves. Combined with their humanoid emotional state, this makes them quite dangerous. People often associated the fire signs with physical aggression, but alongside Gemini, Aquarius is one of the most likely to cause physical harm to people or property.

They refuse to admit to needing help, so either push people away or resort to violence. Their narcissism when combined with their superiority complex make them very sinister- they lack empathy and compassion entirely, which has already been mentioned, but also become dangerously stubborn. You can say anything rational, just, or sane to them. It's like talking to a child or a mental health patient. As a Fixed sign, Aquarius is stubborn beyond belief. The way they show this stubbornness is through their apparent intellectual superiority. An idealistic anarchist with a false sense of superiority is not someone who should be making decisions or guiding others… Unfortunately, many people look up to Aquarius because of their unique and potent sense of idealism. The result? Anarchy. Civil war. Rebellion. Burned down homes. Small businesses or shops destroyed. A total disrespect to the physical foundations real people have devoted their lives to building. What other people have built, Aquarius destroys. Aquarius in this space is a completely devolved version of the Higher Self, which is an amazing leader, teacher, and altruistic way-shower. They live to stand out in shocking and eccentric ways. So they push others away through outrageous behavior, like flirting with other people's partners in front of them or getting involved in sex scandals, just to initiate shock. Aquarius loves to make a scene. Through pretending they're not from this world, existing above laws and sacred law, etc. Aquarius *alien*ates themselves. Ruled by the 11th house of friendship groups and community, they remove themselves from their local circles. Community stands for unity, with "comm" representing many different things; a commune, communication… Well, Aquarius seems not to care or acts like they don't.

This cerebral and overly-analytical air sign is the type of person who will get face tattoos or surgically implanted horns on their head just to show they're different! They'll get a sex change, skin color change, or some other drastic physical alteration just to show their "uniqueness" and "eccentricity." Natural laws are disrespected as well as gone against. Their obsession with being seen as alien makes them go against the parts that make them human. Embarking on a path of potentially life-threatening mind control devices, AI, inorganic technology, or chemical warfare and engineering, synthetic biology, as well as science that limits natural human evolution and potential are part of the Aquarius dark psyche. This all stems from a loss of real joy and human intimacy. Transhumanism, cyborg alterations, and merging with AI are common. A secret need for control is also linked to this theme. Aquarius is the sign who will never verbally express their need for control, however they crave control, as a Fixed sign. They hate being seen as someone who needs control over things, places, and people, and this makes them humanoid and psychopathic in their approach. At their best they are loyal without fault, but in their lower mind they are totally disloyal to people and places.

Serial Killer Vibes?

Due to sociopathic tendencies similar to the other air signs, but combined with a complete disregard to human life on a physical level, Aquarius, unfortunately, is the sign most likely to turn out to be a serial killer. Or at least plot elaborate and evil plans in their heads. Why is this? Because the outside world is a reflection of the inner world- everything we see and perceive externally is a totally reflection of our feelings and impressions inside. Because Aquarius denies and rejects their emotions and feelings, they start to act like robots, quite literally. The empathy code diminishes, and therefore there is little to no compassion, remorse, regard for human life (or animal or plant life), kindness, guilt, morality, or ethics. Integrity coupled with the higher mind dwindles. Aquarius' dark psyche is a merging of Aries' psychopathic ways, Gemini and Libra sociopathy, and Sagittarius' delusional mindsets, with a bit of Scorpio and Pisces depression thrown in too. They feel the world owes them everything while not giving anything back. They don't understand that the world is only a reflection of them, not "them"- Aquarius is one individual amongst millions to billions of people. Not everyone shares the same beliefs and views as them, not everyone possesses their vision. Yet when they are playing out distorted belief systems they forget that certain crimes may only be acceptable in movies or novels. Murder, rape, and other horrific acts, crimes against humanity, are normalized. I am not saying every Aquarius in their dark psyche will become a murderer, but they certainly have more thoughts than the other star signs.

Again, they will sit in their room alone in their bubble dreaming up plots and schemes of revenge, and sometimes for the most simple of things. For instance, someone didn't share their vision or passion for something, so now they're Aquarius' enemy! Or they misheard or misunderstood something and due to a tiny error of miscommunication, they think that person deserves to die. It really is this insane. At a higher vibration, they are masterful and amazingly bright individuals skilled in intellectualism, innovation, inventiveness, higher reasoning, problem-solving, imaginative and creative gifts, skilled perception, and logical and observational skills. At a lower frequency, they become vengeful sociopaths with a total disregard to decency, morals, ethics, natural ways, and basic codes of conduct for living. The "kind" is removed from humankind. It's psychotic too, as they convince themselves they have a right to act in such ways: they play God. Aquarius in this space has a real God complex, believing themselves to be morally superior without actually having any morals. Their thoughts bulldoze over their feelings, thus they move on autopilot. Aquarius gets so lost in the world of dystopian rule, idealized fantasies of murder and justice, and a world rooted in make-belief from various fantasies and illusions, that they give off serial killer vibes. At their worst, they become serial killers or commitors of serious crimes.

Disconnection from Truth and Self-Awareness

With the glyph of the Water-Bearer, Aquarius loses themselves in the realm of the emotions and instincts, unconsciously, and further without actually processing emotions or feelings. How does this happen? Well, if you observe the Water-Bearer symbol, we can see how they pick up on infinite subtle impressions and psychic instincts, through the element water, which symbolizes emotions, depth, sensitivity, soul, subconscious wisdom, and the astral, ethereal, and divine realms. They're deeply in tune with subconscious, spiritual, and astral wisdom and energies, but because they process everything on an intellectual level they can't alchemize the messages properly; not when in their mental health blueprint, at least. Sensory information and wisdom becomes lost in translation. They misperceive and miss out on key teachings, life lessons, and information, as they don't know how to receive it properly. Their channel is faulty, in essence. They try to rationalize every emotion, instinct, and subtle sensation, but this isn't possible. Thus, they become confused, disoriented, and detached from reality including the people and environments they're connected to. Relationships break down, they miss out on financial, cultural, and educational opportunities, and they push their once closest supporters, friends and family, away.

In their dark psyche, Aquarius is completely unconscious of their energy and chaotic state of their inner world. They want so desperately to live in a utopian society with musicians playing liberating songs, flowers and beautiful pastures surrounding them, and hippie-ish laughing people everywhere. This is the Aquarian dream… However, they don't know how to get there or they try to get from A to G, missing out on essential steps, wisdom, qualifications, challenges to strengthen them, life lessons, and so forth. Aquarius isn't that self-honest or self-aware, nor are they accountable. They play victim due to the severe level of denial of their emotions, other people's feelings, and feminine gifts like sensitivity, empathy, etc. Aquarius is a masculine air sign, so feminine instincts don't come too easy for them. They pick up on multiple subtle energies and influences linked to the water element, yet don't know how to alchemize them into proper belief systems or sound rational thought. Their thoughts become clouded. As their entire identity is rooted in the need for community and conscious connections, this makes them question their sanity and the sanity of others, in addition to cutting the bridge between their heart's desires and truth. What is truth? It's all a blur, a cosmic swirling plot of archetypes and energies. In their unwavering desire to live an idealistic life with joy, laughter, and human intimacy, they block themselves from their ultimate goal. Again, this is due to the universal concept of yin and yang; polar opposites, all things have a duality, and you can't remain in one polar opposite forever. The speediness and impatience associated with their core character prevents them from attaining their goals, and further manifesting their vision. When in their mental health blueprint, they are reckless, foolish, and utterly chaotic in their thoughts and actions. They then become a rebel without a cause.

A Rebel Without A Cause

When in their best and evolved self, Aquarius is a rebel on a cause complete with a powerful vision. When not mature or evolved and further with a distorted psyche, Aquarius is on a path of annihilation and extermination, seeing enemies everywhere, and finding faults in every traditional regime or system. Uranus represents change, technology, conscious evolution, and transformation, so Uranus in a low vibration is a type of dystopia brought on by the extreme need for utopia, its polarity. Aquarius is one of the few signs to genuinely believe in parallel universes, time travel, and aliens. Their minds are attuned to a deeply pragmatic and futuristic Self, a Self connected to the multiverse; concepts you might only ponder on from movies and films are taken literally to them. Thus, the darker aspect of Uranus symbolizes turning against tradition, rules and laws, and current systems in place to help our growth. Due to the disillusionment, they see helpful boundaries as life-threatening attacks or restrictions. Aquarius doesn't do well to restrictions or limitations, so much so that they may even threaten others- innocent or not- with death. Physical violence, emotional and psychological violence and abuse, and psychic/spiritual attack are common in Aquarians in their dark psyche. The war they have is with their own mind, which projects out into the world- everything is a mirror. Within to without, as above so below… The Aquarian dark psyche is very dangerous indeed, as they believe they have a duty to protect both humankind and planet earth. They believe with utmost faith that they hold the responsibility to make decisions on behalf of communities, collective, and the planet as whole.

If an individual is in a position of real power and responsibility the results can be catastrophic. Aquarius will hit "kill" on the master switch if their pessimistic dystopian mind outweighs their humanitarian utopian one. A truly disenchanted Aquarius who has simultaneously given up hope sees destructive acts like murder or war paths as integral to the journey back to unity. They understand the following concepts on an intellectual level, not on an emotional one; this means there's an absence of empathy and therefore heart, sensitivity, and soul. Such concepts include the journey from darkness to light, rebirth, destruction making space for creation, and clearing away the old for new life to emerge. This sign would happily trigger a nuclear war if they thought the purging would lead to space for new life and growth! (The only reason this option is not ticked 'absolutely' below is because they are humanitarians, so their conscience will always pull them in between both dualities- high and low.) Aquarius believes fully that purging, cleansing, and eradication of old systems are essential for the new, including rebirth, new societal structures and regimes, and a utopian world. As an unconscious rebel, Aquarius is most likely to vandalize, damage personal property, and act like a teenager with no regards to consideration, kindness, and non-childish antics. There's no maturity nor is there respect for the structures and physical foundations that support them. They will start a riot with no clear outcomes or objectives that are completely immature and unthoughtful; it's just a statement, there's little to no depth or vision in mind. Aquarius is a serial rioter, always looking for ways to spread their "message" while not really meditating, getting clear on, or aligning with a real vision or path to success. It's all in the idealistic stage. Anarchy is an Aquarius concept and construct. Mayhem, turmoil, disorder, no governments, no corporations, lawlessness, and constant revolution are the dark psyche Aquarius ideal. Lower frequency Aquarius thrives on disorder and lawlessness, there's no room for rationality while slowing down to do things the right way is not something they have time or patience for.

They call for no political institutions and no hierarchy on a national and global scale, and in local communities as well as home they prefer the absence of rules entirely. This can drive their family mad, pushing elders, teachers, and parents to issue asbos or call on help from the authorities. This is the problem with the Aquarius personality, they are so extremist in their call for anarchy, etc., that they force their loved ones to go to extreme measures. They create their own downfall, inevitably. If we look at the actual definitions for dystopia and utopia, we can see that they are both imagined. Dystopia is an *imagined* world where there is great suffering and injustice. Utopia is an *imagined* world where there is paradise on earth and all is perfect. Both timelines may be true, but Aquarius clings onto the words themselves, giving them either false disillusionment or false hope. An ideal world, heaven on earth, may be possible, however Aquarius must first come to terms with their own shadow, so it doesn't devolve into a lasting mental health blueprint. This powerfully visionary dreamer with the most altruistic and inventive personality must wade through lots of BS to return to Source, to their soul's blueprint. Once they do so, they will realize that "utopia" is a man-made construct, and the perfect picture for what they hope for humanity, and themselves, is achieved through self-healing. Their *self*-evolution is the key.

Absolute worse crimes possible?

	LESS LIKELY	LIKELY	ABSOLUTELY
MURDER			✓
RAPE			✓
ANIMAL CRUELTY	✓		
CHILD ABUSE		✓	
MOLESTATION		✓	
TORTURE		✓	
HUMAN TRAFFICKING	✓		
SLAVERY	✓		
BESTIALITY		✓	
TERRORISM			✓
KIDNAPPING			✓
GENOCIDE		✓	

NUCLEAR WAR DECIDER		✓	

CHAPTER 12: Pisces the Manic Depressive

House: The 12th house, the house of endings, spiritual illumination, and evolution of the soul.

Planet: Neptune, the planet of dreams, mysticism, psychic instincts, and spiritual powers (positive), and fantasy, illusions, addictions, and escapism (negative).

Element and quality: Water and Mutable.

Color: Aquamarine, the color of tranquility, the imagination, angelic and divine contact, and prophecy, and purple, the color of ancient wisdom, intuition, higher truth, and self-knowledge.

Physical area: Feet and the pituitary gland.

Dates: February 20th to March 20th.

Pisces is the 12th sign ruled by Neptune, the planet of illusions and fantasy, yet simultaneously mysticism, psychic instincts, and dreams. Pisces is one of the most evolved signs of the zodiac, but because they pick up on so much through advanced psychic and extrasensory gifts, they lack boundaries. At their worst, Pisces lacks all sense of boundaries and swims with the tide and waves. Their glyph (astrological symbol) is the Fish; one fish swims upwards towards the heavens and celestial bodies, representing transcendence, and the other swims down, symbolizing the need to merge spirit into matter or the material realm. With such an advanced emotional and spiritual frequency, combined with a complete lack of boundaries as well as the tendency to see the world through rose-colored glasses, Pisces can become manically depressed. They become the lone wolf, wanting to spend all their time in isolation. They need to recharge and return back to Source constantly, either through transcendental meditation, sleep, mysticism, astral travel and dream encounters, or addictions like drugs and substances.

At their best, they are powerful mystics, healers, and psychics, moreover natural caregivers and nurturers. Yet, when deep down in their dark psyche they take on the world's pain and suffering, and it can create a spiral of depression verging on suicidal thoughts.

Let's look at the definition of a manic depressive:

A mentally imbalanced person who alternates between highs and lows, living in perpetual mood swings, depression, and unhealthy shifts in energy levels; low self-worth and self-esteem coupled with irrational and suicidal thoughts.

Let's break this main definition down, shall we!

Extreme Dualistic Forces

As one of the three dualistic signs alongside Gemini and Libra, Pisces' entire identity is governed by dualistic forces. These include the eternal and infinite flow of yin and yang, of polar opposites, which can be found in life, Self, and the universe. Yin flows into yang and vice versa, and this gives Pisces an incredibly "up-down" effect that never seems to end. One minute they're joyous, happy, positive, inspired, and full of creative life force and vision; the next, they are down, moody, depressed, withdrawn, and even suicidal. Later in life once grown, evolved, and matured this influence is very manageable, and even a direct cord to the greatest sources of inspiration, moreover peace and solace. But, when in their mental health blueprint it's a gateway to self-sabotage and self-pity. They become completely absorbed in the highs and lows of bliss and trauma, self-realization and suffering, and higher wisdom and taking on the world's pain. Pisces has two planetary rulers, Neptune (current) and Jupiter (ancient), which makes them prone to multiple energies and influences. Neptune makes them extremely psychic, open to dream and subconscious wisdom and guidance, spiritually evolved and perceptive, and gifted in the realms of subtle perception, the imagination, and advanced visionary and creative gifts. But it also leaves them prone to fantasy, illusions, and a lack of boundaries. Jupiter gives the same 'seek higher truth' vibration of Sagittarius, they are wayshowers and changemakers with powerful idealistic tendencies. Also, they are walking truth magnets and repellers when at the top of their game! Pisces is a major BS detector with amazing intuitive as well as higher perspective abilities. They're deeply concerned with the suffering in the world, in addition to living with nobility, honesty, integrity, and a strong sense of devotion to humankind, including exploding hidden truths, humanitarian themes, and universal compassion and justice…

So, when all of these remarkable gifts are twisted, just like with the other star signs, Pisces falls into extremes and the lower manifestation of their planetary rulers. Pisces becomes lost to a world of despair, isolation, and darkness brought on by tuning into the world's suffering. Every single person, animal, energy, collective theme currently occurring, and individual suffering- Pisces can feel. They feel on a deep level, because they are empaths. They're so advanced spiritually with such heightened sensitive, psychic, and telepathic-extrasensory gifts that they pick up on everything. Every single thought, emotion, energy current, intention, vibration, etc.; they are a psychic sponge to the world around. Environmental clues radiate to them in the same way snakes sense vibrations through the ground or dolphins communicate through supersonic waves, which is also considered a form of telepathy. In fact, Pisces is so spiritually aware that there is no such thing as Self. There is a loss of Self, meaning that they- their core, their soul, and their unique blueprint that makes them, them- is absorbed into the world around. They fade into nothingness and everythingness, there are no boundaries whatsoever. This inevitably makes Pisces fall into depression and severe trauma as we explore next. Firstly, they alternate between various polarities in a way that matches a schizophrenic or bi polar depressant. Pisces essentially has bi polar, moreover a mild or major type of schizophrenia when in their low mental headspace. Schizophrenia is a mental condition characterized by the breakdown of sensory information, creating distortion and disharmony between the realms of thought, emotion, and behavior. It creates faulty perception, inappropriate and irrational actions, and a withdrawal from both personal relationships and reality. It further gives rise to delusions combined with mental fragmentation. Well, this is Pisces. Bi polar disorder is ultimately the same as manic depression, and the disorder has in fact recently replaced the term manic depressive in recent years. It's a mental imbalance whereby there are constant and very unusual shifts in a person's mood, energy, and activity levels, so much so that day-to-day tasks are difficult to perform. Young and unevolved Pisces has both mild or major schizophrenia and bi polar.

They shift between high to low and low to high, adapting to the mood and frequencies surrounding them. It's impossible for people closest to them to know whether they're coming or going. As they are a Mutable water sign, this makes them the most adaptable of all. They're deeply open-minded, philosophical, and flexible, but when these qualities are applied in a negative way it opens them up to demonic forces. They cling onto mindsets and belief systems that set them down dark spirals. They enter into toxic and self-destructive cycles in a way very similar, if not identical to, Sagittarius. They become delusional through faulty belief systems and modes of perception birthed from core distortions. Root blockages aren't identified, then perpetuated, until they eventually become poor Pisces' reality. Pisces is overly trusting and overly innocent and naive to the world, they see everything through rose-tinted glasses, which portrays the desire to only look on the bright side. Yet, as everything involves duality, this means they attach onto one extreme to deny or reject the other, and, over time, they start to fall into the extreme polarity. There's no balance. They attach to false positives, choosing optimistic mindsets (Jupiter is their ancient ruler, after all) and dismissing other truths. They live from a sort of "half truth" perspective, continuously spiraling from bright to pessimistic, positive to negative, and overjoyed to utterly depressed in the process. Life becomes a rollercoaster and they themselves become a yo-yo bound to their own ludicrous mood swings. Thus, they become traumatized, but they also enter into a type of psychosis, as well as disillusionment shared by Aquarius the Water-Bearer, the second most visionary sign. This is the only sign to take the concept of *Oneness* too far, whereby they believe that another person's pain, suffering, accomplishment, qualification, or relationship is theirs. They may find the deepest soul resonance or sympathy- they may merge with them on the spiritual dimensions so powerfully that they experience or take on the other person's feelings, but they are *not* that person or achievement. Pisces takes oneness and interconnectedness too far because they are natural mystics. Like Scorpio, Pisces has a deep knowledge of the occult, metaphysics, and ancient wisdom; they are seers and shapeshifters when at their best. Pisces is fully aware that we're all mirrors of one another, we're divine reflections. But, because Pisces is distanced from reality (one Fish is swimming up towards the heavens, trying to escape the material and mundane-earthly realm), they become disassociated. In fact, this sign is a master of disassociation, which is leaving their physical body to astral project into the future, or into a different time or place. Pisces can, quite literally, think they're in a relationship with someone while having only a minor connection or brief moments of emotional and spiritual bonding, chemistry, and so forth. The same applies to real world things like qualifications, achievements, jobs, security, and societal labels. The positive aspect of this is that they are visionaries, they are capable of tuning into a future end goal or vision of their best self; self-evolution on a soul level makes them incredibly advanced and psychic. However, Pisces neglects physical reality altogether, failing to see how 3D concepts and experiences are necessary. They're escapists and illusionists.

So, Pisces lives in a sort of dream-world where they believe things that aren't real. They also create truths that aren't entirely real, merely a figment of their imagination. When older and mature, Pisces is the creative genius of the zodiac. They are amazingly prophetic, gifted in powerful spiritual abilities only real life shamans and mystics possess. Yet, when unhealed and imbalanced they lack the self-awareness to heal and prosper. Their mental health blueprint is completely wrapped up in the loss of Self... where does Self end and begin? Who knows. To Pisces, it's all a game; a free for all. *We're all one,* right? No, well, maybe on an energetic level- there is such a thing as an Oversoul and the Akashic Records are real. But we're also individuals, each with separate bodies, minds, hearts, and souls. Unfortunately, Pisces has a bad habit when in such a low mental headspace to take on other people's karma. In other words, other people's bad habits, actions, and energies become theirs. Alongside Cancer, Pisces is the most likely to get *gaslighted* by narcissistic characters. Pisces is a lover, not a fighter (Venus is exalted in Pisces)... a giver, not a taker (they are more submissive and selfless than dominant and self-centered)... and more concerned with soul that the physical body or realm (they're ruled by the 12th house of endings and completions). Pisces will be selfless to the point of sacrifice, letting others who have done sh*tty things be seen in a positive light. They do this for a few reasons. Either, 1. The pain of accepting harsh truths and realities would destroy them- they're not emotionally strong enough to come to terms with reality. Or, 2. They care so much about someone not good for them, who doesn't have their best interests at heart, through idiot compassion, their extraordinary sense of unconditional love and universal compassion, or sheer faith that the person they love is good, of noble and pure intentions, etc. As the sign associated with seeing the world through rose-colored glasses, Pisces is the only sign to forgive a rapist, murderer, or child abuser! I mean, really forgive them, on a soul level, where they wish them well in a next life while hoping they find love in this one. Some people see them as crazy, other people see this inspirational sign as magical. Both are true, but the problem is that such an apparent lack of boundaries can keep naive and sweet Pisces suffering and in constant pain, while no-one seems to know just how much they're suffering. Pisces will put on a brave face and pretend nothing is wrong, as they are masters of illusion and make-believe. *Pretend* is the keyword here.

Depressed and Traumatized

Pisces becomes traumatized, plagued by ghosts and dark forces. Being ruled by Neptune means they pick up on psychic sensitivities and subtleties in waking life, from living people and animals. But it also means they are able to see, sense, feel, and hear spirits, they are natural mediums, seers, and clairvoyants when on top form. They are one of the few signs who can really, truly, see through and beyond the veil of illusion. Being so open to, well, everythings- every single vibration and energy current possible, makes sweet and sensitive Pisces into an emotional dumping ground. When they're in solitude, they are a psychic sponge, and when they're around people they become doormats and dumping grounds for other people's problems… or abuse. Trauma fuels low vibrational Pisces' life whichever way round we look at it. Lacking boundaries coupled with such extreme illusions due to Neptune's influence opens Pisces up to a world of trauma and terror. They tune in, consciously or unconsciously, to the world's sufferings, evil acts, and brutal crimes committed locally or on a global scale. This is why they can't watch the news, it hits home on a really deep and personal level. They see the world as a reflection of them, everything is a mirror, a reflection, and everyone is an extension of them; Pisces believes every human is their family, that we're all brothers and sisters guiding each other home... They also recognize the interconnected nature of all life, and are further aware of universal and sacred laws, divine cause and effect, and oneness. This means that when in their lower frequency they pick up on all the sadness and pain as if it were their own, experiencing it exactly as if it's "them."

Hence, Pisces become traumatized by every act great or small. Acts of violence and scenes of coldness in movies, on t.v. on the news, or anywhere are taken very seriously, moreover are taken straight to heart. They feel it on a soul level, deep inside their cells, and they become attached to the trauma. Why? Because they are natural healers. Pisces are the healers, empaths, mystics, caregivers, and spiritual teachers of the zodiac. They desire nothing more than to help everyone, yet not everyone can be helped, and this is where their mental health issues arise. Additionally, they possess the "victim-martyr-savior" complex, a deeply ingrained belief that they can and should save everyone. If they fail to save someone, they become a martyr or a victim. These innate motivations originate from a selfless space, genuine and honest in their intentions. But, it's not realistic. This is linked to one of their sets of shadow traits: being impractical, ungrounded, and completely disconnected from physical reality. The material world has little interest to them, and this perpetuates their imbalances. They cling onto extreme notions and belief systems of life and Self, and thus become disconnected from relationships, material things, and places or environments that could help them. They hinder their own growth through misguided or distorted belief systems coupled with such a strong emphasis on healing the world. At their best, they are soul warriors with hearts of gold, who genuinely possess the power, moreover spiritual gifts to heal, teach, guide, inspire, and educate. However, to get there they must come to terms with their own shadow.

And being so sensitive and hyper-emotional means they *succumb* to their shadow, instead of exploring it in a healthy way with rationality and logic, to rise up into their light. Like fellow water sign and empath Cancer, Pisces lacks all sense of logic, reasoning, and rationality- intellectual analysis too. So, they stay hyper-emotional and super-sensitive, which keeps them trapped and blocked from true enlightenment. Pisces sees glimpses of enlightenment when in their low mental headspace; it's true that they are the most advanced souls, wise beyond years, and organically intuitive and psychic, even when young. But being so impractical, ungrounded, and disconnected from the material realm has major setbacks for their ultimate evolution. Trauma and wounds circulate due to becoming so wrapped up in both their inner and outer worlds. When in solitude, they keep picking up on the ill-health, wrongdoings, evil, suffering, and trauma around them. When they're in a public or a social setting, the same occurs; in both situations they attach to the stories they are fed from the ether. It's impossible for them not to, as they confuse 'helping' and 'saving' with a lack of boundaries. Their Self swims back and forth to the divine and the material. Remember that Pisces' glyph is the two Fish, one fish swimming upwards towards the heavens, representing transcendence coupled with soul bonding, and the other fish representing the descent of their spiritual self into the physical plane. Therefore, Pisces is always confused, as well as prone to illusions.

It's true they are incredibly psychic, they're mediumship, clairvoyant, clairsentient, clairaudient, precognitive, prophetic, and extrasensory skills are no joke (although many people do laugh at them, bless their sweethearts). No, Pisces is the *most* evolved sign. But, a lack of boundaries, logic, and self-alignment in their life prevents them from being correct and on point, it's more guesswork and slight psychic powers. The other end of the spectrum is when Pisces actually does go deep into the darkness, making them both shamanic and schizophrenic; this is the dual force that's unescapable. They enter into a type of schizophrenic psychosis to the outside world, where they exist predominantly in the dream, multidimensional, and astral planes. Waking life, this reality, becomes a dream, and their true self feels most comfortable in the ethereal and astral worlds. (As a Pisces with my Venus in Pisces, I can vouch for this!) Pisces in this space will "live" in a supremely-spaced out state for years upon years before *waking up* from their self-induced psychosis. Of course, they don't see it as this, they are spiritual beings, after all, furthermore have a direct link to dimensions and worlds other people do not. Nonetheless, it's a dark spiral to enter, as this world becomes a distant memory while the dream and astral/spiritual planes become their home. *Pisces is a fish who feels most comfortable in water.* Unfortunately, some Pisces drown, staying in perpetual darkness and depression if their mental health blueprint remains unchecked. At their utter worst, Pisces drives themselves into madness, perhaps even committing suicide due to the lack of joy and connection they feel in this plane.

Additionally, Pisces is incapable of accepting responsibility over their lives. Their shadow traits include impracticality and a lack of grounding- this is the worst sign at saving and making good financial decisions. So, in their dark psyche their lack of responsibility devolves into a complete disregard of the practical and material things in life. Pisces will neglect their physical bodies and health and then blame others. They will enter into self-pity and isolation in a way similar to Scorpio the doomed, and then project on others when they leave their cocoon. Projection is something common with all water signs. Furthermore, due to ruling the 12th house of endings, spiritual illumination, and soul completion, Pisces is the total opposite to Aries, the 1st sign ruled by the 1st house. This signifies they neglect all aspects of the 1st house (unless their unique natal chart has one or more strong 1st house placements). Pisces lacks accountability. They're not very grounded, despite being incredibly humble and graceful. Moodiness turns into extreme impracticalities, a love of spirit and subtle and subconscious energy prevents their material evolution, and blocks ensue all around. Pisces will be penniless, quite literally, and wander into the night… This naive and trusting sign believes someone will help them, as they are happy to cut off a body part to help even a stranger in need. Unfortunately, they are ignorant to the coldness and harshness of the world. The very wise saying 'you create your own fortune in life' or 'you can't expect everyone to do everything for you' doesn't apply to Pisces- they see everything as interconnected, which inevitably implies oneness. Pisces doesn't grasp that everyone is *not* an extension of them, at least not in a physical sense. Through lacking material awareness, respect, and maturity, Pisces neglects, dismisses, and rejects core life themes. They are more prone to homelessness, severe addictions, and selling their bodies for the most basic security and survival means than most. I am sorry to share that Pisces is one of the most likely to sell themselves in prostitution or become a servant to an abusive rich wo/man's abuse. Whether it's in love or money after finally realizing they can't be poor forever, Pisces will become subservient to anyone who makes them feel even slightly worthy and understood.

Why? Because Pisces is one of the most misunderstood zodiac signs, and being misunderstood brings someone in their dark psyche to the lowest expression of human behavior. It's ironic, because Pisces is so talented coupled with being a master of manifestation that all they'd have to do is play to their strengths, embrace the unknown in a light way, i.e. aligned to a more connected and joyous worldview (where they see humans as kind, helpful, loving, etc.). Yet in their dark psyche, they believe they need to be subservient and downplay their gifts. On this note, it should be mentioned that despite being one of the most likely to get rich and be abundant when at the top of their game, when healed and evolved later in life, Pisces is prone to poverty consciousness. This is believing there's not enough or that they're not worthy of abundance, prosperity, and financial security. Virgo is their opposite sign, so in their mental health blueprint they neglect or even reject security, practicalities, and fundamental 3D/material things.

Feels the World's Pain and Suffering

Joy, happiness, and a sense of fun and play are very hard to come by. Unlike the fire signs who find these things very easy to experience, which in itself leads to their shadow side of narcissism and self-centeredness, Pisces is the complete opposite. They are so selfless and charitable that they put themselves in isolation, sometimes consciously and sometimes unconsciously. Then, they become addicted to the pain that also brings wisdom in the way that fire signs are addicted to the drama which also brings excitement. In other cases, air signs are addicted to the superficiality that brings sociability, and earth signs become immersed in stubbornness while knowing that their determination keeps them materially secure. Each sign has a light and shadow. In Pisces' case, they take on so much from external clues, subtle sensations, and subconscious triggers that they feel everything. The definition of an empath is someone who feels every emotion, thought, and subtle sensation. They know exactly what it's like to be in another's shoes, and are telepathic, caring, and compassionate beyond belief. At a higher level this makes Pisces one of the most devoted, inspirational, and nurturing friends to have; at a lower vibration, they are disillusioned and delusional as to how much they actually need to take on. Instead of healing themselves, working on their shadow, and engaging in proper self-care, or going outside to mingle with the world, have fun, meet new people, explore, and develop a sense of fun, play, color, and joyous sociability; they become isolated, cut off, and withdrawn. They find more familairy in the darkness and shadow realms which bring out their shamanic self (like Scorpio), and further become scared of people. Unlike others who turn sociopathic, psychotic, or antisocial in a violent and damaging way, Pisces harms themselves. They are certainly not selfish, but they open themselves up to demonic entities, dark forces, and the projections of others. I remember my own mother (Leo, who I saw as incredibly selfish and egotistical) triggering me beyond belief when I would *finally* come out of my introspective bubble and do "normal things." She would call me selfish for, essentially, not being selfish! It is a twisted and cold world, and this is the point.

Pisces either plays victim or is an actual victim, in the latter case more dominant and actually selfish people walk all over them, abuse them, or treat them like their verbal punch bags or doormats. Why does this happen? Well, because Pisces is so infused in a world of introspection, trauma, and taking on everyone else's stuff (wounds, pain, subtle cries for help and healing...) that when they finally put themselves first, people attack them. Poor and vulnerable, totally selfless, and innocent Pisces becomes the target. People gang up on them, victimize them, and traumatize them further. They've been so deep into their polarity, one extreme, that when they finally become brave and face the world, it hits them with their other polarity. Selfishness Vs selflessness, dominance Vs passiveness, power and force Vs receptivity and gentleness, logic Vs feelings, intellect Vs instincts... we are all supposed to find balance and unity within, or at least some aspect of unification of dualistic forces. But Pisces is so spiritual, chameleon-like as a Mutable water sign, and submissive that they always gravitate to their core frequency, which, in astrological terms, is the root of both their best Self and their wounds. Pisces is arguably the *Wounded Healer* of the zodiac; they learn their wounds through years to a lifetime of self-evaluation and spiritual journeying, and then transform their wounds into healing, teaching, and helping others. Their core wounds and blocks become a doorway to their highest potential, which is symbolic of the journey from darkness to light or shadow to self-mastery. As the only sign ruled by the 12th house, Pisces is the most susceptible to soul growth and enlightenment, moreover self-actualization in this lifetime. Referring back to the targeting and bullying, all the people who have gotten so used to them being quiet and submissive "turn on them." They've likely failed to work on their shadow personality traits too, so they have got used to being superficial, selfish, egotistical, narcissistic, and so forth (essentially, qualities very different to the Pisces persona). Now there are two or more worlds existing, and we all have to get along, find harmony, and co-exist without violence or conflict. So how does this manifest? Pisces either becomes the victim, subject to bullying and horrific displays of human aggression and unkindness, which pushes them further back into their bubble of despair and isolation. This, in itself, leads to suicidal and schizophrenic or bi polar tendencies already outlined... Or Pisces plays victim, unconsciously becoming a bully through taking the defensive strategy. Once they choose a path of self-defense, through recognizing that their psychic and intuitive senses were, in fact, true- there are bullies and narcissistic people in this world; all hell breaks loose.

Pisces enters fight or flight mode whereby they feel there is no place for them. They lose all sense of trust and hope in people, they start to see people as monsters. Due to their glyph of the Fish, they naturally try to escape, believing that they don't have security or aren't entitled to it. While dominant and self-serving characters like Aries and Leo may be utterly self-entitled, with strong instincts of survival and self-preservation (due to a me-centered and confident approach) Pisces thinks the opposite. And, let's face it, Fish aren't exactly meant to exist in a world of Rams, Bulls, Lions, Centaurs, or Horned-Goats. All the other animal glyphs would, quite literally, squish and even kill Pisces with one minor movement. Even fellow water sign Scorpio wants to sometimes play around with Pisces for sheer fun (their ancient ruler is Mars, after all...). Pisces really is the most down-trodden and doormat-prone of all the zodiac. Feeling the world's pain and suffering puts them in isolation, like sister sign Scorpio, and they are further the lone wolves of the zodiac. If the world's coldness and mean-spiritedness doesn't drive them into suicide or total despair, they put on this defensive attitude in an attempt to stay strong, and it makes everyone realize just how, 1. Mentally ill Pisces has been, and, 2. They've been mean and heartless bullies. No-one likes being called out or made to be a bully, thus unless these "unconscious perpetrators," through direct abuse or neglect of vulnerable Pisces' needs, are ready to own up to their own shadow and/or mental health issues, it sets off an explosive cycle.

Once again, Pisces is forced further into isolation and depression, or they lose faith in their loved ones, associates, peers, friends, housemates, and family entirely, and feel like they have no home or shelter. In a higher frequency, Pisces symbolizes faith, universal compassion, and unconditional love. They are the angels and saints of the zodiac. A Pisces in such a low mental headspace may act completely irrationally and wander off into the night, quite literally. Results that ensue could be sleeping around for a place to sleep, receiving money in exchange for sexual or illegal favors, or entering into even more dangerous (actually dangerous) living or social situations for a false sense of security. They're so prone to illusion that they misconfuse a little bit of conflict for a full blown death threat. In a way, it is a death threat, it's a threat to their core, personality, soul, identity, and character due to having their entire energetic signature entwined with the world around them. They're selfless to the point of *losing* their Self in others and external environments, so any coldness, attack, or harsh word is received as an actual war, a real threat to their spirit. Therefore, they subsequently choose real-life dangerous situations to replace the hole in their hearts; they did so much for the people they lived with, their family, and loved ones, after all, and this breaks their soft and fragile hearts to the core. It also destroys their souls, although they will rarely if not ever verbalize this.

If usually shy, submissive, and apparently weak and neglected Pisces choose to truly stand up for themselves, embodying what they perceive to be strength and assertiveness, it is met entirely the wrong way. They approach their perpetrators with *defensiveness*, and this then makes others attack them more. Of course, their strength is just an act, they're extremely broken inside, so this pushes them to their deathbed. The manifestation is that they either have an ego death, embarking on a new path that inevitably leads to their healing and wholeness, or they choose suicide through Self or other harm (dangerous situations, addictions, etc.). It's a vicious cycle of self-harm, delusion, and psychosis and it takes a miracle to pull Pisces up from their helplessness. Fortunately, Pisces is the most lucky with Jupiter as an ancient ruler, and with a direct cord to the divine and spiritual realms, they have many unseen and ancient helpers to see them through. The journey is very difficult for them, however, and Pisces suffers more than anyone else.

Illusions, Fantasies, and Isolation

This brings us onto illusions and fantasies. Pisces lives in a make-believe world brought on by picking up on so much. They are the wisest and oldest souls, therefore they do see and sense a lot. They're intuitive, visionary, idealistic, psychic, noble, kind, generous, compassionate, gentle, and a symbol for unconditional love. As deeply magnetic and nurturing creatures who likely wouldn't even kill a mosquito if it needed some human blood to survive, Pisces is bound to entwine themselves to some illusionary stories. *What's real and what's fiction?* Pisces operates from a predominantly emotional frequency, just like Gemini functions psychologically. This signifies that they reject and deny the realm of logic, intellect, higher reasoning, analytical thinking, and scientific and rational thought. It's all about emotions, subtle instincts, sensitivities, feelings, and the inner world of what they pick up on psychically and spiritually. They are so emotionally intelligent, deep, and empathic, moreover soul aligned and spiritually gifted that they totally dismiss the need for their intellectual and rational body. Not only does this make them embody a mild or major form of schizophrenia, but they equally have a hard time ascertaining what is true. With ancient planetary Jupiter, their identity is also wrapped up in desires for higher truth, spiritual and philosophical ideals, and everything related to the higher mind. A disconnection from their true self as well as from their authentic spiritual and balanced nature keeps them trapped, they become trapped to their own stories and the stories, judgements, and projections imposed on them by others. Pisces will believe their persecutor or abuser due to the idiot compassion and blind faith mentioned earlier.

This can give rise to fairytale fantasies of true love and intimacy, which keeps them blocked from true love, marriage, finding a compatible soulmate, etc. For any ex lovers or soulmates who might be reading this, you will be pleased to know my 'Marriage line' (palm reading) is short. Actually, it's so short it's non-existent. I may have a very long Life, Heart, Head, Fate, and Sun line, but I missed out on true love many times… Many Pisces in their mental health blueprint will enter a fantasy world in which they close themselves off to physical intimacy with other humans and only self-pleasure; or play out extremist fantasies in their mind. They *idealize* love. They become attached to people in an extremely unhealthy way without wanting to make it real or even make their affections known. Pisces can be in love, or infatuated, with someone for years to decades before realizing that they've been denying companionship, intimacy, and sex in their life due to remaining in a fantasy world. I used to play out many fantasies while young in my teenage to early adult years, while not being open to intimacy in the physical realm. This influence fades with time as well as when you start to heal your mental health blueprint. Alternatively, they may cling onto a fairytale belief in love and never unite with a soulmate! The real and the illusionary become interchangeable for them... The same illusions can be applied to career, vocation, or life path. Multitalented and multidimensional Pisces will know on an instinctive or intuitive level of all their hidden soul talents and gifts, yet haven't taken steps to perfect or master them. Also, they receive glimpses into their future self and think they can jump from 'A to G,' 7 or any number of years without actually establishing the professional bonds. The world of qualifications, certifications, and traditional routes to professional recognition and victory are void to them- they simply don't see their significance, so deny and thus cling onto notions of their validity in the world. These are, of course, unrealistic, moreover not rooted in reality. Pisces may be a multitalented superstar on an energetic or spiritual level, but they need to take practical steps to manifest their vision on this earth plane. Therefore, they become delusional as to their greatness in a way similar to Sagittarius the delusional. They play the game of life with a sort of cheating attitude, not aware or conscious of how their 'half moves' or 'half effort' doesn't actually give them the status, title, prestige, fame, or recognition they desire. Pisces lives in fantasy-land so much they live, breathe, and act from visions. They are prophetic, this is the sign associated with prophetic vision, yet they don't understand that time is also linear. While other people may have a hard time coming to terms with multidimensionality or the nonlinear nature of time, Pisces adopts the other extreme, and this makes them forget about time cycles and significant life chapters. *Pisces is advanced beyond their years.* In their dark psyche, this plays out in the same way it does for Aquarius, whereby they never actually *live* their lives, they just become disillusioned and glide around like a space cadet.

Neglect of Personal Needs

A total lack of self-care, no life force or passion to heal and change, and a sole commitment to staying addicted to their suffering is Pisces in their lowest vibration. When in their dark psyche, they neglect their personal needs, even normal basic things we would say are essential to human survival. Things like eating, brushing your teeth, sleeping peacefully, being comfortable in their body, watching a film, or laughing are seen as monstrous to the dark Pisces spirit. Oh yes, Pisces is deeply confused, they don't understand that it's ok to laugh, be free, and choose themselves first. Selfishness is seen as *alien* to them while being even slightly negative, bitchy, mean, or self-serving is a crime against humankind… and planet earth. *This is no joke.* Poor Pisces has become so misguided and disillusioned that they've distorted reality, always putting themselves last while letting others outshine them, stomp over them, and dismiss them without kindness or empathy. Yet Pisces is so kind, empathic, and beautiful inside due to their evolved levels of integrity and humility that this is an insane self-evaluation to hold. Self-care and self-love diminishes or is eradicated altogether. Any sign of coldness or mean-spirit on their behalf sends them into deeper isolation and depression. Taking back their power from bullies or oppressors or simply the people who are happy to be dominant, direct, and sociable makes them feel suicidal. Pisces is the most positively whimsical yet equally ungrounded sign. They lack grounding, practical awareness, and respect for their longevity, as well as having a complete disregard to the one philosophy that rules their entire world: *yin and yang*. Yin and yang asks for balance and unification, a wholeness and equilibrium within, yet this can't be achieved when they are so adamant on staying selfless 100% of the time. Pisces takes self-sacrifice to a whole new level of self-destruction; to be self-sacrificing is to literally sacrifice yourself, and this is the next stage from selflessness (a loss of Self). So, Pisces enters into the "victim-martyr-savior" complex mentioned early, whereby they become a victim, try to save everyone, or, at their worst, become a martyr to the ill-health, monstrous acts, and brutality of the world.

Inherently connected to this is the increased capacity for persecutors, because when you try to save people who don't want to be saved, it creates a polarity. Thus, Pisces picks up haters and bullies who try to break their spirit even more. *Their toxicity breeds more toxicity*. At their highest vibration, Pisces is the seer, mystic, spiritual guide, counselor, healer, and powerful clairvoyant, shaman, or visionary. They are so gifted- connected to the divine too, however it is a real journey to get there. Pisces not only has to heal their own shadow and mental health blueprint, but undo (apparently) everyone else's conditioning. They take on virtually "every soul they encounter"-'s trauma, and other people's wounds and hardships become theirs, in addition to taking on collective trauma and pain. Pisces, as the Old Soul and final sign, gives themselves the impossible task of healing humankind. Can it be achieved? Not likely. Luckily, they can rise above the wounds of their own mental health blueprint to find peace, solace, and wholeness, also sparking ancient wisdom, knowledge, and memory of their life path and purpose. Similar to Sagittarius the Archer who sees into the future with potent intuition and vision, mystical Pisces is destined to be a healer in some way, either through their healing gifts blessed by Spirit, divine revelations, music, creativity, ingenious imaginative abilities, or teaching, speaking, and guiding others on a path back to purity and higher spiritual awareness. To get there, they must first accept that they are born into this world, not of it. They are one drop in an infinite ocean, not the ocean itself... although they may be on a metaphorical level. Finally, it should be noted that Pisces is less likely to cause harm to others, even when in a mental space. They are more likely to turn towards addictions and fantasies, in addition to self-harm, suicidal thoughts, and getting lost in the shamanic and astral planes. This is the sign most likely to die in their sleep, drifting off to another world because this world is too harsh and unkind for their sweet souls.

Additionally, you may be wondering if Pisces has a temper? All other signs have been mentioned as being aggressive or self-protective in some way? The astrological answer is: no. Pisces is so selfless and fluid- passive and graceful by nature, that they would swim 'sorry walk' away from a fight. Pisces avoids conflict, and this is due to the escapist nature of their personality. As master escapists, Pisces is the sort of person who will live in a hundred different places before feeling at home. At a higher vibration, they are so adaptable and unconditionally loving that they genuinely see everyone and everywhere as their home. They will fit in and find some level of comfort and joy anywhere, quite literally, anywhere. In a lower frequency, they avoid conflict and confrontation to the point of building up problems, always then repeating the same toxic or self-sabotaging cycles. They're masters of self-sabotage. One could argue it's because their mission is so strong; the 12th house makes them inevitably gravitate toward a path of soul completion and alignment, therefore they are bound to be given more challenges (they are also known as the Old Souls in addition to the Fish!). To add, being so dreamy, impressionable, and anti-conflict makes them act out unconscious dark fantasies from the collective psyche. It's usually done in fantasy such as during solitude in privacy, but it can also be taken to extremes if their mental health blueprint goes unchecked. This is the absolute lowest manifestation and extremely rare, such as engaging in evil behavior to heal it through their participation, believing that by visiting the darkest places of the human psyche they can transcend it. (This is only displayed by real schizophrenics or those who have let their mental health disorder devolve…) The unconscious is a tricky place to navigate, and Pisces has access to it. Defined by purity, goodness, and devotion, least to mention faith and higher aspirations, fortunately, Pisces has many guides and unseen helpers to assist them out of their manic depression so they can fulfill their spiritual mission here. Their faith, trust, and unconditional love see them through, in the end.

Absolute worse crimes possible?

	LESS LIKELY	LIKELY	ABSOLUTELY
MURDER			✓
RAPE			✓
ANIMAL CRUELTY	✓		
CHILD ABUSE	✓		
MOLESTATION		✓	
TORTURE			✓

HUMAN TRAFFICKING		✓	
SLAVERY	✓		
BESTIALITY			✓
TERRORISM		✓	
KIDNAPPING			✓
GENOCIDE	✓		
NUCLEAR WAR DECIDER	✓		

As the 12th and final sign representing the evolution of the soul's journey back to enlightenment, Pisces symbolizes the loss and return of the Self. Pisces is the sign of illusions and mysticism, self-sacrifice and psychic & spiritual gifts, and addiction and multidimensional awareness in equal measure. As the only sign ruled by the 12th house, any Pisces in your natal chart will indicate how you can arise above the depths of the mundane coupled with the material world, to attain true self-realization and enlightenment. ***You can read all chapters to understand your own story by applying the themes to the HOUSES. Each star sign represents a house, so this book also serves as an in depth exploration of your psyche in an all-encompassing way.***

Finally, Pisces represents the super-consciousness or divine within us all, such as the journey of the soul from childhood to resting years, what we have to release or "kill" off inside of us (release, transcend, and let go of), and a return to Source and innocence.

ABOUT THE AUTHOR

Grace Gabriella Puskas is a spiritual author of two groundbreaking collections of poetry and a creative visionary. She is a qualified Reiki Master Teacher, Dream therapist, Crystal & Shamanic Healer, Chi Kung practitioner, Reflexologist, Aromatherapist, and Herbalist. In 2014 she won the Local Legend Spiritual Writing Competition, resulting in the publication of her debut book of poetry, 'A Message from Source.' Throughout her twenties she spent her time volunteering on various projects, spiritual, conscious, eco/sustainable, community, and animal welfare and conservation; she has lived on organic farms, shamanic land communities, and in ashrams, and has created beautiful Medicinal herb gardens, in addition to leading workshops in the Healing Arts & Spirituality. Grace Gabriella works at festivals and conscious community gatherings where she offers therapies, healing, and workshops aimed at spiritual development and accessing creative, soul, and intuitive/psychic gifts. She is a Teacher of the Healing Arts, Reiki, and Creative & Spiritual Development, and a poet, wordsmith, world-class ghost-writer, philosopher, inspired visionary, soul guide, psychic, empathic counselor, and astrologer. She is also a Pisces with a grand water trine and grand earth trine in her birth chart (two rare astrological alignments). Grace believes we can transcend comfort zones by leaving behind a fear timeline, and moving towards a timeline of LOVE. Unity consciousness, authentic and conscious spirituality, holistic health, and healing planetary consciousness as well as Mother Earth, beautiful Gaia, are her main life goals and service. She is a Medicine Woman and free-flow Musician who embodies elements of a modern-day, grounded, mystic.

CONTACT:

gracegabriella33@gmail.com

https://gracegabriella33.wixsite.com/grace
https://www.youtube.com/@TheDreamSpiritWeaver

AFTERWORD

Enjoyed this book? Perhaps, but I intuit you were also triggered. Don't worry, so was I! My Higher Self triggered me during the creation process. *It's natural.* This is what happens when we say no to the easy route and choose the higher path; shadow work is never easy, nor is becoming totally honest and accountable with ourselves.

I have a lot of free videos, both face-to-camera and audio only, available on my Youtube channel, *The Dream & Spirit Weaver.* You might want to visit the 'most popular' to see what can spark your Crown…

My other books:

A Message from Source: 33 poems exploring consciousness, our connection to one another, and the universe as a whole. *My debut book won the Local Legend National Writing Competition in 2014.*

A Story of One: A sequel to *A Message from Source*, which delves into tantra, mysticism, healing, higher consciousness, love, intimacy, friendship, community, and soulmate bonds.

Spirit Animals of the Star Signs: Power Animals of the Zodiac: With 52 reviews at the time of writing this book, this game changing "one-of-a-kind" book on spirit animals and astrology was written during my travels through South America in 2022. I began writing in the sacred Mayan lands of Mexico, continued in the mountainous rainforests of Monteverde Costa Rica, and finished in the Amazon Jungle in Ecuador. This book is so in depth it's been described as the holy grail of guides!

Pisces Dream Astrology: The Dreamer (Old Souls Dreams): A book exclusively on Pisces, the 12th and final sign, the mystic, healer, and dreamer… (I myself am a Pisces Sun with my Venus in Pisces too.) *This book can also be consulted for dream symbolism and exploration.*

52 Tantric Tips for Ultimate Intimacy from an Energy Master: Exploring Tantric Intimacy; Merging the Lower Primal Self and Higher Spiritual Self for Your Best Sex Life!- As the title signifies…

EMPATH Essential Survival Guide!- A Complete Guide to The Empath Blueprint, Overcoming Narcissistic Abuse, Reclaiming Self-Sovereignty, and Color & Chakra Therapy and Healing.

CHILDREN'S BOOKS:

<u>A Zodiac Wisdom Book for Kids!</u>- Children's learning about astrology.

<u>72 Spirit Animals for Children</u>: Children's learning about shamanism and spirit animals.

If you have the paperback copy, all of these books can be found on Amazon! <3

Printed in Great Britain
by Amazon